SEXUAL EXPLOITATION AND ABUSE IN PEACEKEEPING AND AID

Critiquing the Past, Plotting the Future

Edited by
Jasmine-Kim Westendorf and Elliot Dolan-Evans

First published in Great Britain in 2024 by

Bristol University Press
University of Bristol
1–9 Old Park Hill
Bristol
BS2 8BB
UK
t: +44 (0)117 374 6645
e: bup-info@bristol.ac.uk

Details of international sales and distribution partners are available at bristoluniversitypress.co.uk

© Bristol University Press 2024

British Library Cataloguing in Publication Data
A catalogue record for this book is available from the British Library

ISBN 978-1-5292-3840-2 hardcover
ISBN 978-1-5292-3841-9 paperback
ISBN 978-1-5292-3842-6 ePub
ISBN 978-1-5292-3843-3 ePdf

The right of Jasmine-Kim Westendorf and Elliot Dolan-Evans to be identified as editors of this work has been asserted by them in accordance with the Copyright, Designs and Patents Act 1988.

All rights reserved: no part of this publication may be reproduced, stored in a retrieval system, or transmitted in any form or by any means, electronic, mechanical, photocopying, recording, or otherwise without the prior permission of Bristol University Press.

Every reasonable effort has been made to obtain permission to reproduce copyrighted material. If, however, anyone knows of an oversight, please contact the publisher.

The statements and opinions contained within this publication are solely those of the editors and contributors and not of the University of Bristol or Bristol University Press. The University of Bristol and Bristol University Press disclaim responsibility for any injury to persons or property resulting from any material published in this publication.

Bristol University Press works to counter discrimination on grounds of gender, race, disability, age and sexuality.

Cover design: Lyn Davies Design
Front cover image: Jake Lyell/CARE/Alamy Stock Photo

Contents

List of Figures and Tables   v
List of Abbreviations   vi
Notes on Contributors   vii
Acknowledgements   xiv

Introduction: Two Decades of Dealing with Sexual Exploitation   1
and Abuse in Peacekeeping and Aid
Jasmine-Kim Westendorf and Elliot Dolan-Evans

PART I Where We've Been: The Origins and Scope of Protection from Sexual Exploitation and Abuse

1 Reflections on 20-Plus Years of Protection from SEA Work   19
   Sarah Martin
2 United Nations Police as a Double-Edged Sword for   34
   SEA Accountability
   Ai Kihara-Hunt
3 Victims' Rights and Remedial Action   46
   Sabrina White and Leah Nyambeki
4 Sexual Violence against Peacekeepers and Aid Workers   62
   Phoebe Donnelly and Dyan Mazurana

PART II How It's Going: Implementing and Institutionalizing Protection from Sexual Exploitation and Abuse

5 Missing the Mark in PSEA   79
   Asmita Naik and Jasmine-Kim Westendorf
6 The Imperative of Prioritizing Victims' Rights   93
   Jane Connors
6A United Nations Victims' Rights Statement   108
7 Accountability Advocates: Representing Victims   114
   Sabrina White
8 Masculinities and Institutional Blind Spots   130
   Jasmine-Kim Westendorf

9	Power, Consent and Peacekeeping Economies *Kathleen M. Jennings*	143
10	Gender, Race, Sexuality and PSEA *Junru Bian, Megan Daigle, Sarah Martin and Henri Myrttinen*	156
11	'We Don't Have a Word for That': Issues in Translating PSEA Communication *Emily Elderfield and Ellie Kemp*	169
12	From 'Cultural Sensitivity' to 'Structural Sensitivity' *Nour Abu-Assab*	184

PART III Looking Forward: Where to from Here?

13	Agency and Affect in PSEA: Understanding Agency through a Transnational Intersectional Lens *Nof Nasser-Eddin*	195
14	Empowered Aid: Transforming Gender and Power Dynamics in the Distribution of Humanitarian Aid *Alina Potts*	207
15	Rethinking PSEA: Reflections for Policy Makers *Jasmine-Kim Westendorf*	221
Notes		226
Index		231

List of Figures and Tables

Figures

3.1	References to the three-pronged strategy on sexual exploitation and abuse in annual reports of the UN Secretary-General, 2004–21	49
7.1	References to victims in the United Nations Secretary-General's annual reports on 'special measures for protection from sexual exploitation and abuse', 2004–21	117
14.1	Visual for the recommendation in Uganda for women travelling in groups	213
14.2	Visual for the recommendation in Lebanon for distribution in mixed-sex groups at household level	213

Table

14.1	Recommendations of women and girls for making aid distribution safer in both Uganda and Lebanon	214

List of Abbreviations

CEB	Chief Executives Board
CTDC	Centre for Transnational Development and Collaboration
DRC	Democratic Republic of Congo
GBV	gender-based violence
IASC	Inter-Agency Standing Committee
ICAI	Independent Commission for Aid Impact
MONUSCO	United Nations Organization Stabilization Mission in the Democratic Republic of Congo
OIOS	Office of Internal Oversight Services
OVRA	Office of the Victims' Rights Advocate
PSEA	protection from sexual exploitation and abuse/ prevention of sexual exploitation and abuse
RSH EE	Resource and Support Hub for Eastern Europe
SEA	sexual exploitation and abuse
SOGIESC	sexual orientation, gender identity and expression, and sex characteristics
SVRO	Senior Victims' Rights Officers
UN	United Nations
UNGA	United Nations General Assembly
UNHCR	United Nations High Commissioner for Refugees
UNPOL	United Nations Police
UNSG	United Nations Secretary-General
VRA	Victims' Rights Advocate
ZTP	zero tolerance policy

Notes on Contributors

Nour Abu-Assab is a feminist sociologist with a PhD from the University of Warwick. Nour is a multidisciplinary practitioner and academic with over 15 years of experience working on issues related to social justice in the Global South. Her interests include gender, reproductive and sexual justice, diversity and inclusion, feminist governance, safeguarding and protection, education, movement building, and environmental and intersectional feminist justice. Nour's publications address issues around identities, sexualities, migration, postcolonialism, and queer and decolonial methods.

Junru Bian is a doctoral candidate at the School of Political Studies, University of Ottawa. His research focuses on the identities, spaces and practices of peacekeeping, humanitarianism and development. As part of his research, he interviews different conflict interveners to understand how their racial, gender, sexual and classed identities can influence their everyday practices in crisis environments. He has worked in multiple humanitarian relief and development programmes in Tajikistan, Mongolia, Myanmar and Ethiopia. He is also part of the Réseau d'analyse stratégique/Network for Strategic Analysis.

Jane Connors was appointed as the first United Nations Victims' Rights Advocate for victims of sexual exploitation or abuse by United Nations and related personnel, by Secretary-General António Guterres from 2017 to 2024. This role, as set out in the Secretary-General's report on *Special Measures for Protection from Sexual Exploitation and Abuse: A New Approach*, was created to push forward his pledge that the United Nations will put the rights and dignity of victims at the forefront of its efforts to prevent and respond to sexual exploitation and abuse. As Victims' Rights Advocate, Jane supported an integrated, strategic response to victim assistance in coordination with United Nations system actors with responsibility for assisting victims. She worked with government institutions, civil society, and national and legal and human rights organizations to build networks of support and to help ensure that the full effect of local laws, including remedies for victims, were brought to bear. She brought to the position a long and multifaceted career in human rights advocacy as well as human rights and humanitarian assistance in the academic, United Nations and civil society spheres. Prior to joining the United Nations, Jane was the International Advocacy Director Law and Policy for Amnesty International in Geneva. Earlier, she held increasingly responsible posts at the Office of the High Commissioner for Human Rights in Geneva, including in the Human Rights Treaties Division, the Special Procedures Branch and the Research and Right to Development Division. From 1996 to 2002, she was Chief of the Women's Rights Section in the Division for the Advancement of Women in the Department of Economic and Social Affairs in New York. Before joining the United Nations, she was a law teacher in the School of Oriental and African Studies at the University of London, Lancaster University and the University of Nottingham, in the UK, and the University of Canberra and the Australian National University in Australia.

Megan Daigle is Senior Research Fellow in the Humanitarian Policy Group at the ODI. Her research focuses broadly on gender, sexuality, race and disability in humanitarian contexts. She has conducted research on access and attitudes to sexual and reproductive health and rights; LGBTQ+ experiences of conflict, displacement and peacebuilding; sexual and gender-based violence in and out of conflict; gender and disability in humanitarian and post-conflict settings; sex work and sex tourism; and feminist, postcolonial and queer politics. Previously, she has held positions at the University of Birmingham, the Gender and Development Network and the Gothenburg Centre of Globalization and Development, and she has worked as a consultant with International Alert, Christian Aid and Womankind Worldwide. She sits on the board of the *International Feminist Journal of Politics*. Megan holds a PhD from Aberystwyth University's Department of International Politics, with a thesis on sexual politics in Cuba. Her book, *From Cuba with Love: Sex and Money in the Twenty-First Century*, was published by the University of California Press in 2015.

Elliot Dolan-Evans recently completed a PhD in International Relations at Monash University, investigating the impact of international financial institutions' activities during war. His research focuses on the political economy of peacebuilding, the international financial institutions and questions of capitalism and health. Elliot's articles have appeared in journals such as *Security Dialogue*, the *Review of International Political Economy*, *Conflict, Security & Development*, the *Journal of Soviet and Post-Soviet Politics and Society*, the *International Studies Review* and the *Journal of Intervention and Statebuilding*. He also has qualifications and professional experience in law and medicine.

Phoebe Donnelly is Senior Fellow and Head of the Women, Peace and Security programme at the International Peace Institute. She is also Adjunct

Assistant Professor at Columbia University's School of International and Public Affairs. Phoebe's doctoral dissertation on forced marriage by rebel groups won the Peter Ackerman Award for outstanding doctoral dissertation at The Fletcher School at Tufts University in 2019. Phoebe is a Feinstein International Center visiting fellow and was previously a Women and Public Policy research fellow at Harvard Kennedy School and a Stanley Kaplan Postdoctoral Fellow at Williams College. She received her PhD in International Relations from The Fletcher School at Tufts University, a Master of Arts in Law and Diplomacy from The Fletcher School at Tufts University, and a Bachelor of Arts from the University of Wisconsin-Madison.

Emily Elderfield is Advocacy Officer at CLEAR Global, a non-profit formerly known as Translators without Borders, which works to ensure people can get information and make themselves heard, whatever their language. This work has included projects supporting language awareness and inclusion of marginalized language speakers in humanitarian action in Bangladesh, Pakistan, Somalia and Ukraine. Prior to joining CLEAR Global, she supported projects advocating against gender-based violence in Uganda and Honduras.

Kathleen M. Jennings is Research Fellow at the Department of Sociology and Political Science at the Norwegian University of Science and Technology in Trondheim. She was previously head of the section for Research and Development at the Faculty of Social Sciences, Oslo Metropolitan University, and a senior researcher at Fafo Research Institute, Oslo. She has published widely on gendered peacekeeping economies, primarily in Liberia and the Democratic Republic of Congo; sexual exploitation and abuse in peacekeeping operations; disarmament, demobilization and reintegration of ex-combatants; and women's participation in peacekeeping operations. She has fieldwork experience in Liberia, the Democratic Republic of Congo, Uganda and Haiti. Kathleen holds a PhD (political science) from the University of Oslo, an MPhil (politics) from the University of Oxford and a BA (political science, honours) from Stanford University.

Ellie Kemp is Head of Research, Evidence and Advocacy at CLEAR Global, a non-profit formerly known as Translators without Borders, which works to ensure people can get information and make themselves heard, whatever their language. Ellie leads the organization's work to provide humanitarian and development organizations with an evidence basis for more effective, two-way communication with the people they aim to serve. She originally trained and worked as a professional translator before moving into the humanitarian field during the Kosovo crisis in 1999. Her more than 20 years of experience in humanitarian action include 12 years leading programmes, teams and advocacy campaigns in Africa, Central Asia and the Balkans.

Ai Kihara-Hunt is Professor at the Graduate Program on Human Security, Director of the International Law Training and Research Hub and Director of the Research Center for Sustainable Peace, at the University of Tokyo. Her main area of research is on United Nations peace operations, in particular United Nations Police, accountability, human rights law and international humanitarian law. She has worked in Nepal, East Timor/Timor-Leste, Sri Lanka, Indonesia, Bosnia and Herzegovina, Switzerland, the UK and Japan. She was nominated by Japan and served as a member of the United Nations Police Doctrinal Development Group, which drafted the doctrinal framework for the United Nations Police in 2016–17. Prior to that, she worked with the United Nations Office of the High Commissioner for Human Rights in Nepal, where she managed a United Nations Peace Fund project on transitional justice, mapped serious violations of human rights and international humanitarian law, and served as the Security Forces Focal Point/Lead Trainer, undertaking security sector reform initiatives, security forces' curriculum reform and transitional justice-related work, as well as leading capacity building programmes for different stakeholders. Part of her work was published in 2006 as the Armed Police Force (APF) Human Rights Handbook and has been incorporated into the mandatory curriculum of the APF. She has also worked for the United Nations Transitional Administration in East Timor, the United Nations Mission in East Timor and the Organization for Security and Co-operation in Europe.

Sarah Martin has over 25 years of experience in the humanitarian and development sector. She has worked on diverse issues, including supporting front-line workers to respond to gender-based violence, researching the needs of adolescent girls, men and boy survivors, tailoring humanitarian programmes to LGBTQ+ persons and empowering women's leadership. She authored one of the first major sectoral reports on sexual exploitation and abuse, *Must Boys Be Boys? Ending Sexual Exploitation and Abuse by UN Peacekeepers*, which was published by Refugees International. She has also worked to change organizational culture to end sexual harassment, exploitation and abuse. She has worked in a variety of humanitarian organizations, including Médecins Sans Frontières, the Office of the High Commissioner for Refugees, the International Rescue Committee and the United Nations Population Fund. She was Regional GBV in Emergencies Advisor for the United Nations in Asia-Pacific and Capacity Building Advisor for the Resource and Support Hub Eastern Europe. She has field experience in Europe, Latin America, West Africa, the Great Lakes Region, the Horn of Africa, the Middle East, South and Southeast Asia, and the Pacific.

NOTES ON CONTRIBUTORS

Dyan Mazurana is Research Professor at the Fletcher School of Law and Diplomacy, where she co-directs the Gender Analysis and Women's Leadership Programme. She is Research Professor at the Friedman School of Science Policy and Nutrition. She also directs the Feinstein International Center's research programme on Women, Children, and Armed Conflict and co-directs the Master of Arts in Humanitarian Assistance programme. Mazurana's scholarship focuses on gendered dimensions of humanitarian response to conflict and crises, documenting serious crimes committed during conflict, and accountability, remedy and reparation. She serves as an advisor to several governments, United Nations agencies, human rights NGOs and child protection organizations regarding humanitarian assistance and improving efforts to assist youth and women affected by armed conflict. This work includes the protection of women and children during armed conflict, including those people associated with fighting forces, as well as remedy and reparation in the aftermath of violence. She has worked in Afghanistan, the Balkans, Nepal, and southern, west and east Africa. Mazurana has an MA and PhD in women's studies from Clark University.

Henri Myrttinen is Visiting Research Fellow at the University of Bremen, Germany, and has been working on issues of gender, peace and security for two decades, including with a focus on masculinities and diverse sexual orientation, gender identity and expression, and sex characteristics in conflicts and post conflict.

Asmita Naik has an advanced education in law and public policy and over 25 years of experience in international aid. She became an independent consultant in 2002, carrying out assignments across the globe on a wide range of issues related to human rights, protection, aid policy and management. Prior to becoming a consultant, she worked for United Nations agencies in Geneva in the 1990s. Asmita is also a part-time adjudicator on various regulatory and investigatory bodies, including the Independent Press Standards Organisation, various health profession regulators and as a magistrate in the Criminal Courts. She has a background education in law and public policy. Asmita has long-standing experience of safeguarding, having co-authored a report for the United Nations High Commissioner for Refugees/Save the Children UK on the sexual exploitation of refugee children by aid workers and peacekeepers in West Africa which led to global policy on sexual exploitation and abuse for the first time, including the 2003 United Nations Secretary-General's Bulletin. She has been engaged with this issue ever since through independent research and advocacy as well through providing technical services (for example, evaluations, risk assessments, investigations) to multilateral organizations, donor governments and NGOs. Asmita is a recognized expert in the field and has been asked to speak at global events, to be an expert witness to the UK Parliament International Development Committee's enquiry into sexual exploitation and abuse in the aid sector, to provide commentary to the media and to participate in a UK government-facilitated global Cross-Sector Safeguarding Group and United Nations Inter-Agency Standing Committee Technical Expert Groups on this subject.

Nof Nasser-Eddin is a feminist sociologist with a PhD from the University of Warwick. Nof has over 15 years of experience, which extends beyond academia, as she has also worked with different international, national and local NGOs across Arabic-speaking countries. Nof's work and publications focus on issues related to social justice, including environmental feminism, intersectional feminism, sexuality, class, refugeehood, displacement, forced migration, decolonial and queer methods, class, masculinities, sexual practices and gender performances, and agency. Nof's work also investigates the intersections of cultural, economic and political class with gender.

Leah Nyambeki is a human rights lawyer who has pioneered victim rights practice initiatives in Kenya through innovative strategic litigation, technical assistance and advocacy while working with The Victim Protection Board of Kenya, the International Justice Mission and the Kenya Truth Justice and Reconciliation Commission. Leah has translated her domestic experience into working with international NGOs, where she led investigations on sexual exploitation and abuse, child abuse, human trafficking and sexual harassment across Africa and the Middle East. She currently works as the Victim Advocate and In Country Support Coordinator for The Global Fund for HIV, AIDS, Malaria and Tuberculosis, based in Kenya. She received her LLB in Law from Makerere University in Uganda, was admitted to legal practice in Kenya in 2012 and received her LLM in Democracy Law and Governance from the University of Nairobi in 2022.

Alina Potts is a practitioner–researcher who has led programmes responding to gender-based violence in emergencies and now engages in applied research to better prevent violence. As part of the Global Women's Institute at George Washington University, she undertakes feminist participatory action research with women and girls in refugee settings to mitigate the risk of sexual exploitation and abuse in the way aid is distributed (Empowered Aid), and on mental health and psychosocial support for gender-based violence survivors in humanitarian settings. She previously coordinated violence prevention research at Unicef, including examining the intersection of violence against women and children in emergencies. As an aid worker with the International Rescue Committee, Alina led gender-based violence in emergencies programming in Cox's Bazar, Lebanon, Syria, the Democratic

Republic of Congo, Dadaab and Darfur. Her experience in forced migration extends to refugee resettlement in the US, asylum advocacy in Europe and addressing grave violations in conflict. She is actively involved in training, teaching and mentoring gender-based violence responders and researchers.

Jasmine-Kim Westendorf is Associate Professor of International Relations and Australian Research Council DECRA Senior Research Fellow at La Trobe University in Australia. She is the author of *Violating Peace: Sex, Aid and Peacekeeping* (Cornell University Press) and *Why Peace Processes Fail: Negotiating Insecurity After Civil War* (Lynne Rienner) as well as numerous articles in academic journals and public media. Jasmine's research focuses on peace and humanitarian processes – in particular, how the international community supports societies as they respond to conflict and crisis. She is interested in issues of participation and protection, and how the assumptions and behaviours of international interveners affect their capacity and credibility in the countries in which they work. Her current research focuses specifically on the nature, patterns and impacts of sexual exploitation and abuse in peacekeeping and humanitarian operations, including challenges to effective prevention and response. Jasmine has conducted field research in Timor-Leste, Cambodia, Bosnia and Herzegovina, Poland, Moldova, Romania, Sicily, Palestine, Nepal and Cyprus, and she has worked with and advised a range of international organizations on issues related to sexual exploitation and abuse and peace processes. She holds a PhD from La Trobe University.

Sabrina White recently completed her ESRC-funded PhD at the University of Leeds School of Politics and International Studies on victim-centred approaches to accountability to victims of sexual exploitation and sexual abuse perpetrated by United Nations peacekeeping troops and related personnel. She is teaching at the University of Leeds and Leeds Beckett University and is working as a gender consultant in the NGO sector on integrity and accountability in the defence and security sector. Her research focuses on the nexus of gender and anti-corruption in integrity systems in defence and security institutions, particularly responses to sexual exploitation and abuse and sexual forms of corruption. She has also worked with the United Nations Association UK in consultations with the UK government on the development of the Murad Code and improved responses to sexual exploitation and abuse in UN peacekeeping missions through the Protection from Sexual Violence Initiative. This research was funded by the Economic and Social Research Council (ESRC grant 1948667) and involved a collaborative partnership with the United Nations Association UK.

Acknowledgements

The idea for this book came out of rich discussions with practitioners and policy makers over numerous years. Many people around the world have been grappling with the challenges and imperatives of more effectively preventing and responding to sexual exploitation and abuse by peacekeepers and aid workers, and we are profoundly grateful for the ongoing willingness of those at the forefront of this work to remain in conversation with researchers about their work, experiences and ideas on the complex and often personally confronting phenomenon of sexual exploitation and abuse. These discussions are increasingly happening in a politically charged environment where issues of sexual misconduct are being weaponized by certain actors to call into question the legitimacy of, and ongoing funding for, United Nations and humanitarian actors, whose work is absolutely critical globally. We are grateful for the trust that our interlocutors have placed in us, and we hope this book proves to be a valuable contribution to the vital work of the many people within the peacekeeping and aid sectors who are committed to serving communities experiencing conflict and crisis in ways that ensure they do no harm.

We are deeply grateful to Carolyn Bys for her contributions to the conception and early stages of editing this book. We are indebted to our chapter contributors for their willingness to be a part of this book and for their generous participation in multiple workshops through the process to share knowledge and sharpen analyses. We are immensely grateful to Stephen Wenham at Bristol University Press for his enthusiasm for our idea for this book and his support in bringing it to life. Huge thanks are also due to Zoe Forbes at Bristol University Press for her careful shepherding of the book through production, as well as Lee-Ann Ashcroft and her spectacular team. Caitlin Hamilton's comments on several chapters were enormously valuable. Anonymous reviewers provided insightful feedback and advice on both the proposal and the full manuscript – thank you for your generous engagement with the substance and vision of this book.

This book would not have been possible were it not for the generous funding provided by the Australian Research Council to Jasmine's work under a Discover Early Career Research Award (DE DE210101244 – Do No Harm: Sexual Exploitation and Abuse in Humanitarian Missions).

ACKNOWLEDGEMENTS

Jasmine is thankful to Bec Strating, Kristin Bergtora Sandvik, Sara Davies and Pablo Castillo-Diaz for their invaluable advice at various points of this project. She is also indebted, as always, to her kids, Billie and Banjo, and her partner, Jem, for their encouragement, support and companionship not only during intensive work periods but through the field research which underpins her research and this book.

Elliot would like to thank his family, especially his mum, Kym, and sister, Ayla, whose patience and love throughout were immense. Elliot importantly thanks Aisha Ismail for her constant support, assistance and understanding throughout the book project, without whom he could not have completed it.

Jasmine-Kim Westendorf, Melbourne
Elliot Dolan-Evans, Havana
January 2024

Introduction: Two Decades of Dealing with Sexual Exploitation and Abuse in Peacekeeping and Aid

Jasmine-Kim Westendorf and Elliot Dolan-Evans

As this book neared completion in October 2023, the United Nations (UN) reported that nine South African peacekeepers serving in the United Nations Organization Stabilization Mission in the Democratic Republic of Congo (MONUSCO) had been detained and confined to barracks as a result of 'fraternizing, after curfew hours, at an out-of-bounds bar known to be a place where transactional sex occurs' (UN, 2023). The UN further noted that the men involved had been linked to 'systematic widespread violation' of the organization's 'zero tolerance' policy on sexual exploitation and abuse (SEA) and, moreover, that when UN Police attended the premises to assess what had been happening, the peacekeepers involved physically assaulted and threatened them (BBC, 2023). The South African National Defence Force immediately repatriated the implicated soldiers for further investigation, but the case was just the latest in what has become a regular occurrence of sexual misconduct scandals involving peacekeepers, not only in the Democratic Republic of Congo (DRC) but wherever they are deployed.

Although shocking, this case is sadly nothing new. It comes on the heels of news reports and investigations that have demonstrated the persistence of SEA by peacekeepers – including military, police and civilian personnel – and humanitarian aid workers against women, children and men in international missions around the world, despite over 20 years of efforts to prevent and ensure accountability for such misconduct. These behaviours are diverse and have ranged from opportunistic sexual assault and rape to planned, sadistic sexual violence, and from sex trafficking and the production of pornography to transactional sex (Westendorf and Searle, 2017). The latter ranges from consensual adult sex work (Jones and Cole, 2023) to sex-for-jobs schemes (Flummerfelt and Peyton, 2020) to 'survival sex', where individuals barter sex for small amounts of food or money so that they and their families can survive (Holt and Hughes, 2004; Kolbe, 2015). Research has demonstrated the remarkable longevity of the economies and cultures of abuse and exploitation that such behaviours help build in conflict- and crisis-affected societies, the long-term impacts they have for the lives of victims and survivors,[1] and the corrosive effects they have on local and global perceptions of the legitimacy of the international organizations under whose auspices they take place (Koyama and Myrttinen, 2007; Henry and Higate, 2009; Jennings and Nikolić-Ristanović, 2009; Simić, 2012; Jennings, 2015; Kolbe, 2015; Simm, 2015; Westendorf, 2020).

This book builds on the growing body of scholarly and policy literature to look back at the last two decades and ask: What has worked in efforts to prevent and respond to SEA? And what gaps or fault-lines have emerged? We bring together important voices on theory, research and praxis to provide the first comprehensive and intersectional overview of efforts to address SEA by peacekeepers and humanitarian aid workers, two decades on from the adoption of the zero tolerance policy. The book reflects on, and critiques, the challenges that have plagued the implementation of the 'protection from sexual exploitation and abuse' (PSEA; sometimes also referred to as 'prevention of sexual exploitation and abuse') agenda, the unintended consequences of the UN's approach to dealing with 'disgrace', and the missing links between the pursuit of PSEA and broader processes of decolonization, anti-racism and localization. The aim of the book is to support and inform critically important efforts to prevent and ensure accountability for misconduct by presenting clear-eyed analysis alongside practical reflections and policy-relevant conclusions. Through bringing together cutting-edge scholarship and practice-based analysis to consider how effective efforts to prevent and respond to SEA have been to date, this collection identifies key challenges and presents a range of ideas as to how these efforts can be improved in the future, including through a deeper engagement with questions of race, power, politics and governance.

Dealing with 'disgrace'

Two decades ago, the UN adopted what has become known as the 'zero tolerance' policy on SEA. The United Nations Secretary-General's (UNSG's) Bulletin on 'special measures for protection from sexual exploitation and abuse' defined *sexual exploitation* as 'any actual or attempted abuse of a position of vulnerability, differential power, or trust, for sexual purposes, including, but not limited to, profiting monetarily, socially or politically from the sexual exploitation of another', and *sexual abuse* as 'the actual or threatened physical intrusion of a sexual nature, whether by force or under unequal or coercive conditions' (UNSG, 2003: section 1). In broad terms, the Bulletin revolves around three rules: all sexual activity with children is prohibited, regardless of mistaken beliefs of the child's age; exchanging sex for money, employment, goods or services is prohibited; and sexual relationships with beneficiaries of assistance are strongly discouraged because 'they are based on inherently unequal power dynamics' (UNSG, 2003: section 3.2(d)).

The Bulletin was promulgated by Secretary-General Kofi Annan in response to a series of sexual misconduct scandals involving peacekeepers and aid workers in Bosnia, Cambodia and West Africa. The early scandals revolved around the extensive patronage of brothels by military and police peacekeepers. This involved violence and the sexual abuse of girls in Cambodia in the mid-1990s, as well as direct participation in sex trafficking and forced prostitution in Bosnia in the late 1990s, which cultivated strong cultures of impunity for such behaviour (Ledgerwood, 1994; Whitworth, 2004; Simić, 2010; Bolkovac and Lynn, 2011).

In 2001, UNHCR (the Office of the High Commissioner for Refugees) and Save the Children UK staff (including Asmita Naik, co-author of Chapter 5) raised the alarm that personnel in the UN and NGOs were abusing and exploiting women and children in refugee camps in Guinea, Liberia and Sierra Leone (UNHCR and Save the Children UK, 2002). A subsequent UN Office of Internal Oversight Services (OIOS) investigation in 2002 verified that SEA was prevalent, documenting the case of a sexual relationship between a UN civilian staff member and a 17-year-old refugee in exchange for school fees, the violent rape of girls by NGO staff, the rape of boys by UN military peacekeepers in Sierra Leone, the exchange of sex for food by NGO staff, and the refusal of international staff to take responsibility for children fathered with local women (UNSG, 2002). In his introductory comments to the report, Secretary-General Annan declared that

> Sexual exploitation and abuse by humanitarian staff cannot be tolerated. It violates everything the United Nations stands for. Men, women and children displaced by conflict or other disasters are among the most vulnerable people on earth. They look to the United Nations and its humanitarian partners for shelter and protection. Anyone employed by or affiliated with the United Nations who breaks that sacred trust must be held accountable and, when the circumstances so warrant, prosecuted. (UNSG, 2002: 1)

This sparked the first real development of SEA policy at the UN. Prior to this, documents governing peacekeeper behaviour had included broad mandates for peacekeepers to respect and promote human rights and observe the highest standards of conduct to maintain mission integrity, but they were not codified specifically in relation to SEA (Westendorf and Searle, 2017: 377). In response to the OIOS report and the Secretary-General's statements, the United Nations General Assembly (UNGA) adopted a resolution expressing grave concern at incidents of SEA and directed the Secretary-General to establish preventive and accountability measures in all peacekeeping operations and humanitarian operations, establish reporting and investigative procedures, and collect data on SEA. All UN bodies and NGOs were encouraged to do the same (UNGA, 2003). The Secretary-General consequently issued the 2003 Bulletin for all UN staff, which, in addition to delimiting prohibited behaviours, outlined duties of mission leadership to ensure accountability, including through referring cases to national authorities for criminal prosecution. It also mandated that all non-UN entities or individuals working in cooperation with the UN accept and implement those standards. The Bulletin has since been a cornerstone of SEA policy, albeit hotly contested due to its treatment of consent between adults and its implications for understanding the agency of local women involved (Otto, 2007; Simić, 2012; Westendorf, 2023b); these issues are taken up by Kathleen Jennings in Chapter 9.

Since the 2003 Bulletin, SEA policy has been developed over time, although largely in response to SEA scandals rather than proactively. A year after the Bulletin was released, *The Independent* documented the abuse and exploitation of young girls in internally displaced person camps by UN peacekeepers in Bunia, DRC, which jolted the UN into a new wave of investigations and policy development (Holt and Hughes, 2004). These shifted focus from preventive measures, such as education, to policy enforcement. At the request of the Special Committee on Peacekeeping Operations, the Secretary General commissioned a comprehensive report and strategy on peacekeeper SEA by Jordanian Prince Zeid Ra'ad Al Hussein (the Zeid Report). Introducing the Zeid Report to the General Assembly in 2005, the Secretary-General declared existing SEA measures to be 'manifestly inadequate' and called for a fundamental shift in approach (UNSG, 2005: 1). The Zeid Report found that the problem of SEA in peace operations revolved around four issues: rules on standards of conduct; the investigative process; organizational, managerial and command responsibility; and individual disciplinary, financial and criminal accountability (UNSG, 2005). Its recommendations emphasized the need for agency systems and processes to strengthen accountability.

However, while the higher levels of the UN were concerned with enhancing enforcement and accountability mechanisms, field-level staff continued to struggle with basic questions of how to implement the zero tolerance policy. For example, a review of the SEA response of MONUSCO by the former director of MONUSCO's Office for Addressing SEA found that when the office was established in 2005 in response to the Zeid Report, there were no procedures for conducting investigations, the UN's responsibility to victims was unclear and there was no guidance on how to address paternity claims

(Dahrendorf, 2006). It furthermore demonstrated that field managers and commanders did not know how to create and maintain environments that prevent SEA and often tended to 'down play the issue, or even cover up' specific cases. The report called for mission-specific training that addresses the impact and context of SEA (Dahrendorf, 2006: 10).

This call for a grounded, contextual policy approach has gone largely unheeded. Although operational directives such as curfews, non-fraternization policies, requirements to wear uniforms outside compounds and specification of off-limits locations have resulted in a decrease in reported incidents, scholars and UN staff alike have suggested that SEA has simply been pushed underground (Dahrendorf, 2006; Grady, 2010; Deschamps et al, 2015). Further, the focus on procedures for investigation conflicts with the reality that SEA, like other forms of sexual- and gender-based violence, is significantly under-reported and difficult to 'prove' to UN investigative standards (Deschamps et al, 2015; Westendorf, 2023a). There are various reasons for this, including that many victims fear retribution if they give evidence against soldiers – particularly in contexts where conflict-related sexual violence has been prevalent and perpetrated by soldiers. Additionally, witness evidence can be difficult to secure because of people movement in emergency settings, and the quality and admissibility of witness statements collected during initial interviews vary greatly. There is also often confusion, even within the UN, over who is responsible for investigating. These factors are complicated by the departure, rotation or repatriation of alleged perpetrators before investigations are completed and the UN's lack of authority over troop-contributing countries regarding investigative processes. And, finally, the reticence of both UN and troop-contributing countries' military officials to hold perpetrators accountable for SEA (discussed by Sabrina White in Chapter 7) underscores the dangers of focusing on procedural matters at the expense of the broader political factors that shape policy implementation (Bolkovac and Lynn, 2011; Burke, 2012; Deschamps et al, 2015; Stern, 2015).

In 2008, the UN General Assembly adopted a Comprehensive Strategy on Assistance and Support to Victims of SEA by UN Staff and Related Personnel, which aimed to ensure that complainants, survivors and children received appropriate medical, legal, psychosocial and other assistance (barring compensation) in a timely and effective manner (UNGA, 2008). This marked an important shift in policy from a focus on training and administrative accountability toward a victim-centred response to SEA, which was further taken up by Secretary-General António Guterres (unpacked in chapters 3, 6 and 7). However, despite these policy developments, an independent 2010 Inter-Agency Standing Committee (IASC) global review of the extent of policy implementation on SEA post Zeid found that very little had been achieved in both peacekeeping and humanitarian contexts. It found that understanding and acceptance of new policies by staff and managers remained low, leadership by senior managers was critically absent, policies and guidance had generally not been communicated to the field and implementation was 'patchy, poor or non-existent' (IASC, 2010: 7).

It is therefore somewhat unsurprising that SEA remained a significant problem in peacekeeping and humanitarian operations, culminating in both the 2015 child sexual abuse scandal involving French peacekeepers in the Central African Republic, and the subsequent institutional cover-up, and the 2018 sexual exploitation scandal involving Oxfam GB staff in Haiti. Both led again to a flurry of policy development. The scandal in the Central African Republic led to a shift in the UN leadership's action and language around SEA, with Secretary-General Ban Ki-Moon telling Member States at the UN Security Council that the Secretariat alone could not address the 'global scourge' of SEA by peacekeeping troops, demanding that they take responsibility for ensuring justice for victims of their peacekeepers' misconduct (Ki-Moon, 2015). He subsequently committed to naming and shaming in annual reports those countries whose personnel perpetrated SEA, created a new office in the UN for the first Special Coordinator on Improving the UN Response to Sexual Exploitation and Abuse, to streamline SEA policy, and established the Trust Fund in Support of Victims of Sexual Exploitation and Abuse. Secretary-General Guterres undertook further reforms on SEA policy as a priority of his tenure, spearheading a new policy paradigm that revolved around a victim-centred approach, recognizing that the system-wide nature of the problem of SEA required responses from a multistakeholder network (the development of this agenda and its implementation are the subject of chapters 3, 6 and 7). Guterres' new approach also fostered greater transparency of reporting and investigations, to end impunity for perpetrators (UNSG, 2017). In a major departure from previous policy, the report identified gender inequality and discrimination as the root of SEA. As part of efforts to put victims at the heart of UN responses, the Secretary-General established the system-wide role of the UN Victims' Rights Advocate (VRA) and the associated Office of the Victims' Rights Advocate (OVRA), which reports directly to the Secretary-General. Jane Connors, the inaugural Victims' Rights Advocate, reflects on her work and the challenges and opportunities this new approach has presented in Chapter 6.

Against this backdrop, the 2018 Oxfam scandal led to a flurry of work under the banner of 'safeguarding' in the humanitarian sector – a buzzword lifted from the UK child protection context and imported into the international humanitarian space as a new approach to PSEA (Bruce-Raeburn, 2018; Sandvik, 2019). While PSEA efforts largely focused on training and reporting mechanisms, safeguarding has brought end-point accountability into much sharper focus (Sandvik and Westendorf, 2023). One of the main outrages of the Haiti scandal was that not only had the aid workers in question avoided punishment for their sexual exploitation of local women, but they had been able to find work elsewhere in the sector. Consequently, policy work in the aftermath aimed at ensuring that perpetrators would be excluded from the sector, through global mechanisms to facilitate the disclosure of misconduct between aid organizations and police forces. These include the IASC's Misconduct Disclosure Scheme, which introduced minimum standards for the sharing of sensitive information about recruitment of workers against whom allegations of misconduct had been substantiated, and Project Soteria, a UK government-funded Interpol project that aims to bring law enforcement and aid organizations together to detect, investigate and ensure criminal accountability for such behaviour – noting that only some sexual misconduct is in fact criminal, even if all is administratively prohibited in both UN and humanitarian organizations. This work is pursued in tandem with efforts to strengthen the traditional responses to prevention and reporting, including through the establishment of the Resource and Support Hub, and important efforts to improve investigation capacities within humanitarian organizations. The UK's Foreign, Commonwealth and Development Office has been spearheading an initiative to establish a 'Common Approach to Protection from Sexual Exploitation, Abuse and Harassment' across peacekeeping, humanitarian missions and aid agencies.

Around the same time as the Oxfam scandal, the #MeToo movement drew attention to another cycle of misconduct scandals in the aid sector, spurring the #AidToo movement, discussed by Sarah Martin in Chapter 1. This movement highlighted the issue of SEA by aid workers against not only local community members but also their colleagues. #AidToo helped individuals speak publicly about their organizations' failures in relation to preventing and appropriately addressing this issue of 'internal' SEA – which has often been downplayed as 'sexual harassment' despite often reflecting the very same behaviours considered to be SEA when perpetrated against local communities (these dynamics are taken up by Phoebe Donnelly and Dyan Mazurana in Chapter 4 and Junru Bian, Megan Daigle, Sarah Martin and Henri Myrttinen in Chapter 10).

Despite the much greater public and institutional attention to these issues and the efforts to better address them through improved policy and practice, many of which are unpacked in further detail in the chapters that follow, allegations of SEA by peacekeepers and humanitarian aid workers continue apace. The UN now shares information on allegations in almost real time, including information on the UN entity/agency the alleged perpetrator works for and their personnel category, and the gender and age of the victim, the nature of the allegation, whether a paternity claim is associated with the allegation, and the statues of assistance rendered and the investigation.[2] According to this data, between 1 January and 30 October 2023, 171 allegations were reported by non-peacekeeping UN entities – for example, UN departments, agencies and funds – and 48 allegations were made against personnel in peacekeeping or special political missions. The UN now also publishes data on allegations reported by implementing partner organizations – in the same time period, 232 allegations were reported. The personnel involved are not under the authority of the UN, but their work is funded by UN partnerships. Unfortunately, there is no consolidated source of data for allegations in the humanitarian sector, and organizations are not obligated to report such data publicly. Furthermore, it is important to note that it is unlikely that UN statistics reflect the true scale of SEA. Grady's research suggested that UN data is unreliable due to poor data management, potential false allegations and likely under-reporting of SEA (Grady, 2016) – the latter has also been flagged by UN investigators themselves (Dahrendorf, 2006: 13–14; Deschamps et al, 2015: 16). Other studies also suggest rates of SEA are significantly higher than official statistics suggest: a study in Liberia found that an estimated 58,000 women aged 18–30 engaged in transactional sex during the first nine years of the UN Mission in Liberia – this was with UN personnel in more than 75 per cent of cases, and more than half of the women reported their first encounter happened before they were 18 (Beber et al, 2016).

Although allegations are not a sign of failed policy – in fact, they can be understood as proof that victims are more willing to report their experiences of SEA and know how to do so – they do raise the question of whether the now-wide collection of activities to prevent and respond to SEA are working as they should, and what course corrections might be valuable now, two decades after the UN's zero tolerance policy on SEA (and action on it) was institutionalized. The critical backdrop to this question is the broader reckoning the UN and aid sector have been going through with questions of power centring on diversity, equity and exclusion and their corresponding localization, anti-racism and decolonization movements, which have been taken up by organizations with varying intensity (Abrahams, 2023). While significant work has been done in the sector to localize, decolonize and address institutionalized structures of discrimination, there has been a failure to connect these issues with the shortcomings of important efforts to address sexual misconduct. The chapters contained in this book capture and respond to these challenges, building bridges throughout between analysis of the PSEA agenda and these broader processes of reckoning with power. In doing so, they help us to make sense of both the effectiveness and unintended consequences of efforts to date for preventing and responding to SEA and chart a course for scholars and practitioners to better approach this complex and critically important issue from now on.

Overview of the book

In this book, we have assembled a diverse, international group of scholars and practitioners who have cumulatively worked for decades on addressing

SEA in peacekeeping and aid from varied standpoints. We believe that there is a dire need to overcome the structural and systemic obstacles to a local, grounded response in addressing SEA by peacekeepers and aid workers. Moreover, such grounded responses are vital for institutions and practitioners that implement the PSEA agenda to sufficiently engage with the victim perspective, which will subsequently permit more humane and robust strategies in instituting a genuine victim-centred framework. Therefore, this collection is structured around three distinct overarching themes that combine both scholarly perspectives and implications for practice regarding PSEA: the origins and purview of the PSEA agenda; its implementation and institutionalization; and the future directions of PSEA.

Part 1 closely traces the historical beginnings of the PSEA agenda and its evolving scope, with a close analytical engagement with key trends in patterns of SEA and the accountability, prevention and support frameworks that have evolved since the early 2000s. In Chapter 1, Sarah Martin reflects on the progress, lapses and evolution of the UN and humanitarian sector's institutional responses to SEA in the two decades since the publication of her groundbreaking report, *Must Boys Be Boys? Ending Sexual Exploitation and Abuse in UN Peacekeeping* (Martin, 2005). Drawing on her personal and professional experiences in the sector, Martin argues that an ongoing challenge in addressing SEA is the underlying conservative, patriarchal cultures inherent to peacekeeping and humanitarian organizations. She argues that these foster an institutional ignorance to abuses of power within and outside the organization, which are only ever superficially addressed in response to public scandals.

In Chapter 2, Ai Kihara-Hunt spotlights the underexamined role of the UN Police in ensuring accountability and the provision of remedies in SEA. Despite this potential, she argues, UN Police officers are often untrained in democratic policing and are in fact sometimes directly involved in SEA as perpetrators, which erodes trust in both the UN and the broader rule of law that peacekeepers are mandated to support. These implications thus necessitate an engagement by scholars and practitioners in the often overlooked place of UN Police in PSEA responses.

In Chapter 3, Sabrina White and Leah Nyambeki chart the history and development of victim and survivor support frameworks on PSEA, focusing particularly on strategies and practices of remedial action from the 1990s to 2023. Drawing on professional insights from Nyambeki's work as a victims' rights advocate in Kenya for the Global Fund, they illustrate that although the remedial action response has evolved significantly through the development of the UN's integrity system for PSEA, and aligns more closely now with victims' rights frameworks, many old challenges remain. In particular, they argue that inadequate attention has been given to the reasons why victims fear reporting, the obstacles to obtaining substantive assistance, gaps in investigative capacity and the implications of donor expectations on PSEA, and that these challenges intersect to limit the protection of victims' and survivors' rights in practice. These challenges are taken up in greater detail in chapters 6 and 7 by Jane Connors and Sabrina White, respectively, which deal with the realization of the victims' rights agenda.

To round out Part 1 of the book, in Chapter 4, Phoebe Donnelly and Dyan Mazurana begin to unravel the patterns of SEA *within* peacekeeping and humanitarian aid organizations. They trace how SEA has primarily been used to refer to abuses perpetrated by peacekeepers and humanitarian workers against civilian women and children *outside* the peacekeeping mission. Drawing on two surveys conducted with peacekeepers and humanitarian workers, they explore the perpetration of sexual abuse against persons *inside* peacekeeping and aid missions, arguing that abuse is enabled by inequitable and sexist power dynamics and toxic organizational cultures that perpetuate and create impunity for sexual abuse both inside and outside peacekeeping and humanitarian organizations.

Part 2 turns to the implementation and institutionalization of PSEA across different contexts, and considers how the experiences of local communities in PSEA responses are interpreted and expressed *for* them through outsider eyes. The chapters engage deeply with questions of neocolonialism, power dynamics, gender and racial equality, and language in charting the recent 'victim-centred' turn of the international community in response to SEA. In Chapter 5, Asmita Naik and Jasmine-Kim Westendorf demonstrate how PSEA efforts have missed the mark in designing necessary solutions in the two decades since Naik co-authored the UN report *Investigation into Sexual Exploitation of Refugees by Aid Workers in West Africa* (UNGA, 2002). The chapter reveals how policy developments are often reactively driven by well-known SEA cases rather than addressing underlying systemic issues with the complaints, investigative and disciplinary processes at the UN. Naik and Westendorf argue that far from the often repeated claim that the problem lies in 'under-reporting' by victims and difficulties in finding cases, the real issue is 'under-action' by organizations to effectively prevent and ensure accountability for SEA, which in turn contributes to the endurance of cultures of impunity in the sector.

In Chapter 6, Jane Connors, the UN Victims' Rights Advocate, builds on the analysis provided in Chapter 3 of the emergence of victim support mechanisms. Connors provides greater detail and nuance as to how such mechanisms within the UN system have worked in practice since the launch in 2017 of UN Secretary-General Guterres' victim-centred approach to confronting SEA by UN staff and non-staff personnel. She traces the genesis and mandate of the UN Office of the Victims' Rights Advocate and its efforts in embedding a victims' rights approach across the UN system. She maps the multitude of challenges the Office faces in securing a victims' rights approach in SEA prevention and response, especially relating to the differing – and often contested – meanings of accountability and the realities of victim support. Connors makes a powerful case for the transformative role of victims' rights advocates on the ground in UN missions, highlighting the impact of the presence of a person tasked with prioritizing victims' rights and who victims trust and can turn to for individual assistance. Connors' chapter is followed by the UN Victims' Rights Statement, a powerful and groundbreaking affirmation adopted by the UN in 2023 that articulates the rights individuals have as victims of sexual exploitation or abuse committed by UN staff or related personnel.

Continuing the theme of accountability and the work of the Office of the Victims' Rights Advocate, in Chapter 7 Sabrina White brings a critical lens to evaluating the UN's turn to victim-centred approaches. Whereas previous chapters have focused predominantly on victim assistance mechanisms, this chapter turns to the *advocacy* agenda, considering how victims have been discursively represented in official UN policy documents. She demonstrates the necessity of the UN's Office of the Victims' Rights Advocate for advancing political will to pursue prevention of, and responses to, SEA in the UN system while identifying the structural challenges that affect how the voices of victims can be *heard* in UN and other accountability processes. White argues that rather than representing a break with previous approaches, the UN's victim-centred approach to SEA prioritizes procedural accountability over substantive redress for victims and remains in thrall to a lack of political will among Member States to properly provide for the material and accountability needs of victims of SEA. White's analysis complements that of previous chapters addressing victims' rights approaches, by exploring the conceptual and practical limitations facing efforts to advocate on behalf of victims and survivors of SEA and identifying the political and institutional limitations on the form and function of that advocacy.

In Chapter 8, Jasmine-Kim Westendorf picks up the investigation of power dynamics in peacekeeping and humanitarian systems that give rise to the perpetration of SEA. Drawing on interviews with policy makers and practitioners, she explores how institutions and policy makers have often made sense of the causes of SEA in terms of a problem of masculinity among peacekeepers, while concurrently failing to adequately capture the dynamics at play in peacekeeper and humanitarian SEA. Westendorf argues that the dominant narratives that centre masculinity as the cause of SEA are shaped by institutional imperatives in ways that, perhaps inadvertently, render invisible the intersecting local, international, normative and systemic factors that create the conditions in which some personnel choose to perpetrate SEA against local people. Consequently, policy efforts have too often focused on individualized compliance based on a 'bad apple' model of understanding perpetrators rather than addressing the structural, normative and contextual factors that together give rise to SEA.

Kathleen Jennings takes the considerations of power and peacekeeping economies further in Chapter 9 by examining how the UN's zero tolerance policy on SEA regulates idealized, but contested, understandings of sexual intimacy and consent. The chapter problematizes the assumed location of power in the (male) peacekeeper, which often ignores local experiences and interactions, and examines how the contradictions between the zero tolerance policy and the realities of peacekeeping economies risks destroying the entire edifice of PSEA. Jennings argues that the zero tolerance policy writes into regulation narrow understandings of sexual intimacy against puritanical and contested conditions for consent, in contexts characterized by complex power relations between interveners and residents. She demonstrates how, cumulatively, the restrictiveness of the zero tolerance policy's conceptualizations of sexual relations and consent and the way the policy flattens power relations between peacekeepers and locals are often counter to their lived experiences, which undermines the policy's legitimacy and complicates its implementation.

In Chapter 10, Junru Bian et al take up the questions of race, sexuality and gender, examining the colonial–patriarchal, heteronormative foundations of the humanitarian system and how these structures and the associated dominant self-image of the humanitarian sector continue to enable sexual abuse against both beneficiaries of their work and their own colleagues. They argue that to seriously address SEA perpetrated by humanitarians, the sector must address fundamental gendered and racialized power imbalances, practices and structures that permeate the humanitarian sector.

In Chapter 11, Emily Elderfield and Ellie Kemp extend our attention to what and who is excluded in dominant PSEA narratives and practices by exploring the realities of language-related exclusion in the humanitarian system. The authors draw on their work at CLEAR Global (formerly Translators Without Borders), a humanitarian translation organization, to argue that humanitarians are not equipped to design PSEA strategies that communicate on SEA in culturally, contextually and linguistically comprehensible ways. They demonstrate that organizations also do not adequately understand or address the intersections between language and other factors of vulnerability that increase individuals' exposure to SEA and decrease their access to support. Drawing on ground-level evidence from several contexts, Elderfield and Kemp illustrate the need to develop victim-centred approaches to PSEA that focus on meeting material needs and highlight the centrality of language and discourse to PSEA implementation.

Nour Abu-Assab continues the conversation on communication and shared understanding in Chapter 12, interrogating the 'universal' models of safeguarding systems exported by international organizations, which often ignore local contexts. She argues that although international organizations claim their safeguarding systems are culturally sensitive, those systems are usually built around the experience of those inside the international organizations and fail to take contextual understandings of local circumstances and dynamics into account. Abu-Assab demonstrates that instead of an over-determinative focus on 'cultural sensitivity', it would be far more productive for international organizations to address the structural sensitivity of their interventions through an intersectional perspective that does not promote cultural exceptionalism and can provide a more robust foundation for restorative and transformative justice processes in response to SEA.

Part 3 ties together the preceding chapters and charts a way forward for the PSEA agenda and offers concrete recommendations for practitioners and scholars to prioritize the agency and empowerment of survivors in a victim-centred approach. In Chapter 13, Nof Nasser-Eddin draws on her work at the Centre for Transnational Development and Collaboration to problematize the lack of appropriate acknowledgement of agency within victim- and survivor-centred approaches to PSEA. She sets a restorative vision for a transnational approach which understands oppression and violence as shared global phenomena, with regard to which no culture is exceptional – as distinct to merely internationalism – and decentralizes Western understandings of victim-centred approaches to focus on the immaterial needs and reparations of victims, which are often more vital aspects of justice for those affected by SEA. The chapter charts how transnationalism can shift hegemonic understandings of agency and victim-centred approaches to build just accountability frameworks.

In Chapter 14, Alina Potts unpacks the Empowered Aid approach, calling for the shifting of power relations in systems of humanitarian aid provision which currently exclude those receiving humanitarian assistance from efforts to understand and address the risks of SEA in their lives and communities. She argues that unequal power on the basis of heteronormative gender roles – whereby men have more access to and control over resources than women – is a root cause of SEA and that this is entrenched in systems of humanitarian aid, whereby those dependent on aid for survival have the least say in how it is delivered and the least ability to hold aid actors accountable. This chapter utilizes two case studies that demonstrate recipient-informed models of safer and more empowered aid delivery, which also speaks to dismantling the barriers of reporting and addressing SEA in recipient communities.

Finally, the book concludes with reflections on the policy implications of this collection for how we might better understand and respond to SEA in peacekeeping and aid. Jasmine-Kim Westendorf reflects on the fault-lines that have emerged in PSEA, the cumulative lessons posed by the chapters in this volume and the potential for new ways of making sense of and responding to SEA perpetrated by peacekeepers and humanitarian aid workers, against those populations in conflict and crisis that they have been sent to support and protect.

References

Abrahams, J. (2023) 'The end of the NGO?', *Prospect*, 4 October. Available from: www.prospectmagazine.co.uk/world/international-development/63350/the-end-of-the-ngo (accessed 18 October 2023).

BBC (2023) 'South Africa recalls UN peacekeepers accused of sexual misconduct in DR Congo', *BBC*, 15 October. Available from: www.bbc.com/news/world-africa-67115883 (accessed 28 October 2023).

Beber, B., Gilligan, M., Guardado, J. and Karim, S. (2016) 'Peacekeeping, compliance with international norms, and transactional sex in Monrovia, Liberia', *International Organization*, 71(1): 1–30.

Bolkovac, K. and Lynn, C. (2011) *The Whistleblower: Sex Trafficking, Military Contractors, and One Woman's Fight for Justice*, New York: Macmillan.

Bruce-Raeburn, A. (2018) 'Opinion: systemic racism and sexism undermine efforts to make aid sector safer', *Devex*, 12 October. Available from: www.devex.com/news/sponsored/opinion-systemic-racism-and-sexism-undermine-efforts-to-make-aid-sector-safer-93608 (accessed 15 August 2022).

Burke, R. (2012) 'Attribution of responsibility: sexual abuse and exploitation, and effective control of Blue Helmets', *Journal of International Peacekeeping*, 16(1): 1–46.

Dahrendorf, N. (2006) *Sexual Exploitation and Abuse: Lessons Learned Study, Addressing Sexual Exploitation and Abuse in MONUC*, New York: United Nations Department of Peacekeeping Operations.

Deschamps, M., Jallow, H. and Sooka, Y. (2015) *Taking Action on Sexual Exploitation and Abuse by Peacekeepers: Report of an Independent Review on Sexual Exploitation and Abuse by International Peacekeeping Forces in the Central African Republic*, New York: United Nations External Independent Panel.

Flummerfelt, R. and Peyton, N. (2020) 'More than 50 women accuse aid workers of sex abuse in Congo Ebola crisis', *The New Humanitarian*, 29 September. Available from: www.thenewhumanitarian.org/2020/09/29/exclusive-more-50-women-accuse-aid-workers-sex-abuse-congo-ebola-crisis (accessed 24 May 2022).

Grady, K. (2010) 'Sexual exploitation and abuse by UN peacekeepers: a threat to impartiality', *International Peacekeeping*, 17(2): 215–28.

Grady, K. (2016) 'Sex, statistics, peacekeepers and power: UN data on sexual exploitation and abuse and the quest for legal reform', *The Modern Law Review*, 79(6): 931–60.

Henry, M. and Higate, P. (2009) *Insecure Spaces: Peacekeeping, Power and Performance in Haiti, Kosovo and Liberia*, London: Zed Books.

Holt, K. and Hughes, S. (2004) 'Sex and death in the heart of Africa', *The Independent*, 25 May. Available from: www.independent.co.uk/news/world/africa/sex-and-death-in-the-heart-of-africa-564563.html (accessed 29 June 2016).

IASC (Inter-Agency Standing Committee) (2010) *2010 IASC Global Review of Protection from SEA*, Geneva: IASC.
Jennings, K.M. (2015) 'Life in a "peace-kept" city: encounters with the peacekeeping economy', *Journal of Intervention and Statebuilding*, 9(3): 296–315.
Jennings, K. and Nikolić-Ristanović, V. (2009) *UN Peacekeeping Economies and Local Sex Industries: Connections and Implications*, MICROCON Research Working Paper No 17. Available from: http://papers.ssrn.com/sol3/papers.cfm?abstract_id=1488842 (accessed 1 July 2016).
Jones, S. and Cole, N. (2023) 'Business as usual for Sierra Leone sex workers despite aid sector bans', *The New Humanitarian*, 19 April. Available from: www.thenewhumanitarian.org/news-feature/2023/04/19/aid-industry-sex-workers-sierra-leone (accessed 10 October 2023).
Ki-Moon, B. (2015) 'Full transcript of Secretary-General's remarks to press on the Central African Republic', United Nations Secretary General, 12 August. Available from: https://www.un.org/sg/en/content/sg/press-encounter/2015-08-12/full-transcript-of-secretary-generals-remarks-press-the-central-african-republic (accessed 15 March 2024).
Kolbe, A. (2015) '"It's not a gift when it comes with price": a qualitative study of transactional sex between UN peacekeepers and Haitian citizens', *Stability: International Journal of Security and Development*, 4(1): 1–26.
Koyama, S. and Myrttinen, H. (2007) 'Unintended consequences of peace operations in Timor Leste from a gender perspective', in A. Chiyuki, C. Cedric and T. Ramesh (eds) *Unintended Consequences of Peacekeeping Operations*, New York: United Nations University Press, pp 23–43.
Ledgerwood, J. (1994) 'UN peacekeeping missions: the lessons from Cambodia', *Analysis from the East-West Center*, 11: 1–10.
Martin, S. (2005) *Must Boys Be Boys? Ending Sexual Exploitation and Abuse in UN Peacekeeping*, Washington, DC: Refugees International.
Otto, D. (2007) 'Making sense of zero tolerance policies in peacekeeping sexual economies', in V. Munro and C. Stychin (eds) *Sexuality and the Law*, Abingdon: Routledge, pp 259–82.
Sandvik, K. (2019) '"Safeguarding" as humanitarian buzzword: an initial scoping', *Journal of International Humanitarian Action*, 4: 3. doi: 10.1186/s41018-019-0051-1
Sandvik, K. and Westendorf, J.-K. (2023) 'Safeguarding sex: the technopolitics of humanitarian genomic accountability', *Global Studies Quarterly*, 3(2): 1–13.
Simić, O. (2010) '"Boys will be boys": human trafficking and UN peacekeeping in Bosnia and Kosovo', in L. Holmes (ed) *Trafficking and Human Rights*, Cheltenham: Edward Elgar Publishing, pp 79–94.
Simić, O. (2012) *Regulation of Sexual Conduct in UN Peacekeeping Operations*, New York: Springer.

Simm, G. (2015) *Sex in Peace Operations*, Cambridge: Cambridge University Press.

Stern, J. (2015) *Reducing Sexual Exploitation and Abuse in UN Peacekeeping: Ten Years after the Zeid Report*, Washington, DC: Stimson Centre.

UN (United Nations) (2023) 'DR Congo: UN peacekeepers suspended over serious misconduct charges', *United Nations*, 12 October. Available from: https://news.un.org/en/story/2023/10/1142247 (accessed 28 October 2023).

UNGA (United Nations General Assembly) (2003) *Investigation into Sexual Exploitation of Refugees by Aid Workers in West Africa*, UN Doc A/RES/57/306.

UNGA (United Nations General Assembly) (2008) *United Nations Comprehensive Strategy on Assistance and Support to Victims of Sexual Exploitation and Abuse by UN Staff and Related Personnel*, UN Doc A/RES/62/214.

UNHCR and Save the Children UK (2002) *Sexual Violence & Exploitation: The Experience of Refugee Children in Guinea, Liberia and Sierra Leone*, London: UNHCR.

UNSG (United Nations Secretary-General) (2002) *Investigation into Sexual Exploitation of Refugees by Aid Workers in West Africa*, UN Doc A/57/465.

UNSG (United Nations Secretary-General) (2003) *Secretary-General's Bulletin: Special Measures for Protection from Sexual Exploitation and Sexual Abuse*, UN Doc ST/SGB/2003/13.

UNSG (United Nations Secretary-General) (2005) *A Comprehensive Strategy to Eliminate Future Sexual Exploitation and Abuse in United Nations Peacekeeping Operations*, UN Doc A/59/710.

UNSG (United Nations Secretary-General) (2017) 'Note to correspondents: the Secretary-General's report on Special Measures for Protection from Sexual Exploitation and Abuse: A New Approach', *United Nations*, 9 March. Available from: www.un.org/sg/en/content/sg/note-cor respondents/2017-03-09/note-correspondents-the-secretary-general's-rep ort-special-measures-for-protection-sexual-exploitation-and-abuse-new-approach (accessed 12 June 2017).

Westendorf, J.-K. (2020) *Violating Peace: Sex, Aid, and Peacekeeping*, Ithaca, NY: Cornell University Press.

Westendorf, J.-K. (2023a) 'A problem of rules: sexual exploitation and UN legitimacy', *International Studies Quarterly*, 67(3): 1–13.

Westendorf, J.-K. (2023b) 'Sex on mission: care, control and coloniality in peacekeeping and humanitarian operations', *International Affairs*, 99(4): 1653–72.

Westendorf, J.-K. and Searle, L. (2017) 'Sexual exploitation and abuse in peace operations: trends, policy responses and future directions', *International Affairs*, 93(2): 365–87.

Whitworth, S. (2004) *Men, Militarism, and UN Peacekeeping: A Gendered Analysis*, Boulder, CO: Lynne Rienner Publishers.

PART I

Where We've Been: The Origins and Scope of Protection from Sexual Exploitation and Abuse

1

Reflections on 20-Plus Years of Protection from SEA Work

Sarah Martin

Introduction

In 2005, in my report *Must Boys Be Boys? Ending Sexual Exploitation and Abuse in UN Peacekeeping*, I quoted Jean-Marie Guéhenno, the then head of the UN Department of Peacekeeping Operations, who said: 'If we fail ... to approve decisive and visible steps to limit sexual abuse, then it will have serious implications for the future of peacekeeping' (Martin, 2005). Two decades have passed since I first went to Liberia and became aware of the problem of sexual exploitation and abuse (SEA[1]) by UN peacekeepers and humanitarian aid workers. In this chapter, I reflect on the time I have spent working for humanitarian NGOs and UN agencies to address gender-based violence (GBV) and the evolution of the SEA response in that time. Using my personal experiences in the sector, I argue that the sector needs to focus more on prevention and that a central challenge is conservative patriarchal cultures in peacekeeping and humanitarian organizations. These cultures catalyse a wilful ignorance to rampant abuses of power involving men who sexually harass and harm women – their co-workers, job applicants, patients or employees of other agencies, fellow refugees and affected community members. As a result, organizations often prefer to sanction the whistle-blowers than remove the perpetrator or change the status quo.

In this chapter, I first detail my experiences as a whistle-blower in humanitarian organizations. From first-hand experience, I detail how efforts to deal with internal patriarchal cultures are limited and, with few exceptions, tend to occur in a flurry in the aftermath of a media scandal. Second, I suggest that subsequent responses do not support survivors or whistle-blowers and only make superficial changes rather than systematically addressing the underlying power imbalances at play. Even the language used is evolving to further obscure the problem and harm survivors. Finally, this chapter demonstrates that unsupportive systems within humanitarian organizations can actually be hostile to survivors and that the current technocratic response is insufficient to address SEA.

My experience as a whistle-blower

Must Boys Be Boys? addressed the widespread problem of peacekeepers sexually abusing women and children in UN peacekeeping missions in Liberia, Sierra Leone and Haiti, and also in the Democratic Republic of Congo (DRC). I had hoped that the report would generate sufficient attention to make the UN act on the 'code of conduct' violations that were rife among troops. Awareness of the problem seemed low. Due to the report's focus on peacekeeping, I only briefly touched on the issue of SEA by humanitarian aid workers, but examples were everywhere in West Africa and Haiti. Although the West Africa 'food for sex' scandal was only a year old (Gillan and Moszynski, 2002), I noticed during my 2003 visits to Liberia and Sierra Leone that the positions created to address SEA were already running out of funds and being phased out. It was a sign of things to come.

I have since grown accustomed to watching the cycle around SEA repeat itself. There is a familiar pattern to how SEA scandals emerge: The act of harm takes place. It is either covered up or ignored by relevant personnel or authorities. Someone gets tired of the hypocrisy and leaks information to the media, who then report on it. There is subsequently a bright spotlight of attention and scolding from donors, which leads to statements of regret from the organization. There is sometimes a flurry of activity to assure donors and concerned parties that the problem is being addressed, including hiring consultants or creating positions or 'focal points' to address the issue (Westendorf and Searle, 2017). There is a 'boom' in SEA response, usually focused on improving reporting mechanisms or providing training for staff designed to improve reporting. Prevention is almost always ignored in favour of response, which is usually designed to protect the organization's reputation and ensure continued funding. The survivors are irrelevant.[2] For instance, when Anders Kompass courageously blew the whistle on French troops sexually abusing children in the Central African Republic, the media attention quickly turned to how he was treated rather than on providing support to the survivors (Laville, 2016). There was little follow-up in the media on the fate of the abused children.

Over the years, in my work to prevent and respond to GBV, including SEA in humanitarian emergencies around the world, I have seen this cycle repeatedly. Processes are developed, then training manuals and reporting forms grow dusty on bookshelves and broken links clutter websites. What has been missing throughout are concerted efforts to improve the political will to address the root problems that underpin the perpetration of SEA: namely, ending gender inequality in the neocolonial peacekeeping and humanitarian systems that are rife with sexism, racism and abuse of power (see Bian and colleagues in Chapter 10). Despite a proliferation of communications using buzzwords like 'survivor centred', the focus is rarely on the survivor (and children she may have). Organizations instead choose short-term Band-Aid solutions. This was not inevitable, however. There was a moment in 2018 when it seemed like things were changing.

In 2017, after spending many years working with NGOs and the UN to improve GBV response in Afghanistan, Pakistan, Nepal, Syria, Jordan and Myanmar, I moved to Europe and began working in Germany, Greece and Serbia with Afghan and Syrian refugees arriving in Europe. The European response to GBV seemed different to what I had seen in Haiti, West Africa, and the Great Lakes in the early 2000s. It was easier to talk about GBV, including sexual violence against men and boys. The GBV sector was bigger. There was programming in Syria and the refugee-hosting countries to support Syrian GBV survivors, unlike in the dark days of the early 2000s, when no one spoke about the abuse of Liberian and Sierra Leonean girls. GBV was not as invisible as it had been in my first years of humanitarian aid work, though we were not yet talking about SEA by aid workers. We were, however, starting to talk about sexual harassment. In 2015, I joined the board of Report the Abuse, a small NGO that was documenting sexual harassment and abuse in the aid sector. I also connected with the Humanitarian Women's Network, which was conducting a survey on gender discrimination and harassment in the aid worker sector.

In October 2017, I was idly scrolling through Twitter when Alyssa Milano's infamous #MeToo tweet came up. I froze, unsure whether to retweet. Like most women my age, I had experienced some GBV. But this tweet made me feel like change was in the air. I hit retweet. Then I called my friends – women aid workers – and we began to talk about what to do about sexual harassment in the aid sector, the 'twin' to SEA that I wrote about in 2005. It is always a topic of discussion after the GBV training sessions that I lead, but typically with a sort of exasperated acknowledgement that little will change. In response to the burgeoning #MeToo movement, I wrote an anonymous piece with a friend that was published on a humanitarian website (Anonymous, 2017). We were optimistic. Things were different; women were speaking out. By the time the Oxfam scandal hit the media in February 2018, the invigorated women of the humanitarian sector were ready to seize the moment. Sexual harassers, like Brendan Cox at Save the Children, were being pushed out (Simpson, 2018).

Emboldened, I decided to write a 'tell-all' blog about the patriarchal and abusive culture and the men who benefited from it at a respected medical humanitarian organization where I had worked (Martin, 2018). I was unprepared for the backlash to the article within the organization, naively believing it would not be widely read and that my colleagues who had been there would recognize the few (thinly veiled) abusers I mentioned and support me. At first it went well. The leaders of the organization called me and arranged meetings to discuss the problem. Yes, they acknowledged, it has been a problem and they wanted to do something about it. What did I think they should do? I spoke at length about culture change in the organization's headquarters and ideas such as survivor panels to vet actions. I urged sanctions against the men who felt empowered to make the organization their private sexual playground. I felt heartened by the meetings and received support from the women leaders with whom I spoke.

Then the media pressure started, and it became obvious that funding could be impacted. Save the Children and Oxfam were being pilloried daily and donors were halting funding. I declined to talk to the media, preferring to stay silent. The tone of the organization's engagement with me shifted significantly, and, unwilling to engage with aggressive investigators, I declined to formally participate in the investigation, which felt like a defensive, rather than investigative, endeavour.

The BBC ran a story that identified eight whistle-blowers. But it focused on allegations of staff using prostitutes and trading medication for sex, not on the workplace culture within the headquarters that I had written about. It did, however, reference an internal report that said a third of female employees it had spoken to had been touched inappropriately at work (Adams, 2018). When the programme was aired, it did not have much impact, and the organization issued an apology expressing 'regret that the whistle-blowers had not felt able to voice their concerns directly' (Preston, 2018). The BBC report had the misfortune of airing around the time that Donald Trump was enacting executive orders separating children seeking asylum in the US from their parents (Gonzales, 2018). This showed that the power of the media is fickle, and timing is everything.

While my personal attempt at activism did not immediately appear successful, the #AidToo movement did inspire some change. There were efforts to strengthen investigations, oversight and data collection. There was independent scrutiny from the UK Parliament's International Development Committee (see House of Commons International Development Committee, 2021). In autumn 2018, the UK government hosted a Safeguarding Summit, but forgot to ask any of the activists to speak at the event, so Alexia Pepper de Caires, a whistle-blower at Save the Children, had to interrupt the UK Secretary of State in the middle of her speech to be heard (Abrahams, 2018). Every organization was terrified that they would be the next Oxfam – which was ironic as prior to the 2018 scandal, Oxfam was seen as one of the few organizations that took SEA seriously (Abrahams, 2023). Donors spent millions on programmes like CLEAR Check, aimed at preventing perpetrators from being hired in the sector. Capacity building efforts, like the Resource and Support Hub, were initiated to help small organizations address SEA. Training sessions from UN actors were ubiquitous.

With very few exceptions, however, the media focused on sexual harassment survivors who were middle class and mostly White European or North American women, as had been the case with the stories on Save the Children UK. The stories told by African and Asian colleagues did not receive the same attention, nor were the links to the abuse of local women and children drawn out in these stories (Daigle et al, 2020). The voices of women and girls who had been sexually exploited by humanitarians were not the focus of the mainstream media.

Yet the problem was not going away. The 'solutions' still ignored prevention. On women aid workers' Facebook groups, people mentioned problems with the Ebola response in the DRC. The news broke in 2020 (Flummerfelt and Peyton, 2020). Over 50 women spoke out and at least 30 women said workers from the World Health Organization were involved in SEA. Then a report came out about unchecked sexual abuse by aid workers in camps in South Sudan (Medneck and Craze, 2022). In 2022, Russia invaded Ukraine and women and children poured across the borders into neighbouring Eastern European countries, where human traffickers lined up to meet them. In Poland, men volunteered to help refugees and explicitly told workers at reception points that they sought to help young childless Ukrainian women (Pertek et al, 2022). In the UK, some Ukrainian women received suggestive messages, requesting sexual favours from British men in return for a place to stay (Syal, 2022). There was little analysis of why the humanitarian sector was not making progress to prevent SEA.

So why is nothing changing? Based on my 25 years of experience as a woman humanitarian aid worker, specializing in preventing and responding to GBV, and based on conversations with like-minded colleagues, I offer here a few thoughts and ideas for enacting change.

Existing systems do not support survivors or whistle-blowers

The system places too much pressure on survivors, the most vulnerable people involved. SEA responses continue to focus on increasing reporting by survivors and communities rather than on prevention. The response to sexual harassment in the sector is the same: there is no action without a report. But what does reporting look like to a survivor of SEA? A survivor must summon their nerve and navigate a mysterious, opaque and often hostile process in an elusive quest for justice. Rather than supporting survivors, investigation processes impose a pseudo-criminal investigation process, looking for weaknesses in the survivor's report, assessing the credibility of witnesses and finding ways to exclude cases from organizational responsibility, as the independent investigation into the World Health Organization scandal in the DRC illustrated (Mukundi and Flummerfelt, 2023). For SEA survivors who are reliant on the organization in question for ongoing humanitarian support, there is little incentive to report, and many opt to withdraw their complaint when the process begins. Indeed, Lucy Heaven-Taylor, an SEA investigations specialist, in a private conversation noted that one of the most common questions in her training sessions is what to do if the survivor does not want to cooperate. Even if they do cooperate, survivors are often abandoned once the system takes over, with many never informed about the outcome of the investigation (Westendorf, 2020).

My own experience as a whistle-blower showed me how difficult and harmful reporting can be – and it likely would have been worse had I still been employed at the organization and dependent on my salary to survive. I was a relatively privileged North American woman who was no longer working for the organization, and even I felt bulldozed by the process. Survivors of sexual harassment have spoken publicly about how demoralizing the process of seeking accountability is – examples are Martina Broström, who was fired from UNAIDS after blowing the whistle on sexual and financial misconduct (Broström shared her story in Gender-based Violence Area of Responsibility Commnity of Practice, 2023; see also Ratcliffe and Beaumont, 2019), and Miranda Brown, who was pushed out of the Office of the High Commissioner for Human Rights for her role in revealing the sexual abuse of children by peacekeepers in the Central African Republic (Edwards, 2018).

A survivor-centred approach to responding to SEA complaints must recognize the potential harms reporting can result in for survivors and that mandatory reporting can thus be detrimental (International Committee of the Red Cross and British Red Cross, 2020; Heaven Taylor and Broström, 2023). When it comes to stopping perpetrators, to take the pressure off survivors, there must be more bystander and third-party reporting. There are approaches for linking complaints to the perpetrator rather than relying on the survivor. For example, if there are enough complaints about someone (even if they do not trigger a formal complaint), the organization should be pushed to investigate the behaviour of the alleged perpetrator without compelling survivors to come forward to tell their story. Another system tries to connect survivors who complain. We have seen from the high-profile cases of Harvey Weinstein, Brett Kavanaugh and Russell Brand that learning the perpetrator is being accused can encourage other survivors to find strength in numbers and realize that they are not alone. I certainly saw this in the response to my blog. However, these examples demonstrate that reporting still relies on survivors engaging in a damaging process and speaking about their experiences.

Additionally, survivors need more support throughout the reporting process – particularly for sexual harassment reporting internal to their organization – which is often held to the standard of a criminal justice proceeding. Organizations are often required by labour law to document a specific policy violation and provide evidence before terminating employment of a perpetrator, and many of the humanitarian organizations have not put in place the policies and procedures that can support that. Organizational responses are usually quite cautious and driven by lawyers seeking to ensure that the organization is not sued by the perpetrator for improper termination. There is little support for the survivor, and it seems that whistle-blowers and survivors end up leaving the organization or are pushed out while the perpetrator hides behind 'due process'. Action Against Prohibited Conduct is a small organization trying to change that.[3] They bill themselves as 'activist lawyers with a rights-based and survivor-driven approach to justice and accountability' and offer up their services to support humanitarian and development workers seeking justice (Action Against Prohibited Conduct, nd). But the cases are many and the activist lawyers are few. They receive far more requests for help than they can address. Too often, women who try to report sexual harassment are discouraged and pressured to drop the case. Attitudes of victim blaming and 'himpathy' are rampant in this sector.[4]

For SEA survivors living in humanitarian emergencies, the situation is even more grim. They rarely have access to support for the physical, emotional and legal ramifications of speaking out about violence. 'They said they'd help us with psychosocial support. We haven't seen it. They said they will bring financial support. We haven't seen it', SEA survivors in the DRC told *The New Humanitarian* (Mukundi and Flummerfelt, 2023; see also Sabrina White in Chapter 7 and Jasmine-Kim Westendorf in Chapter 8 on this point). Guidelines say to refer SEA survivors in humanitarian emergencies to services by local women's organizations offering physical and emotional health (and sometimes legal) support. The women working in these local women's organizations understand the needs of the women living there, and they are aware of struggles that survivors face in lodging a criminal complaint and know what the women and children that they serve need to survive. Yet it has been well documented that women's organizations are not sufficiently resourced (International Rescue Committee, 2020). For the cost of the salary of one senior P5 professional in a UN office, a small local women's organization could provide support to many survivors, yet the money is just not there. 'Honestly, the budget was really very small', said a project manager of a local organization managing a nine-month project to support survivors of the DRC Ebola scandal, noting that they had received funding of roughly US$65,000 to support the survivors they could reach (Mukundi and Flummerfelt, 2023).

Language obscures the problem

There is a trend in the sector to introduce new, less explicit language that obscures the problem of sexual exploitation, abuse and harassment behind acronyms and buzzwords. Historically, this area of work has been framed in terms of sexual exploitation and abuse, foregrounding the harm done to the survivor, but since 2018 there has been an effort by predominantly British-based organizations, funded by the UK government and charity sector, to introduce the term 'safeguarding' (Sandvik, 2019). This term supposedly shifts the focus to what humanitarian aid workers should do, but it further obscures the issue of sexual exploitation or sexual abuse and the harm done to the survivor. It conflates traditional protection programming (abuse happening inside the communities) with abuse happening inside and by the humanitarian sector. Almost everything – from bullying by a co-worker to the rape of children by aid workers – becomes a 'safeguarding issue'. I agree with one critic who called out the

> fusion of abuses against beneficiaries with abuses against staff resulting in a detraction in focus from those most vulnerable and lacking in recourse; the pursuit of criminal justice solutions for behaviours that either do not reach the criminal threshold or do not have a realistic prospect of criminal conviction; and the blind transference of approaches used in stable Western democracies for tackling child abuse and sexual violence into war-torn contexts without any semblance of the rule of law. (Naik, 2022)

I had my own experience working to promote 'safeguarding' at the Resource and Support Hub for Eastern Europe (RSH EE) from 2022 to 2023. RSH EE's country assessments in Moldova, Poland and Romania found that the local organizations that they wanted to target were mystified by the term 'safeguarding'. Civil society organizations could speak about discrimination against refugees and eloquently list the many hurdles refugees were facing that they need to be 'safeguarded' against, but no one seemed to be able to discuss humanitarian actors forcing women into sex or women refugees being pressured into having sex to survive (RSH EE, 2023). In some training sessions, there was a backlash against the idea that kind-hearted aid workers might harm refugees. While conservative societal taboos around sex, alongside participants' understandable sense of pride about supporting their neighbours, may contribute to this reluctance, the confusing and vague language of 'safeguarding' also seems to be a factor. It is reminiscent of the problems we have experienced in the sector with 'doing gender mainstreaming' – the language is confusing and it is everyone's problem but no one's responsibility.

Finally, I have encountered new and mystifying acronyms springing up around the issue of SEA and sexual harassment. I was recently asked about 'pruseah', a word I did not recognize. The humanitarian sector has always had a love affair with acronyms, and the graphic term 'sexual exploitation and abuse' has turned into the innocuous acronym SEA. The acronym further evolved to PSEA (variously spelled out as 'preventing' or 'protection from' SEA), sometimes amended with an 'H' (for harassment) to become PSEAH, or recently with an 'R' (for 'responding') to become PRSEAH, the troublesome new 'word' that I learned recently. I have even seen PRSEAHIE used (for the unwieldy 'preventing and responding to sexual exploitation, abuse and harassment in emergencies'). To the uninitiated, it is completely unclear what acts of harm are being discussed that should be prevented or responded to. The voices of survivors and the harm that they experience is erased as humanitarian organizations focus on forms, procedures and acronyms rather than treating the issue as the human rights violation that it is and addressing the very real pain that survivors and their children endure.

The insufficiency of technocratic responses

In the Ukraine refugee response, there was a flurry of media articles about traffickers gathering at the Polish–Ukraine border, ready to grab women fleeing the war. The sexualization of women from Ukraine is particularly visible on social media, where Ukrainian women and girls are objectified and described as more beautiful, attractive and obedient than 'western' women. Commenters in Facebook groups freely mention their belief that Ukrainian women are submissive and would not refuse sex with them, indirectly inciting abuse (Pertek et al, 2022).

Humanitarian aid workers are not immune to the social norms of their communities. Ingrained tendencies towards 'victim blaming' can lead to a blindness around seeing risks or even cases of sexual exploitation and abuse. Moldova, Romania and Ukraine have all been cited as high-risk trafficking countries. Reports show that GBV and gender inequality are rampant in the refugee-hosting countries of Poland, Romania, and Moldova (OSCE, 2019). Pregnant women are denied access to reproductive health and abortion in Poland. The restriction on Ukrainian men leaving the country meant that most of the refugees would be households headed by single women along with vulnerable persons with disabilities, older persons and unaccompanied children – those that we know are most vulnerable to 'safeguarding' risks. But despite these well-publicized risks, it has been difficult to discuss SEA in the Ukraine refugee response with any clarity. Very few reports of SEA exist. While innovative people have developed apps, websites and other technological ways for women to report, the barriers that women face in taking the first steps to reporting have not changed. Technology will not solve the patriarchal systems that blame women survivors and excuse their male abusers. It will not solve the fact that when Ukrainian women and children became vulnerable, many men around the world saw this as a great opportunity to abuse them (Pertek et al, 2022). In fact, technology seems to be finding new ways to abuse women and attack feminists en masse (United Nations Population Fund, 2023).

Change will require broader transformations in culture within the humanitarian sector. The culture is very patriarchal, and much of the change since the #AidToo movement began has been window dressing. A central challenge is the conservative, risk-averse patriarchal power structures that turn a blind eye to rampant abuses of power among their friends (Spencer, 2018; Martin, nd). These abuses of power involve men who sexually harass and harm women and vulnerable people living in humanitarian settings. Rather than be appalled at the rampant hypocrisy of deploying men who cause harm to the women, men, boys, girls and non-binary people trying to survive natural disasters, war zones and infectious diseases, the leaders of these organizations prefer to sanction the whistle-blowers. It is too difficult to remove the perpetrators or change the status quo.

With few exceptions, the overwhelmingly male leadership structure of the humanitarian world supports the 'old-boy network' and uses all the tools in the book to resist real change. In 2017, Kate Gilmore, a senior UN official, called out the 'systemic calamity' and 'hypocrisy' in the humanitarian sector, noting that it would be very difficult 'to change the status quo within humanitarian NGOs and agencies, which she described as dominated by a "culture of toxic tolerance" towards sexual aggression, homophobia, sexism, and racism' (in Edwards, 2017). Despite claims to change the culture, perpetrators are reinstated to their duties due to loopholes (Dodds, 2023), while survivors like Martina Broström wait years to hear the results of their reports.

Although the UN seems particularly toxic, the culture of international NGOs is not too dissimilar. Indeed, the 'myth of own innocence' often has them convinced that they do not need to work on changing (Bruno-van Vijfeijken, 2019). The problem is that 'silence creates tacit approval' (Bruno-van Vijfeijken, 2019: 4, quoting Rock et al). Despite cosmetic changes like lunchtime discussions for employees to talk about racism, harassment and empowerment in the workplace (and using worrisome acronyms like GEDI in relation to their 'gender, equality, diversity and inclusion' initiatives), many things seem to stay the same. When I spoke out about the toxic workplace cultures in 2018, I was told repeatedly 'don't worry, things are changing', yet issues continue to arise. In 2020, Arnab

Majumdar, an employee at a major international NGO that I had worked at previously, was compelled to write to *The Guardian* to complain about the rigid resistance to change around addressing diversity – particularly racial diversity – in hiring, which resulted in him being accused of 'reverse racism' by the predominantly White men he was trying to engage in discussion. Elsewhere, he referred to the toxic culture at this organization, this time around racism (Majumdar, 2020), and this was very familiar to me. While the organization claimed things had changed since my time there, it seems that the people in power had not.

One solution that many discuss is having women in charge for a change. I considered satirically proposing that we ban all men from deploying into humanitarian emergencies; however, patriarchal cultures also include women. Women play a role in upholding these abusive systems in the humanitarian sector, because that is how the patriarchy works. Despite the many women in the sector, there are many who still believe that they must promote men's interests to succeed and generally use the patriarchal systems to support themselves. Hiring women is not enough to take down this culture.

Conclusion

Perhaps only the public drubbing that Oxfam took in 2018 can trigger any real change, though I am not convinced that truly addressed the problem. For a short time, I had an optimistic view that things could change. Donors were fighting to fund SEA programmes and the number of job announcements for SEA consultants were soaring. Opportunities to work as SEA investigators, coordinators and reporting specialists seemed to be everywhere as organizations sought expertise to help them. But money to support SEA prevention and response seems to be running out again.[5] The attention, like the money, is, as always, going elsewhere.

A truly feminist approach in action, not just words, is needed. Keeping silent maintains the status quo. Feminists have known this for years and continuously shout about the issue, to the displeasure of those who would like to keep the status quo in place. So, we have spoken out – but this is not enough. Despite the co-option of feminist language to proclaim feminist foreign policies and feminist humanitarian aid, the humanitarian system has not actually done the feminist work of challenging abuses of power and racial and gender inequality. The language changes but the faces of power do not. There remains little appetite to destroy the old guard in power and replace it with something radical and new. The humanitarian system seems to prefer a facelift with new buzzwords instead.

One promising feminist approach is the work of the Global Women's Institute's Empowered Aid project, which centres the voices of the women and girls who are targeted for sexual exploitation and abuse (see Alina Pott's work on this in Chapter 14). Listening and talking to the women and girls themselves and using their experiences to develop the programme fulfils an actual feminist principle and could potentially change the way that humanitarian aid is delivered.

However, I do not feel very optimistic for any wholesale change in the sector at this point. Efforts to deal with this toxic culture continue to be limited and, with few exceptions, only occur in a flurry in the aftermath of a media scandal. The spotlight on sexual harassment in humanitarian aid sectors and the ongoing problem of sexual exploitation and abuse has moved on for the time being. Organizations have made some superficial changes rather than addressing this in a systematic way that addresses the underlying power imbalances at play. The gender equality and diversity positions and programmes that were initiated in the aftermath of #AidToo seem to be withering away. Unfortunately, it seems the humanitarian sector will continue to do business as usual, as it has for the last two decades. Perhaps artificial intelligence and drones will replace aid workers and end the scourge of sexual exploitation and abuse of vulnerable women, girls, boys and others. But, then again, maybe technology will just figure out better ways to exploit them.

References

Abrahams, J. (2018) 'Controversy as investigated charity takes on key role in UK safeguarding scheme', *Devex*, 18 October. Available from: www.devex.com/news/controversy-as-investigated-charity-takes-on-key-role-in-uk-safeguarding-scheme-93698 (accessed 25 October 2023).

Abrahams, J. (2023) 'The end of the NGO?', *Prospect*, 4 October. Available from: www.prospectmagazine.co.uk/world/international-development/63350/the-end-of-the-ngo (accessed 25 October 2023).

Action Against Prohibited Conduct (nd) 'Take action', *Action Against Prohibited Conduct*. Available from: www.aapc.legal/action (accessed 29 February 2024).

Adams, A. (2018) 'Médecins Sans Frontières staff "used local prostitutes"', *Civil Society*. Available from: www.civilsociety.co.uk/news/msf-apologises-after-bbc-reports-widespread-sexual-misconduct-issues.html (accessed 25 October 2023).

Anonymous (2017) '#MeToo in the humanitarian world: the humanitarian world is not populated by saints', *The New Humanitarian*, 20 October. Available from: www.thenewhumanitarian.org/opinion/2017/10/20/metoo-humanitarian-world (accessed 25 October 2023).

Bruno-van Vijfeijken, T. (2019) '"Culture is what you see when compliance is not in the room": organizational culture as an explanatory factor in analyzing recent INGO scandals', *Nonprofit Policy Forum*, 10(4): 20190031. doi 10.1515/npf-2019-0031

Chotiner, I. (2020) 'Kate Manne on the costs of male entitlement', *The New Yorker*, 4 September. Available from: https://www.newyorker.com/news/q-and-a/kate-manne-on-the-costs-of-male-entitlement (accessed 15 March 2024).

Collins, L. (2021) 'Exclusive: "I thought I'd be killed"', *Mail Online*, 8 February. Available from: www.dailymail.co.uk/news/article-9211953/Hotel-maid-sparked-international-scandal-accused-Dominique-Strauss-Kahn-speaks-out.html (accessed 24 February 2024).

Daigle, M., Martin, S. and Myrttinen, H. (2020) '"Stranger danger" and the gendered/racialised construction of threats in humanitarianism', *Journal of Humanitarian Affairs*, 2(3): 4–13.

Dodds, P. (2023) 'WHO calls in experts to decide on conflicting Ebola sex abuse reports', *The New Humanitarian*, 1 March. Available from: www.thenewhumanitarian.org/news/2023/03/01/who-calls-experts-decide-conflicting-ebola-sex-abuse-reports (accessed 25 October 2023).

Edwards, S. (2017) 'UN must end "toxic tolerance" of sexual abuse of aid workers, top official says', *Devex*, 27 June. Available from: www.devex.com/news/un-must-end-toxic-tolerance-of-sexual-abuse-of-aid-workers-top-official-says-90534 (accessed 25 October 2023).

Edwards, S. (2018) 'The high price of being a UN whistleblower', *Devex*, 24 May. Available from: www.devex.com/news/sponsored/the-high-price-of-being-a-un-whistleblower-92752 (accessed 25 October 2023).

Flummerfelt, R. and Peyton, N. (2020) 'More than 50 women accuse aid workers of sexual abuse in Congo Ebola crisis', *The New Humanitarian*, 29 September. Available from: www.thenewhumanitarian.org/2020/09/29/exclusive-more-50-women-accuse-aid-workers-sex-abuse-congo-ebola-crisis (accessed 25 October 2023).

Gender-Based Violence Area of Responsibility (GBV AOR) Community of Practice (2023) 'Shifting the focus: applying the survivor-centered approach to PSEA in the aid sector' [video], *YouTube*. Available from: https://youtu.be/PswxED7bsqk (accessed 25 October 2023).

Gillan, A. and Moszynski, P. (2002) 'Aid workers in food for sex scandal', *The Guardian*, 27 February. Available from: www.theguardian.com/society/2002/feb/27/voluntarysector (accessed 25 October 2023).

Gonzales, R. (2018) 'Trump's executive order on family separation: what it does and doesn't do', npr, 20 June. Available from: www.npr.org/2018/06/20/622095441/trump-executive-order-on-family-separation-what-it-does-and-doesnt-do

Heaven Taylor, L. and Broström, M. (2023) *Victim/Survivor-Centered Approach to Protection from Sexual Exploitation, Abuse and Harassment in the Aid Sector*, Geneva: CHS Alliance. Available from: www.chsalliance.org/get-support/resource/victim-survivor-centred-approach-pseah/ (accessed 25 October 2023).

House of Commons International Development Committee (2021) *Progress on Tackling the Sexual Exploitation and Abuse of Aid Beneficiaries: Government Response to the Seventh Report of the Committee, Session 2019–21*, HC 1332. Available from: https://committees.parliament.uk/publications/5347/documents/53234/default/ (accessed 24 February 2024).

International Committee of the Red Cross and British Red Cross (2020) *Forced to Report: The Humanitarian Impact of Mandatory Reporting on Access to Health Care for Victims/Survivors of Sexual Violence in Armed Conflict and Other Emergencies*, London: International Committee of the Red Cross.

International Rescue Committee (2020) *Where Is the Money? How the Humanitarian System Is Failing in Its Commitments to End Violence against Women and Girls*, International Rescue Committee.

Laville, S. (2016) 'UN whistleblower who exposed sexual abuse by peacekeepers is exonerated', *The Guardian*, 18 January. Available from: www.theguardian.com/world/2016/jan/18/un-whistleblower-who-exposed-sexual-abuse-by-peacekeepers-is-exonerated (accessed 25 October 2023).

Majumdar, A. (2020) 'Bearing witness inside MSF: "I resisted the idea that I could be significantly hampered by my race"', *The New Humanitarian*, 18 August. Available from: www.thenewhumanitarian.org/opinion/first-person/2020/08/18/MSF-Amsterdam-aid-institutional-racism (accessed 25 October 2023).

Martin, S. (2005) *Must Boys Be Boys? Ending Sexual Exploitation and Abuse in UN Peacekeeping*, Washington, DC: Refugees International.

Martin, S. (2018) '"Holier than thou" MSF needs its own #MeToo moment', *Cassandra Complexity*. Available from: https://cassandracomplexblog.wordpress.com/2018/05/12/holier-than-thou-msf-needs-its-own-metoo-moment/ (accessed 25 October 2023).

Mednek, S. and Craze, J. (2022) 'Alleged sex abuse by aid workers unchecked for years in UN-run South Sudan camp', *The New Humanitarian*, 22 September. Available from: www.thenewhumanitarian.org/2022/09/22/exclusive-alleged-sex-abuse-aid-workers-unchecked-years-un-run-south-sudan-camp (accessed 25 October 2023).

Mukundi, R. and Flummerfelt, R. (2023) 'WHO sex abuse victims say help is too little too late', *The New Humanitarian*, 8 March. Available from: www.thenewhumanitarian.org/investigations/2023/03/08/exclusive-who-sex-abuse-victims-say-help-too-little-too-late (accessed 25 October 2023).

Naik, A. (2022) 'Tackling sexual exploitation and abuse by aid workers: what has changed 20 years on?', *Humanitarian Practice Network*, 81: 4. Available from: https://odihpn.org/publication/tackling-sexual-exploitation-and-abuse-by-aid-workers-what-has-changed-20-years-on/ (accessed 25 October 2023).

OSCE (2019) 'OSCE-led survey on violence against women - main report'. Available from: https://www.osce.org/secretariat/413237 (accessed 26 March 2024).

Pertek, S., Kuznetsova, I. and Kot, M. (2022) 'Not a Single Safe Place': The Ukrainian Refugees at Risk of Violence, Trafficking and Exploitation. Findings from Poland and Ukraine, Birmingham: University of Birmingham.

Preston, R. (2018) 'MSF apologises after BBC reports "widespread" sexual misconduct issues', Civil Society, 21 June. Available from: www.civilsociety.co.uk/news/msf-apologises-after-bbc-reports-widespread-sexual-misconduct-issues.html (accessed 25 October 2023).

Ratcliffe, R. and Beaumont, P. (2019) 'UN #MeToo whistleblower sacked for alleged sexual and financial misconduct', The Guardian, 16 December. Available from: www.theguardian.com/global-development/2019/dec/16/un-metoo-whistleblower-sacked-for-alleged-sexual-and-financial-misconduct-unaids-martina-brostrom (accessed 25 October 2023).

RSH EE (2023) 'Poland country assessment: safeguarding support for Ukrainian refugees'. Available from: https://easterneurope.safeguardingsupporthub.org/documents/poland-country-assessment-safeguarding-support-ukrainian-refugees (accessed 26 March 2024).

Sandvik, K. (2019) '"Safeguarding" as humanitarian buzzword: an initial scoping', Journal of International Humanitarian Action, 4(1): 1–6.

Simpson, S. (2018) 'Save the Children dismissed staff over sexual harassment allegations, charity boss confirms', The Standard, 20 February. Available from: www.standard.co.uk/news/uk/save-the-children-dismissed-staff-over-sexual-harassment-allegations-charity-boss-confirms-a3771331.html (accessed 25 October 2023).

Spencer, D. (2018) Cowboys and Conquering Kings: Sexual Harassment, Abuse and Exploitation in the Aid Sector, Global Interagency Security Forum. Available from: www.gisf.ngo/wp-content/uploads/2020/02/2241-Danielle-Spencer-2018-Cowboys-and-Conquering-Kings.pdf (accessed 25 October 2023).

Syal, R. (2022) 'Stop matching lone female Ukrainian refugees with single men, UK told', The Guardian, 13 April. Available from: www.theguardian.com/world/2022/apr/13/stop-matching-lone-female-ukraine-refugees-with-single-men-uk-told (accessed 25 October 2023).

United Nations Population Fund (2023) Measuring Technology-Facilitated Gender-Based Violence: A Discussion Paper, University of Melbourne, United Nations Population Fund and kNOwVAWdata. Available from: www.unfpa.org/publications/measuring-technology-facilitated-gender-based-violence-discussion-paper (accessed 25 October 2023).

Westendorf, J.-K. (2020) Violating Peace: Sex, Aid, and Peacekeeping, Ithaca: Cornell University Press.

Westendorf, J. and Searle, L. (2017) 'Sexual exploitation and abuse in peace operations: trends, policy responses and future directions', International Affairs, 93(2): 365–87.

2

United Nations Police as a Double-Edged Sword for SEA Accountability

Ai Kihara-Hunt

Introduction

United Nations Police (UNPOL) is a distinct component of United Nations (UN) peace operations, which has the potential to play a significant role in delivering accountability for sexual exploitation and abuse (SEA), although there is often a gap between this and the actual role UNPOL plays. This chapter focuses on the potential and actual roles that UNPOL plays in achieving accountability for SEA. SEA includes crimes, such as rape or sexual violence, abusive behaviours and consensual sexual relationships, including transactional sex, if they are based on the abuse of a position of power (UN, 2003: section 3.2b). Naturally, there is a wide variety of SEA, and responses should differ. Therefore, accountability has multiple different paths.

Peace operations include operations focusing on unarmed monitoring of ceasefire agreements, robust and comprehensive peacekeeping that emerged after the end of the Cold War, peace enforcement operations without full consent of the host state, operations that have the rule of law and state building as the central aim, UN's transitional administrations and, recently, after entry into the 21st century, more robust stabilization-style operations (De Coning, 2020).[1] Increasingly, UN peace operations are deployed in fragile situations and have protection of civilians mandates, which have become the main aim of several missions (Andersen, 2007), including protecting children and protecting against conflict-related sexual violence. There has also been a trend towards more implicit authorization of the use of force (Andersen, 2007) and increasing partnership between the UN and regional organizations and coalitions of states. There are three categories of peacekeeping personnel – military, police and civilian – though UNPOL did not exist in early missions. While UN peace operations started in 1948, UNPOL – previously the Civilian Police – began in the 1960s in the United Nations Operation in the Congo. Out of the approximately 90,000 personnel who currently work for UN peace operations, there are around 9,000 UNPOL personnel (UN Peacekeeping, nd).

UNPOL personnel are deployed either in state-based units under national command or individually. 'Formed police units' undertake tasks that require a robust posture or coherent response, and they generally work for protection of VIPs and mission installations, protection of civilians and tasks that require rapid and coherent responses, such as riot or crowd control. 'Individual police officers' are employed directly by the UN and work on reforming, restructuring and rebuilding a host state's police and other law enforcement agencies through training and advising. They also take up interim law enforcement tasks and work on the protection of mission personnel and installations. Tasks related to protection of civilians are also partly delivered by individual police officers. 'Specialized police teams' are small teams of police with specific expertise, seconded by Member States. Other than the recruitment process, specialized police teams are generally organized within the individual police officers' framework (UN Department of Peace Operations, 2019). Formed police unit personnel are selected and sent by UN Member States. The majority of them come from African and South Asian states. Some individual police officers are selected and seconded by the sending state; others apply directly to the UN. A small number of personnel, for example, some staff officers, work for UN Headquarters and are sent on missions (UNPOL, nd).

This chapter focuses on UNPOL's roles – in both their institutional function and individual conduct – in achieving accountability for SEA. This is vitally important for UN peace operations because the rule of law is set as the UN's central aim and accountability is an essential element for the rule of law. The UN sets out police as a key actor for building or rebuilding the rule of law, and that makes it imperative that UNPOL makes positive contributions in delivering SEA accountability in peace operations. Paying attention to the unique and important role that UNPOL plays in SEA accountability, the chapter seeks to answer the following question: what are the positive and negative roles that UNPOL plays in accountability for SEA in UN peace operations? The next section elaborates on the link between the rule of law and accountability, including by making the definition of accountability clear, and places UNPOL in that picture. The section after that discusses how allegations and information regarding SEA incidents are treated in UN peace operations and highlights the central role that UNPOL plays, or can play. The section that follows assesses how well UNPOL as an institution, comprising individual personnel, has functioned in relation to

SEA accountability. The chapter reveals that UNPOL has been expected to play a significant role in SEA accountability and has been contributing greatly to investigations and other aspects at the structural level, but that the behaviour of individual officers and commanders has sometimes posed risks to UNPOL's contribution. In addition, UNPOL's contribution varies quite a lot, depending on the nature of particular police units and their operations on the ground.

UNPOL in the rule of law and accountability

By 2004, the UN formally recognized the importance of the rule of law in its broader mission, including in peace operations. Rule of law is defined as:

> a principle of governance in which all persons, institutions and entities, public and private, including the State itself, are accountable to laws that are publicly promulgated, equally enforced and independently adjudicated, and which are consistent with international human rights norms and standards. It requires, as well, measures to ensure adherence to the principles of supremacy of law, equality before the law, accountability to the law, fairness in the application of the law, separation of powers, participation in decision-making, legal certainty, avoidance of arbitrariness and procedural and legal transparency. (Annan, 2004: 4)

Its importance has since been reinforced by UN Member States (UNGA, 2012) as well as by the Secretary-General. The rule of law is one of the UN's universal and indivisible core values and principles (UNGA, 2012), 'fundamental to lasting peace and security', and thus 'foundation[al] for conflict prevention, peace-making, sustaining peace and peacebuilding' (Guterres, 2023: 3–4).

Within the rule of law, accountability is a key principle (Bural and Neligan, 2005). In the context of UN peace operations, this term has several different meanings. In this chapter, the term is used in a restrictive way to mean responsibility of various actors to hold wrongdoers to account and provide redress to the victims following particularized or general allegations of SEA incidents. Effective accountability mechanisms create a deterrent effect.

The Secretary-General's approach is that the rule of law is central to all UN activities and that accountability as part of the rule of law is important for serious crimes and breaches of international law, including sexual violence (Guterres, 2023: 2, 4). While SEA is not only sexual violence, holding SEA abusers to account in order to live up to the rule of law standard that the UN preaches, and to provide redress for the victims – beyond treating the abusers as mere 'bad apples' – is therefore vitally important for the UN.

In delivering SEA accountability, UNPOL is in a key position. It is the main actor that can collect information about the local environment and about particularized SEA allegations, which it does through patrols, community policing and protection of civilians, all of which involve direct communication with local people. UNPOL also has expertise in criminal investigation. Specialized police teams are often involved in specific types of investigation, such as organized crime or sexual violence. Protection of victims and witnesses is also part of police tasks. In fact, UNPOL's functions have been transformed significantly since its foundation, when these were restricted to monitoring and training local police. The early role meant that UNPOL kept its distance from local institutions and the population. UNPOL was under military command until 1974 when the UN Peacekeeping Force in Cyprus established policing as an independent unit so that police could respond to communal tension. This meant that UNPOL started to interact with the local population. Since the mid-1990s, UNPOL has also delivered policing services itself, including investigations, searches, arrests, detention and crowd and riot control (for example, in the UN Transitional Authority in Cambodia, the UN Mission in Haiti and transitional administrations in Kosovo and Timor-Leste). When delivering policing tasks, UNPOL acted as a role model. In some missions, such as the UN Observer Mission in El Salvador and the UN Mission in Haiti, reforming the local police was the central aim. There, UNPOL directly created local police forces (Durch, 2010). Where the UN was the transitional government in a post-conflict society in Kosovo and Timor-Leste, UNPOL led the establishment of the local police at the same time as delivering policing tasks. In these missions, the power and practice of law enforcement derives from the assumption that the UN is the sovereign authority (Dwan, 2002). At the same time, formed police units came into existence (Kihara-Hunt, 2017).

In the 21st century, the (re)establishment of rule of law has become the central aim and a major element of UN peace operations' exit strategy. UNPOL has gained a more central role in achieving the UN's mission. This means that UNPOL has gained influence over the operation and behaviour of local police – it has started to focus on restructuring, training and reforming local police forces – as well as the future of the rule of law institutions in host states (Kihara-Hunt, 2017). Protection of civilians mandates require UNPOL to be involved in all phases, with formed police units delivering a central role in physical protection of civilians facing imminent threats and individual police officers working on the establishment of safe environments. Because protection of civilians requires an understanding of the people who need protection, and because it involves direct physical protection, UNPOL works very closely with the protected population. In more recent stabilization-type missions, the situations that UNPOL personnel are deployed into may make it harder for them to contribute to the rebuilding of rule of law institutions, because of the fragile situation on the ground. In a recent development, a new police mission was established in October 2023 in Haiti to provide security against gangs (UN, 2023). Even in such stabilization or security operations, UNPOL still works alongside local police to rebuild national legal institutions and nurture respect for the rule of law.

Because of the roles that UNPOL plays, it is able to influence not only the process of (re)building but also the future of the rule of law institutions in host states. They also have influence over the local rule of law personnel – over their values and behaviour – which will in turn affect respect for the rule of law in the local population. The Secretary-General acknowledges this trust factor: 'Community-oriented policing and integrated security and crime prevention plans that address discrimination, and that incorporate community engagement and local ownership, will help build trust between justice and security institutions and the people they serve' (Guterres, 2023: 4).

One would think UNPOL can make a significant contribution to SEA accountability. To examine whether this is the case, the next section examines UN peace operations' SEA accountability processes and mechanisms and UNPOL's relationship to accountability.

Mapping SEA accountability and UNPOL

There are four possible types of proceedings for holding individual wrongdoers to account: criminal, disciplinary, administrative and civil proceedings. For each type, there are multiple forums. Military personnel can be held to account for their actions through criminal proceedings in the state of nationality.[2] They can also be held accountable through disciplinary proceedings by the state of nationality or by the military, as well as by the UN. Police and civilian personnel can be called to account through criminal proceedings both in the state of nationality and the host state. UNPOL can also be held accountable through disciplinary proceedings at the UN, by the contributing state or by the national police. Civilian personnel can be held accountable through UN disciplinary proceedings.

In these processes, UNPOL plays various roles. At the stage of gathering information, UNPOL personnel, especially those who are engaged in community policing and patrols and have daily communication with the local community, can be the ones to detect the occurrence of SEA.[3] UNPOL's relationship with the local community determines the extent to which they can contribute in this regard. A report by Guterres on UNPOL positively evaluated their engagement with the local community, including through community policing (2018: paras 6–7). Through community policing, they can provide protection to actual and potential victims of SEA. And they may be able to do the same where they are engaged in protection of civilians. Sometimes, such as when local people seek refuge at a UN base, the UN declares that such sites are protected – the sites are known as 'protection of civilians camps'. Provision of safe environments also helps witnesses and local actors. This is important, as in the new approach introduced by Guterres, local actors help the UN communicate with the local population in relation to SEA. International and national civil society actors are also able to operate more effectively in assisting victims, witnesses and, more generally, the local population if there is a safe environment.

UNPOL advise and reform the local police and justice systems. Through this, UNPOL can assist the work of local police by gathering information on particular cases or by providing advice or assisting in the creation or implementation of relevant policies. In this capacity, UNPOL may be able to contribute to the victim-centred approach through compliance with human rights and protection of victims and witnesses in the local justice system. Further, in the long term, by contributing to a culture of respect for the rule of law (Hunt, 2023), UNPOL can support SEA accountability in the host state. UNPOL are also in a very influential position with regards to the future of a host state's rule of law institutions, as well as the values and behaviour of local police personnel. It follows that how UNPOL deliver functions related to the rule of law, and how individual UNPOL personnel behave, affect SEA accountability in the short term and the long term.

As well as the role played by UNPOL, UN investigations can be conducted by the Office of Internal Oversight Services (OIOS), the special investigation units in the missions, which specialize in investigation of misconduct in the missions, military police and ad hoc mission-based panels (UN, nd-b). UNPOL actors are often directly involved in preliminary or formal investigations. UNPOL officers are active members of national police services, and some are assigned specifically to carry out investigation or provide expertise in investigation. Even where other entities, including the OIOS, are in charge of investigations, UNPOL officers in the mission assist by securing evidence, conducting a preliminary investigation, facilitating or assisting further investigations, conducting follow-up investigations and providing protection to victims and witnesses. UNPOL can also assist national investigation officers (who are appointed by governments in troop-contributing countries) in their investigations, whether or not they are investigating jointly with the UN. In addition, where a UNPOL officer is the one accused of SEA, UNPOL as an institution has a responsibility to act (Boutros-Ghali, 1994; OIOS, 2015, nd).

In processes of a civil nature, proceedings start with information gathering, which UNPOL may contribute to. The success of civil claims depends on the initial information gathered (Ferstman, 2017). UNPOL also contributes to creating a sufficiently safe environment, protecting victims and other people involved, and providing guidance and technical support to relevant actors when a victim pursues a civil route for accountability.

UNPOL is also in a position to assist in ensuring that the human rights of all are protected in SEA accountability. The victim-centred approach includes the principle that accountability should be guided by victims' informed choices. In that respect, UNPOL works with senior victims' rights officers (UN, 2017) to ensure that human rights standards are complied with by investigators and other actors involved in the process of SEA accountability. This includes not only victims' rights but also the human rights of the accused personnel in any proceeding against them. The last point is that UNPOL can contribute to appropriate SEA accountability by demonstrating their model of policing. This is achieved not only through UNPOL delivering their mandate and carrying out set roles, but also by working professionally and acting with integrity at all times, on and off work.

How UNPOL is doing in SEA accountability

At the institutional level, UNPOL is well suited to providing professional services to support the rule of law and, more specifically, SEA accountability. UNPOL can contribute to collecting information, ensuring two-way communication with the local community, providing safe environments, conducting investigations, assisting in investigations led by other actors, such as the host or contributing state, and conducting joint investigations. For this purpose, UNPOL as an institution has been tailoring how they operate – for example, by using more specialized police officers in certain types of investigation.

However, issues persist. One problem relates to the quality of personnel, both in terms of the expertise they bring to the mission and their personal qualities. In relation to expertise, evidence shows that people other than police officers have joined missions. Moreover, people who failed to meet minimum standards, such as being able to speak the mission language, have also joined missions. Indeed, being able to communicate within the mission is vital for all stages of UNPOL's role in SEA accountability. Individuals have also joined the UN Protection Force without having basic monitoring skills, and in Sierra Leone without policing experience. Past police commissioners and commanders have acknowledged the poor quality of UNPOL personnel (Kihara-Hunt, 2017). In contributing to SEA accountability, it is crucial that members of UNPOL can detect potential SEA incidents as well as environments that allow SEA to flourish. It is also important that UNPOL are in fact capable of quality policing, not only in seeking accountability for particular SEA incidents, but also in establishing the foundation for longer-term SEA accountability by actively demonstrating how SEA should be treated. In Haiti, there was criticism centred on the poor quality of some UNPOL officers, the insufficient number of French-speaking members of UNPOL and the lack of certain specialized skills, including those relevant to dealing with sexual and gender-based violence (Mobekk, 2017). This is an obvious obstacle for delivering SEA accountability.

Another issue is the personal qualities of UNPOL personnel. My previous research has concluded that whether or not UNPOL personnel commit crimes during a mission is not so much dependent on the environment where the mission operates or the mandate they are given, but rather on their personal qualities (Kihara-Hunt, 2017). In UNPOL's selection process, required personal qualities include professionalism and integrity, and candidates must not have any allegations against them of criminal or disciplinary offences, other than minor traffic offences (UNPOL, nd). It is important that UNPOL personnel contribute to a culture and understanding that considers SEA as a serious problem and recognizes the need to hold perpetrators to account. Nine out of the top ten countries contributing UNPOL personnel in 2013 were subject to clear criticism by the Human Rights Committee and the Universal Periodic Review process for failing to meet fair trial standards. In addition, nine out of the same ten countries were criticized, based on the same human rights procedures, for not holding their police officers to account for their own crimes (Kihara-Hunt, 2017). This suggests there is a high possibility that the police personnel are not accustomed to acting in support of SEA accountability, especially if fellow UNPOL personnel are the ones accused of SEA.

On the issue of quality of UNPOL personnel, several practical barriers exist. One is to do with the way personnel are selected. UNPOL personnel are appointed through voluntary contributions by Member States. Former UN Secretary-General Ki-Moon (2016) identified the deployment process and insufficient financial incentives as obstacles for securing high-quality personnel, acknowledging the mismatch between tasks that UNPOL are expected to deliver and the resources provided. However, evaluation in 2021 by the OIOS of the UN's approach to SEA found that vetting of UNPOL personnel has improved (OIOS, 2021).

There is also evidence that UNPOL officers are not sufficiently equipped with the skills needed to deliver their roles in SEA accountability. In the external review of UNPOL, the process for recruiting UNPOL personnel was severely criticized due to its being ineffective and lacking integrity and strategic direction (UN, 2016). This resulted in an insufficient number of qualified personnel for specific tasks. Recruitment of good-quality police personnel specialized in investigation, more precisely in SEA-related investigation, is needed, but this aspect of recruitment has not been reformed since the review (Møller, 2023).

One way that the officers' personal qualities can be assessed is through their behaviour. When I conducted research into allegations of crime against UN peace operations personnel, I found that military personnel had the highest number of allegations of criminal behaviour, though between 2007 and 2014, there was a slightly higher rate of allegations per capita against police personnel compared to military personnel. For sexual offences during the same period, the rate per capita was the highest amongst civilian personnel, then UNPOL personnel, followed by military personnel (Kihara-Hunt, 2017). This may indicate that the more contact personnel have with the local population, the more opportunities arise to engage in this type of criminal behaviour. The rate of SEA allegations has decreased since, but SEA allegations continue to be lodged against UNPOL personnel. From 2018 to 2022, UN data shows there were 31 allegations against UNPOL personnel (UN, nd-a), although actual numbers are likely to be higher. A more worrying potential development would be a UNPOL unit-wide involvement in SEA. Although this was evident in missions to former Yugoslavia in the 1990s, with UNPOL units involved in sexual offences and human trafficking, there is no recent evidence of unit-wide involvement in such crimes. It is important to ensure that this does not happen again.

An additional issue concerns the broader policing culture UNPOL brings to UN peace operations. Where police personnel come from an authoritarian policing culture and bring that culture with them, problems arise with UNPOL's engagement with the local community. This is because authoritarian policing seeks to control people, in contrast to democratic policing, which serves people based on the principle of equality. Scholars have found that police personnel from countries that use an authoritarian policing model often do not measure up to the standards set by UNPOL (Costa, 1996; Hansen, 2002; Greener, 2011). This is problematic for the collection of information regarding SEA and specific SEA incidents, as UNPOL's relationship with the local community will determine the extent to which they can contribute in this regard. In addition, where UNPOL personnel operate an authoritarian policing model, the negative effect on SEA accountability extends into the long term, as they are modelling how police should act in relation to SEA, and this impacts how the local police and population view the appropriate response.

Finally, UNPOL personnel also bring their beliefs and behaviours regarding gender into the broader peacekeeping culture. As with other militarized actors, the masculinities expressed by UNPOL personnel (Higate, 2007) may have a significant impact on SEA accountability (see Jasmine-Kim Westendorf's contribution in Chapter 8). Their attitude toward women in general or toward victims and witnesses is important, as SEA is about power relationships.

Conclusion

This chapter has addressed how UNPOL contribute to SEA accountability. Recent reports commend the UN's effort in putting in place rules, policies and structures to practise 'zero tolerance' of SEA (OIOS, 2021). Since Secretary-General Guterres' 'game change', it is apparent that the UN is making a good effort to change at the structural level.

However, at the implementation level, issues persist. In relation to UNPOL, two main issues remain. One is that some individual UNPOL officers – though a limited number – themselves engage in SEA. This is particularly serious because the UN is trying to restore faith in the machinery that delivers the rule of law, accountability and security. In some states, the UN is attempting to build the rule of law for the first time, based on the belief that establishing peace and stability are reliant on this. If, in the process of preaching the values of good governance, the rule of law and accountability, there were to be a mismatch between these values and the way in which UNPOL personnel behave, it would have serious adverse effects on SEA accountability.[4] Further, it would obstruct the establishment of the rule of law – in particular, accountability among multiple elements – in the host state, and the culture of the rule of law would not be absorbed by the local communities. SEA happens in the context of abusers exploiting the power they have over victims. When UNPOL personnel commit SEA, they show that power can be abused. Another factor is that if UNPOL abusers come from a state where police are authoritative, they may transfer their power dynamics to the host state. This is made worse if no form of accountability is delivered in relation to SEA committed by UNPOL personnel.

Another issue is the personal qualities of UNPOL personnel. One issue is the authoritarian posture of some UNPOL officers who carry their national police model and culture to the mission. This results in distance to the community, which makes it impossible for good relationships to develop. Without a good relationship with the community, UNPOL cannot contribute effectively to SEA accountability. Indeed, research suggests that UNPOL are not well equipped with the skills needed to deliver their roles in SEA accountability.

In sum, UNPOL is in a good position to make a significant contribution to SEA accountability if the quality and integrity of personnel is maintained at a high level through an effective recruitment system. However, UNPOL can also negatively impact SEA accountability if the quality and integrity of personnel is insufficient and when individual officers are involved in SEA. UNPOL, thus, represents a double-edged sword for SEA accountability. They can affect SEA accountability to a great degree, either positively or negatively, depending on how the individuals involved behave.

References

Andersen, L. (2007) *UN Peace Operations in the 21st Century: State-Building and Hybridity*, Copenhagen: Danish Institute for National Studies.

Annan, K. (2004) *The Rule of Law and Transitional Justice in Conflict and Post-Conflict Societies: Report of the Secretary-General*, UN Doc S/2004/616.

Boutros-Ghali, B. (1994) *Secretary-General's Bulletin on the Establishment of the Office of the Oversight Services*, UN Doc ST/SGB/273.

Bural, S. and Neligan, C. (2005) *Accountability of International Organizations*, Berlin: Global Public Policy Institute.

Costa, G. (1996) 'The United Nations and the reform of the police in El Salvador', in N. Azimi (ed) *The Role and Functions of Civilian Police in United Nations Peace-Keeping Operations: Debriefing and Lessons*, London: Kluwer Law International, pp 51–89.

De Coning, C. (2020) 'Stabilization and the UN' [video], *EPON*. Available from: https://effectivepeaceops.net/video/stabilization-and-the-un-cedric-de-coning-nupi/ (accessed 20 August 2023).

Durch, W. (2010) *United Nations Police Evolution, Present Capacity and Future Tasks*, Tokyo: GRIPS Policy Research Center.

Dwan, R. (2002) *Executive Policing: Enforcing the Law in Peace Operations*, Oxford: Oxford University Press.

Ferstman, C. (2017) *Sexual Exploitation and Abuse in Peace Operations: Improving Victims' Access to Reparation, Support and Assistance*, London: REDRESS.

Greener, B.K. (2011) 'The rise of policing in UN peace operations', *International Peacekeeping*, 18(2): 183–95.

Guterres, A. (2018) *United Nations Policing*, UN Doc S/2018/1183.

Guterres, A. (2023) *New Vision of the Secretary-General for the Rule of Law*, New York: United Nations.

Hansen, S. (2002) *From Congo to Kosovo: Civilian Police in Peace Operations*, Oxford: Oxford University Press.

Higate, P. (2007) 'Peacekeepers, masculinities, and sexual exploitation', *Men and Masculinities*, 10(1): 99–119.

Hunt, C. (2023) 'International policing and/as the future of UN peace operations', in A. Gilder, D. Curran, G. Holmes and F. Edu-Afful (eds) *Multidisciplinary Futures of UN Peace Operations*, Cham: Palgrave Macmillan, pp 43–68.

Kihara-Hunt, A. (2017) *Holding UNPOL to Account: Individual Criminal Accountability of United Nations Police Personnel*, Leiden: Brill Martinus Nijhoff.

Ki-Moon, B. (2016) *Report of the Secretary-General on United Nations Policing*, UN Doc S/2016/952.

Mobekk, E. (2017) *UN Peace Operations: Lessons from Haiti: 1994–2016*, London: Routledge.

Møller, J. (2023) 'Revitalizing the external review of UN Police Division', *Linkedin*, 15 March. Available from: www.linkedin.com/pulse/revitalizing-external-review-un-police-division-jon-christian-m%C3%B8ller (accessed 31 August 2023).

OIOS (Office of Internal Oversight Services) (2015) *Investigations Manual*, New York: Office of Internal Oversight Services Investigation Division.

OIOS (Office of Internal Oversight Services) (2021) *Evaluation of the Prevention, Response and Victim Support Efforts against Sexual Exploitation and Abuse by United Nations Secretariat Staff and Related Personnel*, UN Doc A/75/820.

OIOS (Office of Internal Oversight Services) (nd) 'About OIOS', *United Nations Office of Internal Oversight Services*. Available from: https://oios.un.org/about-us (accessed 21 January 2022).

UN (United Nations) (2003) *Secretary-General's Bulletin on the Special Measures for Protection from Sexual Exploitation and Sexual Abuse*, UN Doc ST/SGB/2003/13.

UN (United Nations) (2016) *External Review of the Functions, Structure and Capacity of the UN Police Division*, New York: United Nations.

UN (United Nations) (2017) 'Victims' Rights Advocate', *United Nations*. Available from: www.un.org/preventing-sexual-exploitation-and-abuse/content/victims-rights-advocate (accessed 30 June 2022).

UN (United Nations) (2023) 'Security Council authorizes "historic" support mission in Haiti', *UN News*, 2 October. Available from: https://news.un.org/en/story/2023/10/1141802 (accessed 19 October 2023).

UN (United Nations) (nd-a) 'Conduct in UN field missions: data', *United Nations*. Available from: https://conduct.unmissions.org/data (accessed 1 June 2023).

UN (United Nations) (nd-b) 'Conduct in UN field missions: investigations', *United Nations*. Available from: https://conduct.unmissions.org/enforcement-investigations (accessed 19 October 2023).

UN Department of Peace Operations (2019) *Specialized Police Teams on Assignment with United Nations Peace Operations*, 2019.34, New York: United Nations.

UNGA (United Nations General Assembly) (2012) *Declaration of the High-Level Meeting of the General Assembly on the Rule of Law at the National and International Levels*, UN Doc A/67/L.1.

UN Peacekeeping (nd) 'Our history', *United Nations Peacekeeping*. Available from: https://peacekeeping.un.org/en/our-history (accessed 23 August 2023).

UNPOL (United Nations Police) (nd) 'UN Police selection and recruitment – at a glance', *United Nations Police*. Available from: https://police.un.org/en/un-police-selection-and-recruitment-glance (accessed 19 October 2013).

3

Victims' Rights and Remedial Action

Sabrina White and Leah Nyambeki

Introduction

This chapter traces the emergence of victim and survivor support mechanisms in protection from sexual exploitation and abuse (PSEA), particularly through strategies and practices on remedial action from the 1990s to 2023. Remedial action, which centres on the response to allegations, constitutes the third prong of the United Nations' (UN's) long-standing strategy on PSEA (the first and second being prevention and enforcement of the zero tolerance policy). The remedial action response evolved throughout the development of the UN's integrity system for PSEA, aligning more closely with victims' rights frameworks following a series of public scandals in 2015. Yet many old challenges remain. Responses that inadequately address factors constraining victims' access to justice and assistance – including political priorities, organizational reluctance, investigative capacity, resourcing and donor expectations – limit protection of victims' and survivors' rights.

First, we situate victims' rights frameworks in international instruments and establish how the integrity system emerged around sexual exploitation and abuse (SEA). Second, we analyse the status of remedial action strategy with respect to victims' rights over time. Third, we highlight enduring challenges for organizations and victims in access to justice and provision of assistance and support. Analysis of the challenges draws on professional insights from the co-author of this chapter, Leah Nyambeki, who works for the Global Fund as a victims' rights advocate in Kenya and has more than decade of experience in victims' rights. She has worked with diverse victims/survivors of sex trafficking, child sexual abuse and SEA in the transitional justice, criminal legal, and humanitarian spaces in cases in the Middle East and across Africa. We identify how practices are beginning to change, but conclude that the gaps identified here remain as long-standing challenges to protection of victims' rights.

Victims' rights and the UN's SEA integrity system

Victims' rights are derived from human rights law, and the right to a remedy is embedded in a range of international, regional and national legal frameworks. State responsibilities for protection of victims' rights are also embedded in the International Covenant on Civil and Political Rights (United Nations General Assembly – UNGA, 1966: article 2.3), which recognizes the right to an effective remedy before competent authorities. Two UNGA resolutions address victims' rights: the Declaration of Basic Principles of Justice for Victims of Crime and Abuse of Power (1985) and the Basic Principles and Guidelines on the Right to a Remedy and Reparation for Victims of Gross Violations of International Human Rights Law and Serious Violations of International Humanitarian Law (2006). The 1985 Declaration focuses on victims of domestic crimes and acknowledges the duty of states to provide remedies to individual victims, and the 2006 principles on international crimes include both individual and collective rights (Bassiouni, 2006). The right to a remedy includes equal and effective access to justice, reparations for harm suffered, access to information on reparation mechanisms, and necessary material medical, psychological and social assistance (UNGA, 1985: para 14, 2006: para 11). Further, the Protocol to Prevent, Suppress and Punish Trafficking in Persons, Especially Women and Children, Supplementing the United Nations Convention against Transnational Organized Crime (UNGA, 2000) includes state duties to provide remedies to victims. Victims' right to a remedy has been granted increased attention in SEA scholarship, particularly following the adoption of victim-centred initiatives (REDRESS, 2017; Grover, 2018; Ferstman, 2020; Anania, 2022). Yet, until 2017, little attention to this right has been granted by the UN across the history of its policy agenda and integrity system on SEA.

Integrity systems refer to a combination of 'institutions, laws, regulations, codes, policies and procedures' (Aulich, 2016: 119) that are meant to improve accountability and integrity in decision-making. The principle of integrity relates to establishing rules, norms, standards and processes for promoting ethical behaviour and addressing violations. It can also be understood as a moral aspect of governance (Huberts, 2018). Core components of integrity systems include policies, ethical or normative frameworks, risk assessment and mitigation strategies, transparency mechanisms, oversight bodies and safeguarding measures (Six and Lawton, 2013).

Internal issues of sexual misconduct led to reforms in the 1980s and 1990s (for instance, the United Nations Secretary-General – UNSG, 1989a, 1989b;

Assistant Secretary-General for Human Resources Management, 1992) that suggest some awareness regarding the behaviours of UN personnel. Indeed, evidence was found indicating *decades* of peacekeeper sexual misconduct, including 'demanding sexual favours in return for food or employment, sexual assault, rape and paedophilia' (Group of Legal Experts, 2006: para II.12). Extensive evidence of violations perpetrated by peacekeeping and humanitarian personnel in the 1990s, including complicity in sex trafficking in the Balkans (Whitworth, 2004; Bolkovac and Lynn, 2011), raised public concern about the integrity of UN missions. UN action did take place in the 1990s, with efforts made to clarify a code of conduct and expected standards of behaviour (see United Nations Department of Peacekeeping Operations and UNAIDS, 1998; UNSG, 1999). However, these actions largely focused on protecting peacekeepers rather than the victims of abuse of power at the hands of peacekeepers and humanitarian personnel. It was not until sexual exploitation of children by UN personnel hit international headlines in the early 2000s that a dedicated policy agenda establishing an integrity system on SEA formed (UNHCR and Save the Children-UK, 2002; see also Asmita Naik and Jasmine-Kim Westendorf in Chapter 5).

What is widely known as the 'zero tolerance' policy (UNSG, 2003) serves as the foundation for the integrity system initiated in 2003, by establishing a code of conduct and expected standards of behaviour. The policy has been extensively criticized for failing to acknowledge the range of asymmetric power relations shaping consent and the various forms of SEA, and for its efforts to hold perpetrators accountable (Otto, 2007; McGill, 2014; Westendorf, 2023). Implementation of the policy has also been plagued with challenges.

Following public scandals involving the peacekeeping mission in the Democratic Republic of Congo (Milmo, 2004; The Independent, 2005), the UN took greater efforts to ascertain and address what was happening (UNSG, 2005; Dahrendorf, 2006). This work coincided with the production of the Zeid Report, which constituted a public oversight and transparency initiative that framed SEA as an integrity problem for the UN (UNGA, 2005). The Zeid Report was commissioned to comprehensively assess the status of SEA prevention and response measures, and to propose reforms. The report evidenced poor compliance with the zero tolerance policy (UNGA, 2005: para 39) and proposed reforms aiming to improve support and outcomes for victims, which led to the establishment of remedial action as one strategic area of focus.

Remedial action

By 2006, Member States and military and humanitarian communities had negotiated ten principles in a Statement of Commitment on Eliminating

VICTIMS' RIGHTS AND REMEDIAL ACTION

Sexual Exploitation and Abuse by UN and Non-UN Personnel, which included duties to protect from retaliation and assist victims (Inter-Agency Standing Committee – IASC, 2006). The SEA integrity system expanded to include a three-pronged strategy centred on prevention, enforcement of the zero tolerance policy and remedial action (UNSG, 2006b; UNGA, 2010). Prevention pertains to efforts to raise awareness of SEA and the zero-tolerance policy, and enforcement largely deals with enforcing the zero tolerance policy and holding perpetrators accountable. Remedial action, by contrast, has had a few different meanings over the course of the SEA policy agenda and has been prioritized differently in official policy documents. There have been multiple challenges to the political will behind remedial action, as disagreements have emerged regarding priorities in remedying the harm done.

Remedial action is closely linked to the concept of a remedy which seeks to correct a wrong or harm done. Compared to the prevention and enforcement prongs, remedial action, especially remedies for victims, were the least mentioned of the three prongs of the SEA strategy in the UNSG's annual reports on SEA produced during 2004–21 (see Figure 3.1).

Shortly after the Zeid Report, efforts were made to raise the voices of victims, signifying a connection to victims in accountability relationships, but this was short-lived. In 2006, remedial action began as a focus on improving investigations and a public information campaign for peacekeeping components to help 'restore the reputation of alleged perpetrators and the image and credibility of the United Nations and Member States' in unfounded and false allegations (UNSG, 2006a: para 23). Guidance materials covering reporting mechanisms and updating victims on the status of their allegations were shared with media, UN personnel and the host populations.

Figure 3.1: References to the three-pronged strategy on sexual exploitation and abuse in annual reports of the UN Secretary-General, 2004–21

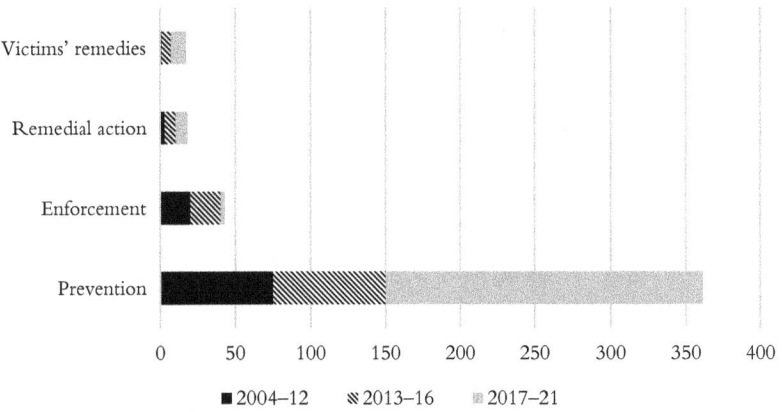

The concern with false allegations was raised by the office established to address SEA in the UN peacekeeping mission in the Democratic Republic of Congo, as were a range of challenges for victims' access to accountability and recommendations to provide redress and compensation to victims (Dahrendorf, 2006). In subsequent years, the question of false allegations saw a ripple effect across UN committees and bodies, which transitioned from references to victims' rights to discourse seeking to preserve the image and credibility of the UN. Indeed, between 2006 and 2016, there were only two occasions when SEA by peacekeepers was highlighted as an international human rights issue, and both mentions were made by the Committee on the Elimination of Discrimination against Women in their recommendations (concluding observations) to states (Mudgway, 2017).

However, from 2008 onwards, in pursuit of implementation of the victim assistance strategy, the focus of remedial action shifted towards providing assistance and support to victims (UNGA, 2007; UN, 2015). The adoption of the UNGA (2007) resolution on the Comprehensive Strategy on Assistance and Support to Victims of Sexual Exploitation and Abuse by United Nations Staff and Related Personnel established what is known as the 'victim assistance mechanism'. This mechanism seeks to coordinate victims' access to pre-existing services and assistance via a referral system (IASC, 2016: 30). The UN and humanitarian and aid organizations are meant to provide support services for survivors, including services for emergency needs, medical and psychosocial support services, safety and security services, and legal support services. This scope of services has borrowed significantly from the gender-based violence prevention and case management work over the past decades. The support services for survivors are based on the guiding principles that a survivor must feel they are safe, respected and receiving equal treatment, and that their information will be kept confidential (United Nations Office for Drug Control and Crime Prevention, 1999). Victims will likely require multiple forms of assistance, including while they are participating in legal processes and in the long term. Support for dealing with what happened to them, medical assistance and a clear understanding of how legal processes are handled can have profound benefits for victims, their participation in legal processes and what happens to them when legal processes are finalized. Yet, by 2013, limited progress had been made in this regard.

The first substantial integrity review of action on SEA was released internally within the UN in 2013. This damning expert report, which investigated the four peacekeeping missions with the highest numbers of allegations (Democratic Republic of Congo, Haiti, Liberia and South Sudan), found that complainants and investigators 'often remain unaware of final decisions, leading to frustration and even insecurity due to the presence of the potential perpetrator in mission even after several years'

(Awori et al, 2013: 13–14). The zero tolerance policy was not taken seriously, and impunity was common. Further, it found 'a culture of silence around reporting and discussing cases, and a culture of extreme caution with respect to the rights of the accused, and little accorded to the rights of victims' (Awori et al, 2013: 3). The review criticized the failure of the UN's strategy *'to protect the most vulnerable'* and argued that the organization was 'more focused on UN personnel than on victims' (Awori et al, 2013: 15, original italics).

This prompted a shift whereby there were no longer references made in UN bodies to the need to combat false allegations and restore the image and credibility of UN personnel. Rather, language calling for improvement in reporting and investigations reintroduced (indirectly) a discourse of rights by referring to the need to 'maintain the dignity of victims at all times' (Special Committee on Peacekeeping Operations, 2014: para. 191), suggesting a values-based approach connected to human rights norms. Further, in 2013, remedial action integrated issues with reporting, piloting community-based complaints mechanisms, addressing the conduct of investigations with respect to victims and, finally, considering paternity claims (UNSG, 2013), which had been raised as a key issue five years prior (UNGA, 2007). After the fallout from the 2015 scandals in the Central African Republic, the UNSG announced the introduction of a victim-centred approach to SEA (UNSG, 2017), which has led to increased focus on resourcing assistance and support for victims (as discussed by Jane Connors in Chapter 6).

Yet, despite the expansion of remedial action and the expectation that all UN entities were responsible for implementing the victim assistance mechanism (UNSG, 2012: para 130), progress has been slow.

Enduring challenges for victims

Two key areas characterizing limitations in advancing remedial action and promoting victims' rights are constraints on access to justice as well as assistance and support for victims.

Victims, survivors and paternity claimants face a range of challenges in reporting SEA in the first place. The main issue for victims deciding to report is fear. They may fear a range of repercussions, including stigmatization by their entire community and retaliation from family, friends and senior authorities (Csáky, 2008; Lattu, 2008; Human Rights Watch, 2014; Kleinfeld, 2018). Victims in rural communities are especially at high risk of ostracization, and this can have long-term impacts on a victim's life. Fear of not being believed can also serve as a strong deterrent, which can be especially profound for single parents, who, when comparing the loss likely to happen from reporting versus remaining silent, often choose silence. Boys can be especially at risk of not being believed, because of stigmas and taboos (Hilton, 2008). Other reports have provided evidence of UN agency workers threatening and pursing retaliation or bribing victims not to make complaints (Csáky, 2008; IASC and CEB, 2019).

Every time a victim speaks out, it is highly significant, and the imputed organization(s) has a responsibility to provide any support they need and to protect them from retaliation as much as possible. Yet there is often a lack of information for victims regarding what they can expect through response processes that accompany remedial action, including regarding their participation in justice processes. Survivors 'are often left on their own to navigate and cope' with accountability processes and consequences that follow reporting, which can also erode community trust in response processes (Heaven Taylor and Brostrom, 2023: 5). Where legal representation is available to victims, unfortunately there is little awareness regarding the quality of this representation nor the extent to which it is victim-sensitive or victim-centred.

Approaches to PSEA and sexual harassment tend to take a compliance-based approach reflecting the organization's needs rather than victims' and survivors' perspectives as a starting point (Heaven Taylor and Brostrom, 2023). In her work as a victim rights advocate, Leah has found that one of the main accountability challenges for organizations in the response to allegations is the high burden of proof required to substantiate allegations of sexual misconduct. Criminal cases are required to prove beyond any reasonable doubt that the criminal act was committed against the victim by the perpetrator in question. Organizations in the humanitarian space often try to reach the same level of proof through human resources departments, which is often impossible. Organizations do not usually work with professional investigative authorities, and while some are developing competencies, they tend to lack investigative capacity themselves and often outsource this work. A key challenge in non-criminal cases is to understand the threshold of what needs to be investigated and how, plus what levels of evidence are required to justify disciplinary accountability action. Further, often the most an organization can do is dismiss the perpetrator. Where the perpetrator in substantiated allegations comes from an organization working in their own community, Leah has observed that on dismissal, they may go back to the community and retaliate against the victim.

In Leah's experience, victim- and gender-sensitivity and trauma-informed support is key to promoting victims' rights and helping meet their needs. Helping victims to better understand the legal process can help build their confidence. There are a range of additional challenges victims may face through their participation in legal proceedings. Different approaches on the part of investigators will be required where the perpetrator is known to victims. Their safety and well-being may be at risk, and family and community members may try to persuade them to drop their case, including through obstructing their arrival at court. Even in cases of long-term pro bono legal support, survivors have faced traumatization and mistreatment in court (REDRESS and Childs Rights International Network, 2020). Survivors may need access to a range of assistance and support to deal with participation in these processes as well as the longer-term effects and harms that may come from them, which leads to a second challenge.

The victim assistance mechanism has never had any regularly allocated budget (an issue further taken up in Chapter 6 by the UN's Victims' Rights Advocate Jane Connors.) Instead, missions and agencies have had to pool woefully inadequate resources (UNSG, 2015). The mechanism's resourcing demands on agencies were a point of concern from the beginning, particularly as the content of the policy strategy was poorly understood (Reddick, 2010). The mechanism has also been guided by assumptions that assistance and support to victims 'could cost no money at all' (Executive Committees on Humanitarian Affairs and Peace and Security and NGO Task Force on Protection from Sexual Exploitation and Abuse, 2009: 15). And so, the minimum standard for victim assistance by UN agencies was merely having written guidance on victim assistance. By 2010, only 2 out of 14 surveyed UN agencies had this guidance with victim assistance policies, and overall there were 'extremely low' levels of implementation as agencies were working out how to resource this (Reddick, 2010: 54). In 2015, in response to poor realization of the mechanism, proposals were made to develop a common funding instrument for the victim assistance strategy (UNSG, 2015: para 65), yet by 2021 resourcing challenges remained (Office of International Oversight Services, 2021; Reddick, 2021).

Carla Ferstman (2020) has argued that victim assistance and support was never understood as a requirement, but rather as an appropriate action and good practice. One of the challenges in encouraging assistance and support for victims is based on the perception held by organizations that if they provide support to a victim, they are accepting liability for the conduct of their employee and thus opening themselves up to legal ramifications. This is part of wider issues balancing an organization's duty of care with acceptance of liability. Organizations are generally averse to accepting liability in such circumstances and, specifically, with the inherent risks of such cases where it is difficult to pre-empt outcomes. This is particularly problematic in paternity cases, where there are unclear responsibilities for maintenance of a child fathered by an organization's personnel while legal proceedings are underway.

Many organizations claim they want to provide support services for victims/survivors of SEA. However, they often lack the capacity and resources to do so. Victims may need support going to the police station to report criminal acts, somewhere to go for shelter and safety, medical assistance and so on. Specialist expertise is also needed to respond to complainants in a gender- and victim-sensitive manner. In criminal and civil cases, there are significant challenges to securing access to legal services for victims. Many organizations involved in allegations lack resources or do not take responsibility for providing legal services for victims. Some do pay in criminal cases, but not in civil cases – for instance, cases involving paternity claims. Outside of this, there may not be public defenders or a legal aid service, nor NGOs working in the legal space that could provide support.

Another common argument against providing victim/survivor support services is the fear of creating dependency. As Leah observes, organizations may fear that victims become dependent on temporary support systems. Indeed, the expert report from 2013 even evidenced that for this reason, some staff were intentionally discouraging 'too much assistance to victims' beyond meeting minimum immediate needs (Awori et al, 2013: 15). This attitude towards providing assistance indicates that some staff may hold negative views or perceptions of complainants. Yet where there are longer-term psychosocial, medical or other support needs, particularly in paternity cases, victims and their dependants may well have longer-term support needs.

Overall, there remains a 'lack of adequate and sustainable funding and resourcing to provide for the assistance and support to victims' (Office of the Victims' Rights Advocate, 2020: 3). Evaluations on victim assistance in 2015 and 2021 found that very few victims of SEA had received any form of assistance (OIOS, 2015, 2021). This is in part attributed to under-resourcing, despite the introduction of the long-awaited Trust Fund in Support of Victims of Sexual Exploitation and Abuse in 2016, which was designed to help address resourcing gaps but is not a source of compensation for victims (UNSG, 2016).

Many organizations, donors and state entities have produced guidance and policies on victim- and survivor-centred approaches to PSEA (see UN, 2019; UNHCR, 2020; USAID, 2020; World Bank, 2020; Foreign Commonwealth & Development Office, 2022; IASC, 2023), but the resources for implementation lag behind, particularly in terms of assistance and support to promote and protect the rights of victims and survivors as they seek remedy for the harm they experienced. Donors may bind themselves to policies and set out guidelines for a response without investing in either.

Although there has been increasing awareness of the issue, support services for survivors of SEA are still lacking in many countries. The implementation of comprehensive support services for victims/survivors is hindered by the lack of resources and infrastructure in many countries. Even in countries where such services exist, they are often underfunded, understaffed and inadequate. Additionally, cultural and societal norms that victim blame and stigmatize survivors hinder their access to both justice and support.

Human and financial resource capacity are in part a key problem of donor priorities. If donors were to make it a requirement for their implementers to have certain capabilities and provide funding to support these capabilities, that would help fill the resourcing gap. Deliberate prioritization of SEA resourcing from donors can go a long way in improving the response to victims and ensuring that SEA is a core component of risk assessments – for instance, if, to secure donor funding, an implementing partner needs to access an SEA investigator or, especially for larger organizations, have a department on SEA. Donors may also support SEA professional networks that can develop communities of practice.

Organizations must also be willing to accept a level of liability and come up with specific strategies and mechanisms to respond to SEA allegations in a holistic manner, including providing victim/survivor support services when and where needed. This is essential to overcoming challenges in providing assistance and support and promoting and protecting victims' and survivors' rights.

Conclusion

This chapter has outlined how concerns with victims' rights have emerged in the UN's integrity system on SEA, particularly through the remedial action strategy. It has analysed how challenges in prioritizing and resourcing remedial action inhibit realization of victims' rights. Remedial action is meant to promote access to a remedy which seeks to correct a wrong or harm done. The SEA integrity system, which has now expanded beyond the UN to include a range of state and non-state entities and organizations, has a long way to go in ensuring that victims' rights, including to a remedy, are integral to SEA strategies and responses.

Integrity systems are meant to promote ethical behaviour and reflect moral aspects of governance. Victims' access to justice and assistance and support are part of realization of their rights and promotion of ethical behaviour and moral governance. Responses to victims which fully support their rights should be a required and consistently actioned and resourced component. States, donors and organizations have a significant role to play in establishing priorities, cultivating robust integrity systems and supporting adequate resourcing of strategies to support realization of victims' rights.

References

Anania, J. (2022) 'Transitional justice and the ongoing exclusion of sexual exploitation and abuse by international intervenors', *International Affairs*, 98(3): 893–913.

Assistant Secretary-General for Human Resources Management (1992) *Guidelines for Promoting Equal Treatment of Men and Women in the Secretariat*, UN Doc ST/IC1992/67.

Aulich, C. (2016) 'Integrity and public sector governance: a democratic deficit?' in C. Aulich (ed) *From Abbott to Turnbull: A New Direction? Australian Commonwealth Administration 2013–2016*, Victoria: Echo Books, pp 119–41.

Awori, T., Lutz, C. and Thapa, P. (2013) *Final Report: Expert Mission to Evaluate the Risks to SEA Prevention Efforts in MINUSTAH, UNMIL, MONUSCO, and UNMISS*, United Nations. Available from: https://static1.squarespace.com/static/514a0127e4b04d7440e8045d/t/55afcfa1e4b07b89d11d35ae/1437585313823/2013+Expert+Team+Report+FINAL.pdf (accessed 1 October 2022).

Bassiouni, M. (2006) 'International recognition of victims' rights', *Human Rights Law Review*, 6(2): 203–79.

Bolkovac, K. and Lynn, C. (2011) *The Whistleblower: Sex Trafficking, Military Contractors, and One Woman's Fight for Justice*, New York: Palgrave Macmillan.

Csáky, C. (2008) *No One To Turn To: The Under-Reporting of Child Sexual Exploitation and Abuse by Aid Workers and Peacekeepers*, London: Save the Children. Available from: https://resourcecentre.savethechildren.net/document/no-one-turn-under-reporting-child-sexual-exploitation-and-abuse-aid-workers-and-peacekeepers/ (accessed 1 October 2017).

Dahrendorf, N. (2006) *Lessons Learned Study: Addressing Sexual Exploitation and Abuse in MONUC*, United Nations Department of Peacekeeping Operations. Available from: www.peacewomen.org/assets/file/Resources/UN/dpko_addressingsexualviolenceinmonuc_2006.pdf (accessed 1 October 2023).

Executive Committees on Humanitarian Affairs and Peace and Security and NGO Task Force on Protection from Sexual Exploitation and Abuse (2009) SEA victim assistance guide. Available from: https://pseataskforce.org/en/tools/search/--3----.html (accessed 1 October 2021).

Ferstman, C. (2020) 'Reparation for sexual exploitation and abuse in the (post) conflict context: the need to address abuses by peacekeepers and humanitarian aid workers', in C. Ferstman and M. Goetz (eds) *Reparations for Victims of Genocide, War Crimes and Crimes against Humanity*, Leiden: Brill Nijhoff, pp 271–97.

Foreign Commonwealth & Development Office (2022) 'Safeguarding against sexual exploitation and abuse and sexual harassment: due diligence guidance for FCDO implementing partners', *Gov.uk*, 7 November. Available from: www.gov.uk/government/publications/dfid-enhanced-due-diligence-safeguarding-for-external-partners/safeguarding-against-sexual-exploitation-and-abuse-and-sexual-harassment-seah-due-diligence-guidance-for-fcdo-implementing-partners (accessed 4 October 2023).

Group of Legal Experts (2006) *Report of the Group of Legal Experts on Ensuring the Accountability of United Nations Staff and Experts on Mission with Respect to Criminal Acts Committed in Peacekeeping Operations*, UN Doc A/60/980.

Grover, S. (2018) 'Children's participation in holding international peacekeepers accountable for sex crimes', *Children's Legal Rights Journal*, 38(1): 1–38.

Heaven Taylor, L. and Brostrom, M. (2023) *Victim/Survivor-Centred Approach to Protection from Sexual Abuse, Exploitation and Harassment in the Aid Sector*, Geneva: CHS Alliance. Available from: https://safeguardingsupporthub.org/documents/victimsurvivor-centred-approach-protection-sexual-abuse-exploitation-and-harassment-aid (accessed 7 June 2023).

Hilton, A. (2008) *'I Thought It Could Never Happen to Boys': Sexual Abuse & Exploitation of Boys in Cambodia: An Exploratory Study*, Social Services of Cambodia, Hagar and World Vision. Available from: https://data.opendevelopmentmyanmar.net/en/library_record/i-thought-it-could-never-happen/resource/21566d12-9b74-4c1c-a578-6fe425e16d6c (accessed 21 September 2021).

Huberts, L. (2018) 'Integrity: what it is and why it is important', *Public Integrity*, 20(suppl 1): S18–S32.

Human Rights Watch (2014) '"The power these men have over us": sexual exploitation and abuse by African Union forces in Somalia', *Human Rights Watch*, 8 September. Available from: www.hrw.org/report/2014/09/08/power-these-men-have-over-us/sexual-exploitation-and-abuse-african-union-forces (accessed 1 April 2022).

IASC (Inter-Agency Standing Committee) (2006) *Statement of Commitment on Eliminating Sexual Exploitation and Abuse by UN and Non-UN Personnel, 4 December 2006*, IASC. Available from: https://interagencystandingcommittee.org/focal-points/documents-public/statement-commitment-eliminating-sexual-exploitation-and-abuse-un-and (accessed 26 February 2024).

IASC (Inter-Agency Standing Committee) (2016). *Guideline: Inter-agency community-based complaint mechanisms, April*, IASC. Available from: https://interagencystandingcommittee.org/sites/default/files/migrated/2019-02/best_practice_guide_inter_agency_community_based_complaint_mechanisms_1.pdf (accessed 14 July 2021).

IASC (Inter-Agency Standing Committee) (2023) *IASC Definition & Principles of a Victim/Survivor Centred Approach*, IASC. Available from: https://psea.interagencystandingcommittee.org/sites/default/files/2023-06/IASC%20Definition%20%26%20Principles%20of%20a%20Victim_Survivor%20Centered%20Approach.pdf (accessed 4 October 2023).

IASC (Inter-Agency Standing Committee) and CEB (United Nations Chief Executives Board) (2019) *Inter-Agency Standing Committee and United Nations Chief Executives Board Task Force on Addressing Sexual Harassment in the Organizations of the UN System: Second Meeting of Investigatory Bodies on Protection from Sexual Exploitation, Abuse and Sexual Harassment*. Available from: https://psea.interagencystandingcommittee.org/sites/default/files/2020-06/SummaryRecord_IASCCEB%20investigatory%20bodies%20on%20%20PSEAH%20Nov2019.pdf (accessed 23 November 2022).

Kleinfeld, P. (2018) 'Central African Republic, part 3: "I have no power to complain"', *The New Humanitarian*, 25 July. Available from: www.thenewhumanitarian.org/special-report/2018/07/25/central-african-republic-peacekeeper-sexual-abuse-investigation (accessed 30 January 2021).

Lattu, K. (2008) *To Complain or Not to Complain: Still the Question*, Geneva: Humanitarian Accountability Partnership. Available from: https://pseataskforce.org/uploads/tools/tocomplainornottocomplainstillthequestion_hapinternational_english.pdf (accessed 11 March 2022).

McGill, J. (2014) 'Survival sex in peacekeeping economies', *Journal of International Peacekeeping*, 18(1–2): 1–44.

Milmo, C. (2004) 'UN soldiers "buy sex" from teenage refugees in Congo', *The Independent*, 25 May. Available from: www.independent.ie/world-news/africa/un-soldiers-buy-sex-from-teenage-refugees-in-congo-25915804.html (accessed 6 February 2021).

Mudgway, C. (2017) 'Sexual exploitation by UN peacekeepers: the "survival sex" gap in international human rights law', *The International Journal of Human Rights*, 21(9): 1453–76.

Office of Internal Oversight Services (2015). *Evaluation of the Enforcement and Remeidial Assistance Efforts for Sexual Exploitation and Abuse by the United Nations and Related Personnel in Peacekeeping Operations*, UN Doc IED-15-001.

Office of Internal Oversight Services (2021) *Evaluation of the Prevention, Response and Victim Support Efforts against Sexual Exploitation and Abuse by United Nations Secretariat Staff and Related Personnel*, UN Doc A/75/820.

Otto, D. (2007) 'Making sense of zero tolerance policies in peacekeeping sexual economies', in V. Munro and C. Stychin (eds) *Sexuality and the Law*, Abingdon: Routledge-Cavendish, pp 259–82.

OVRA (Office of the Victims' Rights Advocate) (2020). *Summary notes: 'Voices from the Field' briefing by United Nations Field Victims' Rights Advocates and Dedidcated Protection from Sexual Exploitation and Abuse Coordinators*, 28 October. Available from: https://www.un.org/preventing-sexual-exploitation-and-abuse/sites/www.un.org.preventing-sexual-exploitation-and-abuse/files/summary_notes_-_voices_from_the_field.pdf (accessed 1 September 2023).

Reddick, M. (2010). *Global Synthesis Report: IASC Review of Protection from Sexual Exploitation and Abuse by UN, NGO, IOM and IFRC Personnel*, Geneva: IASC. Available from: https://www.unocha.org/sites/unocha/files/dms/Documents/PSEA_Synthesis_Report_-_submitted_to_IASC_WG_Jul10_mtg_-_FINAL.pdf (Accessed 17 July 2023).

Reddick, M. (2021) *Global Report on Protection from Sexual Exploitation and Abuse and Sexual Harassment*, Geneva: IASC. Available from: https://psea.interagencystandingcommittee.org/sites/default/files/2022-01/IASCExternalReview_GlobalReportPSEAH_2021.pdf (accessed 20 February 2023).

REDRESS (2017) *Sexual Exploitation and Abuse in Peacekeeping Operations, Improving Victims' Access to Reparation, Support and Assistance*, London and The Hague: REDRESS and Child Rights International Network. Available from: www.refworld.org/pdfid/59c383034.pdf (accessed 1 October 2018).

REDRESS and Childs Rights International Network (2020) *Litigating Peacekeeper Child Sexual Abuse*, REDRESS and Child Rights International Network. Available from: https://redress.org/wp-content/uploads/2020/01/LitigatingPeacekeeperChildSexualAbuseReport.pdf (accessed 24 March 2022).

Six, F. and Lawton, A. (2013) 'Towards a theory of integrity systems: a configurational approach', *International Review of Administrative Sciences*, 79(4): 639–58.

Special Committee on Peacekeeping Operations (2014). *Report of the Special Committee on Peacekeeping Operations*, 1 April, U Doc A/69/19.

The Independent (2005) 'Sex and the UN: when peacemakers become predators', *The Independent*, 11 January. Available from: www.independent.co.uk/news/world/africa/sex-and-the-un-when-peacemakers-become-predators-486170.html (accessed 6 February 2021).

UN (United Nations) (2015) *Accountability for Conduct and Discipline in Field Missions*, United Nations Department of Political Affairs, Department of Peacekeeping Operations and Department of Field Support. Available from: https://unmil.unmissions.org/sites/default/files/policy_on_accountability_for_conduct_and_discipline_in_field_missions_30-07-2015.pdf (accessed 1 May 2022).

UN (United Nations) (2019) *United Nations Protocol on the Provision of Assistance to Victims of Sexual Exploitation and Abuse*, 12 December. Available from: www.un.org/en/pdfs/UN%20Victim%20Assistance%20Protocol_English_Final.pdf (accessed 7 June 2023).

UNGA (United Nations General Assembly) (1966) *International Covenant on Civil and Political Rights*, 16 December, UN Doc A/RES/2200A(XXI).

UNGA (United Nations General Assembly) (1985) *Declaration of Basic Principles of Justice for Victims of Crime and Abuse of Power*, 29 November, UN Doc A/RES/40/34.

UNGA (United Nations General Assembly) (2000) *Protocol to Prevent, Suppress and Punish Trafficking in Persons, Especially Women and Children, Supplementing the United Nations Convention against Transnational Organized Crime*, UN Doc A/RES/55/25.

UNGA (United Nations General Assembly) (2005) *A Comprehensive Strategy to Eliminate Future Sexual Exploitation and Abuse in United Nations Peacekeeping Operations*, UN Doc A/59/710.

UNGA (United Nations General Assembly) (2006) *Basic Principles and Guidelines on the Right to a Remedy and Reparation for Victims of Gross Violations of International Human Rights Law and Serious Violations of International Humanitarian Law*, UN Doc A/RES/60/147.

UNGA (United Nations General Assembly) (2007) *United Nations Comprehensive Strategy on Assistance and Support to Victims of Sexual Exploitation and Abuse by United Nations Staff and Related Personnel*, UN Doc A/RES/62/214.

UNGA (United Nations General Assembly) (2010) *Cross-Cutting Issues*, UN Doc A/RES/64/269.

UNHCR (2020) *Policy on a Victim-Centred Approach in UNHCR's Response to Sexual Misconduct*, UNHCR. Available from: www.unhcr.org/media/39118 (accessed 7 June 2023).

UNHCR and Save the Children-UK (2002) *Note for Implementing and Operational Partners by UNHCR and Save The Children-UK on Sexual Violence & Exploitation: The Experience of Refugee Children in Guinea, Liberia and Sierra Leone*. Available from: www.unhcr.org/media/note-implementing-and-operational-partners-unhcr-and-save-children-uk-sexual-violence (accessed 1 October 2018).

United Nations Department of Peacekeeping Operations and UNAIDS (1998) *Protect Yourself, and Those You Care About, against HIV/AIDS*. New York: United Nations. Available from: www.navedu.navy.mi.th/stg/databasestory/data/laukniyom/workjob/bigcountry-workjob/UN-Publications/033-hiv-aids_protect_yourself-English.pdf (accessed 25 November 2018).

United Nations Office for Drug Control and Crime Prevention (1999) *Handbook on Justice for Victims: On the Use and Application of the Declaration of Basic Principles of Justice for Victims of Crime and Abuse of Power*, New York: United Nations Office for Drug Control and Crime Prevention. Available from: www.unodc.org/pdf/criminal_justice/UNODC_Handbook_on_Justice_for_victims.pdf (accessed 1 October 2023).

UNSG (United Nations Secretary-General) (1989a) *Administration of Justice in the Secretariat*, UN Doc A/C.5/44/9.

UNSG (United Nations Secretary-General) (1989b) *Amendments to the Staff Rules*, UN Doc A/C.5/44/2.

UNSG (United Nations Secretary-General) (1999) *Observance by UN Forces of International Humanitarian Law*, UN Doc ST/SGB/1999/13.

UNSG (United Nations Secretary-General) (2003) *Special Measures for Protection from Sexual Exploitation and Abuse*, UN Doc ST/SGB/2003/13.

UNSG (United Nations Secretary-General) (2005) *Investigation by the Office of Internal Oversight Services into Allegations of Sexual Exploitation and Abuse in the United Nations Organization Mission in the Democratic Republic of the Congo*, UN Doc A/59/661.

UNSG (United Nations Secretary-General) (2006a) *Comprehensive Report Prepared Pursuant to General Assembly Resolution 59/296 on Sexual Exploitation and Sexual Abuse, Including Policy Development, Implementation and Full Justification of Proposed Capacity on Personnel Conduct Issues*, UN Doc A/60/862.

UNSG (United Nations Secretary-General) (2006b) *Special Measures for Protection from Sexual Exploitation and Sexual Abuse*, UN Doc ST/SGB/2003/13.

UNSG (United Nations Secretary-General) (2013) *Special Measures for Protection from Sexual Exploitation and Sexual Abuse*, UN Doc A/67/766.

UNSG (United Nations Secretary-General) (2014). *Overview of the financing of the United Nations peacekeeping operations: budget performance for the period from 1 July 2010 to 30 June 2011 and budget for the period from 1 July 2012 to 30 June 2013*, UN Doc A/66/679.

UNSG (United Nations Secretary-General) (2015) *Special Measures for Protection from Sexual Exploitation and Sexual Abuse*, UN Doc A/69/779.

UNSG (United Nations Secretary-General) (2016) *Combating Sexual Exploitation and Abuse*, UN Doc A/71/97.

UNSG (United Nations Secretary-General) (2017) *Special Measures for Protection from Sexual Exploitation and Sexual Abuse: A New Approach*, UN Doc A/71/818.

USAID (2020) *Policy on Protection from Sexual Exploitation and Abuse (PSEA)*, Washington, DC: USAID. Available from: www.usaid.gov/sites/default/files/2022-05/PSEA_Policy_Digital.pdf (accessed 4 October 2023).

Westendorf, J. (2023) 'A problem of rules: sexual exploitation and UN legitimacy', *International Studies Quarterly*, 67(3): 1–13.

Whitworth, S. (2004) *Men, Militarism, and UN Peacekeeping: A Gendered Analysis*, Boulder, CO: Lynne Rienner.

World Bank (2020) *Addressing Sexual Exploitation and Abuse and Sexual Harassment in Investment Project Financing Involving Major Civil Works* (2nd edn), Washington, DC: World Bank.

4

Sexual Violence against Peacekeepers and Aid Workers

Phoebe Donnelly and Dyan Mazurana

Introduction

Women's and children's rights activists, scholars and practitioners have drawn increasing attention to peacekeepers and humanitarian aid workers sexually exploiting and abusing civilians, primarily women and children, in the countries where they are working (Higate, 2007; Nordås and Rustad, 2013; Karim and Beardsley, 2016; Westendorf, 2020; Wheeler, 2020). Thus, the term sexual exploitation and abuse (SEA) has primarily been used to refer to SEA by peacekeepers and aid workers against members of the local population. Specifically, United Nations Peacekeeping (nd) describes SEA as including

> any sexual activity with minors or any actual or threatened physical intrusion of a sexual nature, whether by force or under unequal or coercive conditions; any actual or attempted abuse of position of vulnerability, differential power, or trust, for sexual purposes, including, but not limited to, profiting monetarily, socially or politically from the sexual exploitation of another. This includes acts of transactional sex, solicitation of transactional sex, and exploitative relationships. In addition, military and police personnel have non-fraternization policies making relations with beneficiaries of assistance a breach of the standards of conduct.

Despite the fact that power differentials also occur *within* peacekeeping and humanitarian aid organizations, SEA has primarily been used to refer to abuses perpetrated by peacekeepers (notably almost all allegations are against men peacekeepers) against civilian women and children *outside* of the peacekeeping mission. While scholarship continues to explore how peacekeepers and aid workers abuse host populations (Higate, 2007; Westendorf, 2020; Mednick and Craze, 2022), there has been almost no research examining the patterns of perpetration of sexual abuse against persons *inside* peacekeeping and aid missions – a gap we seek to fill in this chapter.

Due to increased reports of sexual abuse (a term we use in this chapter as a catch-all to refer to sexual discrimination, harassment and assault) from women peacekeepers and women aid workers who experienced sexual abuse while on mission and are fighting for prevention and redress, the United Nations (UN) and its partners have been forced to act. As part of this action by the UN to acknowledge sexual abuse experienced by peacekeepers, the UN and its partners have begun to use the acronym SEAH (sexual exploitation, abuse and harassment). Using this acronym could be a way to augment the 'SEA' category of abuse (which is used in reference to violence committed against women and children outside missions) to denote sexual harassment that occurs internally against peacekeepers and aid workers (UN Women, 2020). One problem with the use of SEAH is that it can lead to the treatment of all forms of sexual abuse against women peacekeepers and aid workers as sexual harassment. This reduction of all forms of sexual abuse to sexual harassment is inaccurate and results in misidentifying and too often downplaying the range and severity of sexual abuse that is occurring (primarily) against women inside peacekeeping and humanitarian missions.

In this chapter, we analyse patterns of sexual abuse perpetrated by peacekeepers and aid workers against other peacekeepers and aid workers. We review data from two original studies we conducted on peacekeepers' and aid workers' experiences of sexual abuse while on mission (Mazurana and Donnelly, 2017; Donnelly et al, 2022). Our first study collected data on the experiences of sexual abuse of women, men and LGBTQ+ humanitarian aid workers while on mission. Our second study focused on military and police UN peacekeepers' self-reported experiences and witnessing of sexual abuse while on peacekeeping missions.

In exploring the dynamics that create and facilitate conditions for this sexual abuse, we find similarities in the overarching dynamics that lead to sexual abuse against two otherwise different populations that operate in conflict areas. In examining the distinct forms of sexual abuse in settings of peacekeeping and humanitarian aid missions, we find that abuse is enabled by inequitable and sexist power dynamics and toxic organizational cultures that perpetuate sexual abuse both inside and outside peacekeeping and humanitarian organizations. We argue that similar phenomena enable the sexual abuse of primarily women peacekeepers and aid workers by their men colleagues. Importantly, these factors also lead to sexual abuse of LGBTQ+

individuals, a dynamic that has not yet received sustained attention in the literature on sexual abuse within peacekeeping and aid work (and is further taken up in Chapter 10 by Junru Bian and colleagues). These interlinked and mutually reinforcing phenomena include patriarchal and sexist power dynamics, toxic organizational cultures[1] and cultures of impunity. We demonstrate the ways they combine to create environments in which sexual abuse against (primarily) women peacekeepers and aid workers takes root and spreads.[2]

Patriarchal power dynamics

While people of any gender can perpetrate sexual violence, research finds that, overwhelmingly, men are the perpetrators and women are the victims of gender-based and sexual violence (True, 2012). Furthermore, scholars demonstrate how militaries are gendered institutions created, established and dominated by men (Szitanyi, 2020). The association of war with 'real men' and the reinforcement of these gendered ideals lead to what Megan Mackenzie (2015: 4) describes as a 'militarized-masculinity complex'. Military organizations operate within a framework that elevates the positions of men and creates male-dominated and male-privileged power structures.[3] In such contexts, a hegemonic militarized masculinity is reinforced as the dominant mode of interaction, in which an exaggerated, male-dominated sexuality is an integral component (Wadham, 2017; Duriesmith, 2017). We can see this same militarized masculinity complex within the uniformed components of peacekeeping missions.

While less research has focused on masculinities within aid organizations, we find similar dynamics exist given that these organizations are operating in similar contexts as peacekeepers, where there is often the presence of a security threat and therefore creation of a securitized and militarized space. In peacekeeping and aid organizations, we see the emergence of different forms of hegemonic masculinities that are militarized and securitized (Duncanson, 2009; Myrttinen, 2019). Gender-based violence is often an inherent part of militarized and securitized institutions, as it serves as a means of reinforcing traditional masculine traits of strength and domination over women and persons deemed feminine (Wadham, 2017).

A person of any gender can be a perpetrator or a victim of sexual abuse. Yet our research found that the survivors and witnesses of sexual abuse stressed that a male-dominated environment was a primary contributor to existing patterns of sexual abuse by men peacekeepers and aid workers against women and children both inside and outside the mission. Our research on peacekeeping and humanitarian organizations found that perpetrators are almost exclusively men and victims are almost exclusively women and, to a lesser extent, persons who identify as LGBTQ+.[4]

In both peacekeeping and humanitarian missions, men are empowered to be dominant through holding positions of authority and having decision-making power over priorities, agenda setting, and material and human resources. Despite the Uniformed Gender Parity Strategy that seeks to increase the number of uniformed women in UN peacekeeping, men far outnumber women, and a heterosexist, male-dominated environment remains.

Among our 457 survey participants in our study of peacekeepers, women and men had different rates of experiencing and witnessing sexual abuse (this included sexual harassment, discrimination and assault) on mission. Men peacekeepers were significantly less likely to report either experiencing (2 per cent) or witnessing (4 per cent) sexual abuse while on mission. In comparison, more than a quarter (28 per cent) of women peacekeepers reported experiencing sexual abuse while on mission and a similar percentage (26 per cent) reporting witnessing sexual abuse. Women peacekeepers also reported experiencing multiple instances of abuse from the same perpetrator. For women peacekeepers who indicated on the survey that they experienced sexual abuse, the most common form of reported was sexual harassment (57 per cent of women respondents who reported experiencing sexual abuse), and this was followed by sexual discrimination (25 per cent) and sexual assault (13 per cent). Among survey participants who said they witnessed sexual abuse, the frequency of types of abuse witnessed was similar. The perpetrators of sexual abuse were overwhelmingly identified as men (94 per cent), including men of a higher rank than their victims (54 per cent) or of a similar rank to their victims (22 per cent), and almost all of the perpetrators were military or police personnel (91 per cent; Donnelly et al, 2022).

The patterns of male perpetration of sexual abuse in peacekeeping are also found in humanitarian organizations. The Humanitarian Women's Network carried out a convenience survey in early 2016, distributed through social media. The survey, completed by a total of 1,005 women from 70 organizations, tracked different forms of sexual abuse. The top three reported abuses women aid workers experienced were persistent unwanted romantic and sexual advances (55 per cent of participants), unwanted touching (48 per cent) and unwanted kissing (27 per cent). All of the reported incidents were perpetrated by men, and over one third were perpetrated by a male supervisor (Mazurana and Donnelly, 2017: 13).

Male dominance through positions of power in peacekeeping and aid missions was repeatedly highlighted in our interviews with peacekeepers and aid workers. Notably, it is the combination of male dominance and the presence of armed conflict, and its associated higher risk levels, that are core components driving a hyper-masculinized environment among peacekeepers and aid workers, which creates an environment conducive to sexual harassment and assault. One peacekeeper explained:

'There is something about the uniformed capabilities that can bring out the worst in people. An element of that is the high-stress environment and the personality types that go into these high-risk jobs, who tend to exhibit high-risk behaviour in all elements of their life'.[5]

Through positions of authority and access to weapons, some men peacekeepers and aid workers foster work environments where sexual discrimination, sexual harassment, discussions and jokes about sex and sexuality, homophobia and a 'boys will be boys' attitude flourish. Under these conditions, perpetrators and their supporters see sexual abuse as permissible. A man working in the humanitarian industry illustrated this phenomenon:

'[Organization name] tends to use insecurity and armed conflict to make the working environment very masculinized. When you go to meetings at high levels, you have an absolute male majority in charge of operations, missions and projects. So this makes reporting [on sexual harassment and assault] very difficult. ... The factors that make it conducive to abuse and hard to report is that it is really masculinized, and male-dominated, operating in situations of conflict and high insecurity, and include[s] staff from anti-gay countries. Male security officers, male health officers, male supervisors. And at the national level, your complaints or reports go to them, and their view on what to do is based a lot on their gender, views, religion, culture, et cetera'.[6]

Women peacekeepers referred to peacekeeping missions as having an environment similar to a "frat party", where male domination over women is celebrated (Donnelly et al, 2022: 13). Women peacekeepers noted that women are in the minority in peacekeeping missions, with one woman describing that she felt like she was an oasis surrounded by thirsty camels.[7] The idea of male dominance and displays of power was also discussed in relation to the perpetration of sexual abuse within the aid industry. Describing perpetrators of sexual abuse, one woman aid worker said, "Males above the age of 30 is what I have encountered, and then the common denominator that they are in some kind of position of power."[8]

In discussing the type of people that perpetrate sexual abuse, one woman peacekeeper explained:

'Those in my organization that were the harassers would harass the cleaning women as much as the parliamentarian. The bad behaviour is inherent. It is access and opportunity, not vulnerable groups. Where there is an opportunity to continue the bad behaviour [they] will exploit [it]. The mission is ripe for that.'[9]

However, our research also found that the rate of sexual abuse against relatively junior level women officers was higher compared to abuse against more senior women personnel (Nobert, 2016; see also Deloitte, 2019: 2), and power imbalance was repeatedly identified as a key factor in perpetrators' ability to commit sexual violence.[10]

Male domination within both types of organization (aid and peacekeeping) – in terms of levels of authority, power, decision making and resources – combined with a macho attitude about providing peacekeeping assistance and humanitarian relief contribute to demeaning and dangerous work and living environments for women, where sexual harassment and assault is much more likely to occur (see also Humanitarian Women's Network, 2016; Nobert, 2016; Deloitte, 2019).

Organizational cultures that promote and condone sexual abuse

In highly masculinized environments that promote and or condone sexual harassment, discrimination and assault, sexual abuse becomes normalized as part of the organizational culture (Higate, 2012; Wadham, 2017). Scholars note that while sexual abuse is not authorized within national militaries, it is often tolerated by commanding officers and soldiers and is primarily driven by social dynamics among soldiers rather than individual preferences (Wood and Toppelberg, 2017). Such practices arise through informal socialization processes (such as sexual hazing) that lead to the trivialization of sexual abuse and position it as an appropriate form of punishment for those who transgress military gender norms. Sexual abuse is also used by military men to retaliate against those within their forces who report or push back against sexual abuse (Wood and Toppelberg, 2017).

In our research, women peacekeepers spoke about the levels of sexual discrimination they faced in their role. For example, one woman police peacekeeper, with years of experience as a detective, explained that she was expected to do menial tasks: "There were constantly men from other countries giving me secretarial work. Maybe in their countries women aren't police officers, but of course I refused to do it. … They were used to having women do these things."[11] Another women peacekeeper spoke about receiving marriage proposals from men peacekeepers who hoped to receive citizenship in her country. According to another women peacekeeper, there was a "trivialization of sexual harassment" and the feeling that women's reports of sexual abuse were not important and that the "women didn't have a sense of humour".[12] This notion that sexual harassment was not taken seriously by the UN was also reflected in survey data. Of the people surveyed who reported an incident of sexual abuse, when asked what the official response was to their report, 47 per cent responded 'nothing' (Donnelly et al, 2022). According to our research subjects, sexual abuse was normalized throughout the peacekeeping environment. Women peacekeepers said they were warned by their female colleagues to anticipate sexual abuse and take measures to protect themselves from their male colleagues (Donnelly et al, 2022: 13).

While not comprised of military personnel, aid agencies similarly had cultures of sexual abuse. Our interview participants noted widespread institutional hypocrisy, where the very agencies that are meant to promote gender equality, human rights, and women's and girls' rights have senior staff who are guilty of degrading and violating these same 'standards. One woman humanitarian worker said:

> '[We have] organizations that have mission statements and whose existence is about reducing inequality or women's empowerment, as an example. And then to hear stories about field teams where there is rampant misogynistic, sexually exploitive humour and conversation that goes on a regular basis with no kind of pushback. And then when it gets reported, people are told "That is just life in the field and if you can't hack it, you should get out."'[13]

A culture of sexism and homophobia is strongly related to the prevalence of sexual abuse against LGBTQ+ within the aid sector.[14] Deloitte (2019: 2) found that 'respondents who identified as lesbian, gay, and queer reported the highest prevalence rates (53%, 48.4%, and 48.1%, respectively)' of sexual violence (see also Humanitarian Women's Network, 2016; Nobert, 2016). In our interviews with aid workers, they described working for agencies and in countries where pervasive sexist and homophobic attitudes existed, which contributed to demeaning, unsafe and abusive work environments. A man humanitarian worker said:

> '[LGBTQ+ people] had to put up with negative or harmful comments and a hostile work environment. At that point, when [co-workers] say hurtful things, you have to agree, and having any disagreement over rights of sexual minorities in an environment where people internally could turn against you in your own compound is very tricky. So when in these environments, you have to be quiet or you can put yourself at risk. So you just have to put up with it. You have to then be even more low profile than in your own home environment.'[15]

LGBTQ+ victims often did not report sexual violence within the missions because they feared violence by their colleagues, who often were intensely homophobic and from countries where homosexuality is punishable by imprisonment or death. This resulted in cases we term 'sexual identity blackmail', where perpetrators pressure victims to do what they are told or face having their sexual identity revealed to their homophobic colleagues. For example, we found that threats targeting LGBTQ+ staff meant that the compounds where aid workers live were extremely unsafe for LGBTQ+ aid professionals, a factor their abusers used to mistreat and silence them. This is deeply concerning given that staff compounds are supposed to be places of refuge and security (Mazurana and Donnelly, 2017). Nearly everyone we interviewed reported sexist and homophobic working and living environments while on humanitarian field missions. This atmosphere led to interviewees lacking confidence in agencies' and field missions' abilities to counter sexual abuse against LGBTQ+ aid professionals.

In both peacekeeping and aid organizations, study participants discussed the challenging settings inherent in the environment. Interviewees stated that healthy outlets for stress management and self-care were lacking on mission, and funding was not prioritized to help peacekeepers or aid workers maintain good mental or physical health. Rather, the use of alcohol and drugs was noted as the primary means for peacekeepers and aid workers to socialize and release stress, particularly in areas where they had limited movement. However, this created further insecurity, as perpetrators assaulted victims under the influence of drugs and alcohol. One woman humanitarian worker said: "My attacker was drunk, and [in] the two other instances when he [attacked other women] he was drunk again. There was definitely a pattern."[16]

Victims of sexual abuse who called for assistance from their agencies reported they were immediately interrogated as to their possible consumption of alcohol, regardless of the circumstances of their case. A woman humanitarian worker told us:

'The first question I was asked after my assault – in the middle of the night by the staff person on call for emergencies that week – was "Were you drinking?" As if I were to blame! I had not been drinking. My bedroom door was kicked down in the middle of the night while I was sleeping, by masked men wearing military attire.'[17]

Another woman peacekeeper discussed the ways in which the environment where peacekeepers operate affected incidences of sexual abuse:

'I just think in fast-moving situations, there is a rush to get people in, and they are in a communal living, bathing, eating area where there is a lack of privacy. The physical conditions make inequality even sharper. I have heard of places where they [women peacekeepers] had to go from their room to washing facilities in an area with no lighting. Some of those workers felt particularly vulnerable and women weren't going to the loo at night because they were getting targeted. I am thinking about the haste with which people are taken on without checking their histories, their backgrounds. Who is getting TCCs [troop-contributing countries] to validate that their staff have clean records?'[18]

These findings show that the male-dominated, sexist and homophobic cultures of peacekeeping and humanitarian aid missions are contributing factors to the sexual abuse of women and LGBTQ+ aid workers and peacekeepers by their colleagues.

Impunity

Impunity for sexual abuse is a serious and widespread problem within peacekeeping and the aid industry, resulting in a tolerance for sexual abuse (Neudorfer, 2014; Humanitarian Women's Network, 2016; Nobert, 2016; Mazurana and Donnelly, 2017; Wood and Toppelberg, 2017; Deloitte, 2019; Westendorf, 2020; Donnelly et al, 2022). Research finds that impunity for perpetrators leads to an environment where sexual abuse flourishes (Higate, 2007; Nordås and Rustad, 2013; Neudorfer, 2014).

Our research found that impunity permeates peacekeeping and aid missions. Perpetrators, ranging from staff at headquarters to international and national staff, largely do not face consequences for their actions. There are two interwoven causes for this – the first relates to reporting barriers and challenges and the second relates to organizational responses to reports of sexual violence. Notably, the reasons perpetrators are not held to account differ between peacekeeping missions and humanitarian organizations (see Donnelly et al, 2022).

Looking first at peacekeeping missions, the organization of missions creates a gap in accountability for sexual abuse. Most peacekeepers are from military contingents, and they remain under the exclusive jurisdiction of their national governments while deployed in UN peace operations (United Nations Peacekeeping, nd). Additionally, the UN's Office of International Oversight Services investigates SEA allegations against host populations and follows up with the troop- and police-contributing country on how they respond to SEA allegations. However, we could find no similar centralized reporting system or follow-up response to sexual abuse committed *against* peacekeepers themselves.

Peacekeepers report that peacekeeping missions often operate outside of traditional rules and regulations (Henry, 2012; Freedman, 2018). A senior male peacekeeper stated: "It is like the rest of the world doesn't apply to you."[19] This sense of being outside of the real world can lead to feelings of impunity. This was summed up by one woman peacekeeping expert we interviewed: "Basically most UN personnel are above the law."[20]

In terms of reporting sexual abuse that occurred against peacekeepers within a peacekeeping mission, interview participants found the reporting process unclear, and they had different perspectives on who to report to. Most thought that if they were going to report an incident, they should do so through the military chain of command in their mission. One peacekeeping interviewee shared an example of a friend who was sexually harassed by her supervisor, describing her experience of reporting:

> 'She went to Conduct and Discipline, through the chain of command, and the chain of command said it was up to the sending country to resolve the issue. She had to reach back through her chain of command, her country, explain the situation. And they aren't on the ground to see what is going on. There were other complaints from other members of this guy's country, and he did not get removed until the last day he was there. Chain of command in force structure really can't do anything – they can send a letter saying they don't want this guy back. It is up to the [troop-contributing] country to pull that guy back.'[21]

Several current and former peacekeepers noted that they would not personally report incidences of sexual abuse, because survivors are treated poorly by the mission. One former UN official, a woman, explained:

> 'At the moment, internally in the justice system, those who report and have alleged cases against them are not treated equally. The inequality feeds through every part of the system. Someone who makes a report, alleges a sexual harassment case, is not guaranteed a report of the investigation, they don't get to see it, no right to see it. Those who were alleged to abuse do see it. What's the defence for this? It is scandalous. You say you put victims first. Basically, they go into a black hole. One of the things we need in culture change is organizational transparency. It does not exist ... I gave evidence in a tribunal last year and it was very unpleasant. I don't think you can claim a victim-/survivor-centred approach in a system in which all your staff are out to prove the person is lying and contributing to the problem, not worthy of belief, not worthy of report, waiting four years for an outcome. These can be tidied up procedurally, but the culture in which that exists, in which the organization is infused with the cultural norms obtained outside (on rape culture, et cetera) how do you expect the organization to be different without tackling those bigger issues?'[22]

In comparison to peacekeeping missions, the situation for reporting abuse within the aid industry differs due to more centralized organization and reporting structures. Nevertheless, victims' experiences of reporting were as problematic as those experienced by the peacekeepers in our research. In some cases in the humanitarian sector, interviewees felt that the organization's human resources department treated their case seriously at first, but then they saw no follow-up.[23] Failure to prioritize expert and trained staff to handle incidences of sexual violence resulted in further harm to victims/survivors. Some interviewees noted that their case was not kept confidential. Others complained that they were given no control over the process. One woman aid worker who suffered sexual abuse at the hands of a man aid worker explained:

> 'There was no duty of care at all. If I had to do it over, or advise someone else, I would say get yourself a lawyer, because a lawyer can represent you to say what you need ... there was a tremendously toxic environment and basically it was seen as I was the problem'.[24]

Even if an aid worker wanted to report an instance of sexual abuse to their organization, many did not know the process. Interviewees stated that the mission's security advisor is not the most appropriate person to report an incidence of sexual violence to, though this is the person they were told to relay such experiences to. Most security advisors are men, and frequently ex-military, so have worked within organizational cultures that tend to be masculinized and militarized.[25] Furthermore, security personnel are often not well known to victims/survivors, and many victims said they hesitated to share sensitive or personal details with someone they barely knew. One woman humanitarian worker who was sexually abused explained: "How could I report it on the compound? The bosses were male and were hostile to me. Security would have to let me out. How could I report it? You are traumatized and you are talked to like you are incompetent."[26]

Additionally, victims may have been breaking security protocols or gendered social norms – such as drinking alcohol, going out with a group of locals or frequenting locations that were off limits – when the incident took place. In these types of situation, a victim might be hesitant to report sexual abuse for fear of being blamed for their assault. Concern around reporting instances of sexual abuse can be even more severe for LGBTQ+ individuals, who may fear outing themselves or that their case will not be handled with the appropriate level of sensitivity.[27] For these reasons, victims more frequently share their experience of sexual abuse with someone outside formal security or organizational reporting avenues.

Indeed, victims risk being blamed, sanctioned or fired for reporting their experience of sexual assault (Humanitarian Women's Network, 2016; Nobert, 2016). One interviewee noted that sexual violence is really about "power and extortion, and it can ruin your career and character, so [people] do not speak [out]".[28] Knowledge about victims being fired for reporting experiences of sexual assault was widespread among interviewees. A woman reporter told us:

> 'There was a woman who got raped and then afterwards felt like the NGO she was working for got rid of her because they did not want her to keep talking about it. Even though she was saying they should change their protocol, and she was upset and needing to talk about it with her colleagues, the NGO was saying to just be quiet and not talk about it. When she wasn't [quiet], they ended her contract.'[29]

We found that even if organizations provide information on reporting sexual violence against employees, organizational leadership often does little to respond. As explained by one interviewee, for organizations that do have policies about how to respond to sexual violence, "you have a difference in what happens at the corporate level and what filters down into the field".[30] There is a divide between the written policy and the organizational adoption of the policy. A woman aid worker explained:

> 'some of those who have these policies in place don't, in fact, enact them. So, they've taken measures because, for example, survivors or news agencies have spoken out against them. But these measures are largely in the form of policies or procedural guidelines but have not manifested into concrete change through implementation of policies/procedures, regular trainings, or even efforts toward a cultural shift within the workplace mentality.'[31]

Even when victims/survivors overcome the hurdles to report, they are frequently not taken seriously, and perpetrators do not face consequences (Humanitarian Women's Network, 2016; Deloitte, 2019). A woman security professional noted that sexual violence was not prioritized because it was seen as "someone else's problem" and as something "too difficult to deal with".[32] There was a sentiment throughout interviews that humanitarian organizations are more concerned with their reputation than the well-being of the aid workers. Survivors of sexual violence that did report to their employers felt that the organizations "brushed [their reports] under the carpet" and did not think their complaints "were serious enough".[33] The lack of follow-up on reports of sexual violence creates environments in which perpetrators continue to abuse other victims (Mazurana and Donnelly, 2017).

Conclusion

In this chapter, we have provided detailed insight into the toxic organizational work culture that enables and perpetuates sexual abuse inside peacekeeping and humanitarian aid missions. Based on our research, we conclude that sexual abuse against primarily women peacekeepers and women and LGTBQ+ aid workers by their men colleagues will continue until the organizational culture that fosters sexual abuse is taken seriously and tackled head on, and impunity is ended. It is not the presence of 'a few bad apples' that causes women and LGBTQ+ peacekeepers and aid workers to be sexually abused while on mission. It is the very fabric of the organizational culture itself. The changes needed are clear and leave no room for continued excuses not to enact reforms and stop impunity.

References

Deloitte (2019) *Safe Space Survey Report 2019*, Deloitte. Available from: www.interaction.org/resource-library/un-safe-space-survey-report/ (accessed 12 September 2023).

Donnelly, P., Mazurana, D. and Papworth, E. (2022) *Blue on Blue: Investigating Sexual Abuse of Peacekeepers*, New York and Bahrain: International Peace Institute. Available from: www.ipinst.org/2022/04/blue-on-blue-investigating-sexual-abuse-of-peacekeepers (accessed 12 September 2023).

Duncanson, C. (2009) 'Forces for good? Narratives of military masculinity in peacekeeping operations', *International Feminist Journal of Politics*, 11(1): 63–80.

Duriesmith, D. (2017) *Masculinity and New War: The Gendered Dynamics of Contemporary Armed Conflict*, London: Routledge.

Freedman, R. (2018) 'UNaccountable: a new approach to peacekeepers and sexual abuse', *European Journal of International Law*, 29(3): 961–85.

Henry, M. (2012) 'Peacexploitation? Interrogating labor hierarchies and global sisterhood among Indian and Uruguayan female peacekeepers', *Globalizations*, 9(1): 15–33.

Higate, P. (2007) 'Peacekeepers, masculinities, and sexual exploitation', *Men and Masculinities*, 10(1): 99–119.

Higate, P. (2012) 'Drinking vodka from the "butt-crack"', *International Feminist Journal of Politics*, 14(4): 450–69.

Humanitarian Women's Network (2016) *Full Survey Results*, Humanitarian Women's Network. Available from: https://interagencystandingcommittee.org/system/files/hwn_full_survey_results_may_2016.pdf (accessed 12 September 2023).

Insecurity Insight (nd) 'Aid in danger', *Insecurity Insight*. Available from: https://insecurityinsight.org/projects/aid-in-danger (accessed 12 September 2023).

Karim, S. and Beardsley, K. (2016) 'Explaining sexual exploitation and abuse in peacekeeping missions: the role of female peacekeepers and gender equality in contributing countries', *Journal of Peace Research*, 53(1): 100–15.

Mackenzie, M. (2015) *Beyond the Band of Brothers: The US Military and the Myth that Women Can't Fight*, Cambridge: Cambridge University Press.

Mazurana, D. and Donnelly, P. (2017) *Stop the Sexual Assault against Humanitarian and Development Aid Workers*, Somerville, MA: Feinstein International Center. Available from: https://fic.tufts.edu/publication-item/stop-sexual-assault-against-aid-workers/ (accessed 12 September 2023).

Mednick, S. and Craze, J. (2022) 'Aid sector sex abuse: a common occurrence with reoccurring themes', *The New Humanitarian*, 22 September. Available from: www.thenewhumanitarian.org/2022/09/22/aid-sector-sex-abuse-common-occurrence-reoccurring-themes (accessed 12 September 2023).

Myrttinen, H. (2019) 'Stabilizing or challenging patriarchy? Sketches of selected "new" political masculinities', *Men and Masculinities*, 22(3): 563–81.

Neudorfer, K. (2014) 'Reducing sexual exploitation and abuse: does deterrence work to prevent SEAs in UN peacekeeping missions?', *International Peacekeeping*, 21(5): 623–41.

Nobert, M. (2016) *Prevention, Policy and Procedure Checklist: Responding to Sexual Violence in Humanitarian and Development Settings*, Report the Abuse. Available from: https://safeguardingsupporthub.org/documents/prevention-policy-and-procedure-checklist (accessed 30 October 2023).

Nordås, R. and Rustad, S. (2013) 'Sexual exploitation and abuse by peacekeepers: understanding variation', *International Interactions*, 39(4): 511–34.

Sivakumaran, S. (2007) 'Sexual violence against men in armed conflict', *European Journal of International Law*, 18(2): 253–76.

Sull, D., Sull C., Cipolli, W. and Brighenti C. (2022) 'Why every leader needs to worry about toxic culture', *MIT Sloan Management Review*, 16 March. Available from: https://sloanreview.mit.edu/article/why-every-leader-needs-to-worry-about-toxic-culture/ (accessed 26 February 2024).

Szitany, S. (2020) *Gender Trouble in the US Military: Challenges to Regimes of Male Privilege*, Cham: Palgrave Macmillan.

True, J. (2012) *The Political Economy of Violence against Women*, Oxford: Oxford University Press.

United Nations Peacekeeping (nd) 'Standards of conduct', *United Nations Peacekeeping*. Available from: https://peacekeeping.un.org/en/standards-of-conduct (accessed 30 October 2023).

UN Women (2020) *Bridging the Gap: Sexual Exploitation, Abuse and Harassment (SEAH)*, New York: UN Women. Available from: www.unwomen.org/en/digital-library/publications/2020/09/discussion-paper-bridging-the-gap-sexual-exploitation-abuse-and-harassment (accessed 12 September 2023).

Wadham, B. (2017) 'Violence in the military and relations among men: military masculinities and "rape prone cultures"', in R. Woodward and C. Duncanson (eds) *The Palgrave Handbook of Gender and the Military*, London: Palgrave Macmillan, pp 241–56.

Westendorf, J. (2020) *Violating Peace: Sex, Aid, and Peacekeeping*, New York: Cornell University Press.

Wheeler, S. (2020) 'UN peacekeeping has a sexual abuse problem', *Human Rights Watch*, 11 January. Available from: www.hrw.org/news/2020/01/11/un-peacekeeping-has-sexual-abuse-problem (accessed 12 September 2023).

Wood, E. and Toppelberg, N. (2017) 'The persistence of sexual assault within the US military', *Journal of Peace Research*, 54(5): 620–33.

PART II

How It's Going: Implementing and Institutionalizing Protection from Sexual Exploitation and Abuse

Part I

5

Missing the Mark in PSEA

Asmita Naik and Jasmine-Kim Westendorf

Introduction

In 2001, Asmita Naik, co-author of this chapter, was part of a team of staff from the United Nations High Commissioner for Refugees (UNHCR) and Save the Children which unexpectedly uncovered allegations of sexual exploitation and abuse (SEA) of refugee children by aid workers in West Africa (UNHCR and Save the Children UK, 2001). The allegations spanned several refugee camps, hundreds of miles apart, in three countries: Liberia, Guinea, and Sierra Leone. The scale was truly shocking: some 70 perpetrators and 40 aid agencies were implicated, and 40 child victims were identified. It involved the most egregious abuses, including humanitarian workers demanding sex from children in exchange for desperately needed aid supplies, such as biscuits, soap and medicine. Nearly two decades later, despite efforts to prevent and ensure accountability for sexual misconduct, it was revealed that in 2011 survivors of the Haiti earthquake had been sexually exploited by Oxfam staff. Moreover, not only were the perpetrators from Oxfam not held properly accountable, they were in fact supported to transition to jobs elsewhere in the sector (O'Neill and Haddou, 2018). This was followed in quick succession by allegations engulfing multiple organizations in the aid sector, including Save the Children, UNAIDS, the United Nations Population Fund, UN Women, Médicines Sans Frontières, Plan International, the Catholic Agency for Overseas Development and the International Planned Parenthood Federation.

Protecting recipients of aid from harm caused by aid workers goes to the heart of the ethical responsibility in the aid sector; after all, unless organizations can apply core humanitarian values and human rights principles to their own conduct, how can they hold other actors to account for their behaviour? For a sector that is so dependent on its moral authority to carry out its work (Westendorf, 2020: 110–11), acknowledging and tackling aid worker abuses with integrity is not only the right course of action, but essential to the sector's maintenance of public perceptions of its legitimacy.

However, long-time observers of the aid sector's efforts to manage SEA in aid operations have watched the scandals of recent years with a strong sense of déjà vu and increasing disillusionment. After seeing the inadequacy of the aid sector's response to the cases in West Africa, Asmita argued that a humanitarian watchdog was the only way to provide redress for victims of SEA by aid workers (Naik, 2003). Today, following the 2018 resurgence of the issue on the global agenda and subsequent investment in efforts to prevent and punish SEA, the need for independent accountability mechanisms remains as important as ever. However, the likelihood of such a mechanism being realized is increasingly remote, as political will flags and new initiatives follow the footsteps of past efforts without addressing the reasons why such efforts struggled to effectively prevent SEA, encourage reporting and ensure perpetrators were held accountable for their actions.

While the scandals of recent years have prompted efforts to address the problem, continuing media reports of systematic SEA in the humanitarian sector have shown that real progress is not being made in ensuring accountability for its perpetration.[1] Incidents of SEA in humanitarian and peacekeeping contexts are, to some extent, inevitable given that the roots of sexual violence run deep in all societies and that abuses of power occur in all contexts where there are imbalances of power. Moreover, increased reports are not necessarily a cause for concern: as awareness of SEA is raised, reports will increase, as Sabrina White explores in more detail in Chapter 7. Such reports are a sign of progress. However, cases of systemic abuse continue to be uncovered, demonstrating persistent and unaddressed cultures of exploitation and impunity within particular missions or contexts. For example, *The New Humanitarian*'s 2020 investigation into sexual abuse by aid workers from the World Health Organization and other agencies in the Democratic Republic of Congo illustrated both pervasive cultures of exploitation and efforts by some World Health Organization staff to exclude certain allegations from their organizational responsibility due to deliberate misinterpretations of organizational policy (Flummerfelt and Peyton, 2020). Evidently, the sector has a long way to go in turning rhetoric of zero tolerance for sexual exploitation, abuse and inaction into *action*.

Far from the oft-repeated claim that the problem lies in 'under-reporting' by victims and difficulties in finding cases, in this chapter we argue that the real issue is 'under-action' by organizations to effectively prevent and ensure accountability for SEA, which in turn contributes to the endurance of cultures of impunity in the sector. We first explore the early SEA scandals that have set the scene for policy development in this space since 2002. We then consider the momentum towards the establishment of an independent accountability mechanism, and the reasons why this has not been established. Finally, we consider why efforts to date, despite the commitment and investment of individuals and organizations, have not resulted in significantly improved accountability outcomes for perpetrators of SEA in the aid sector.

Putting abuse on the agenda

The 2001 West Africa report was the first time that abuse perpetrated by aid workers had been identified so publicly. This does not mean it was not happening or known about before; indeed, the investigation uncovered pre-existing reports that this was a known problem in humanitarian operations (Naik, 2002). However, up until that point, aid worker abuse had not come to the fore of the policy agenda. It took a global media scandal to pierce the bubble of sanctity surrounding aid charities, which had benefited from the camouflaging of scandals involving United Nations (UN) peacekeepers over the years (Westendorf and Searle, 2017).

The revelations from the West Africa report were shocking, not least because it involved the exchange of sex for life-saving aid items, which has since become known as 'sextortion' (Transparency International, 2020). This prompted international outcry, and a frenzy of media attention, meetings, missions, working groups and plans of action ensued. Donors and aid agencies alike expressed horror, and stakeholders made a genuine effort to respond to these abuses. For example, the Inter-Agency Standing Committee (IASC) set up the Task Force on Protection from Sexual Exploitation and Abuse in Humanitarian Crises in March 2002 (IASC, 2002). The scandal set in motion a chain of events which led to global policy on this issue for the first time, in the form of a UN General Assembly Resolution (UNGA, 2003), followed by the 2003 UN Secretary-General's (UNSG's) Bulletin on 'Special measures for protection from sexual exploitation and sexual abuse' (UNSG, 2003), which outlined the UN's zero tolerance policy on SEA.

However, there was also a darker side to the response. Those who had exposed the abuse faced a backlash, the victims were denigrated, and some members of the aid community responded with defensiveness to the allegations. This attitude was best exemplified by the UNHCR at the time, as the High Commissioner, Ruud Lubbers, went on public record to dispute the claims of abuse in West Africa, calling them 'hearsay', despite the UN report's findings, and pledging that there would be no further studies or investigations in other places on the topic (Krever, 2002). Lubbers himself left office in 2005 following allegations of sexual harassment (van der Vat, 2018).

Ultimately, although the scandal led to some high-level policy changes, it amounted to little in the way of practical change on the ground. The specific allegations arising from the West Africa report were not promptly or adequately investigated – perpetrators were not sanctioned, no one in management was held accountable, and the victims did not achieve redress (Naik, 2003). Also, there were no wider programmatic measures aimed at preventing or responding to abuse embedded in aid operations. Instead, high-level coordination was facilitated, and policies were developed, under the restructured IASC Task Team on Accountability to Affected Populations and Protection from Sexual Exploitation and Abuse, as well as various NGO initiatives, such as the International Council for Voluntary Agencies' Building Safer Organisations project. The growth of humanitarian standards in this period, from the Humanitarian Accountability Partnership Standard through to its successor, the Core Humanitarian Standard, provided good practice markers to tackle the issue. Periodically, individual organizations placed a heightened focus on the issue; for instance, Save the Children UK drew attention to the problem in a 2008 report (Csáky, 2008). However, while important, these initiatives focused largely on the compliance and accountability of individuals rather than offering sustained engagement with the structural and contextual issues which give rise to SEA and present obstacles to reporting and effective investigation and accountability processes (Westendorf and Searle, 2017).

In 2017, the UNSG launched a reinvigorated programme to tackle the issue, focusing on four pillars: putting victims first; ending impunity; engaging civil society and external partners; and improving strategic communications for education and transparency (UNSG, 2017). This became the cornerstone of the victim-centred approach (explored by Jane Connors and Sabrina White in chapters 6 and 7, respectively). Soon, concerns regarding preventing and addressing the sexual harassment of aid workers were also being added to the policy repertoire (as explored by Phoebe Donnelly and Dyan Mazurana in Chapter 4). Despite these critically important policy developments, the issue of SEA continued to lack the acknowledgement, resources and political capital that it deserved and required for effective policy implementation.

Opportunity for action

When the Oxfam scandal broke in 2018, it bought with it a strong sense of history repeating itself alongside a renewed hope that, finally, something would be done to better prevent SEA and ensure perpetrators were held accountable. The policies and guidelines on SEA which had been developed in the intervening years were ready to be implemented. The time for action had come.

The policy response was swift. The UK aid sector was in the dock given that the two main organizations in the frame, Oxfam UK and Save the Children UK, were British aid agencies. The UK government was central to the response and convened a Safeguarding Summit in London in October 2018, bringing together more than 500 delegates from across the aid world (UK Government, 2018). This resulted in widespread commitments from governments, UN agencies and multilateral institutions, NGOs and the private sector to redouble efforts to address SEA in the sector. It also introduced a new framing for this work – safeguarding – a nebulous concept with origins in UK child protection discourse that was, suddenly, everywhere in the aid sector, supplanting the previous framing of protection from sexual exploitation and abuse (PSEA; Sandvik, 2019). Activity followed at the policy level, with new strategies and multilateral coordinating mechanisms established (UK Government, 2020a and 2020b). Millions were spent on employment cycle schemes aimed at preventing perpetrators from acquiring jobs in the sector, capacity building hubs and training schemes, programmes for victims and survivors, and efforts to strengthen investigations, oversight and data collection. Safeguarding advisors were employed across many organizations. Independent scrutiny was provided by the UK Parliament's International Development Committee, which provided real-time accountability for decisions and actions taken through a series of inquiries (International Development Committee, 2018).

With all this energy and attention, there were some more favourable markers of change compared to the 2002 response by the aid community. In 2002, the very public denials and recrimination by some leaders in the aid community hindered concrete action against the perpetrators and organizations associated with those allegations (Naik, 2003). This time, there were some signs of progress: a handful of high-profile cases saw alleged perpetrators disciplined (Bachelor, 2018); alleged perpetrators were referred for criminal prosecution, including cases where UN immunity was waived (Newsweek, 2018); organizations were held to account through threats of loss of funding (Bulman, 2018) and regulatory investigations (Charity Commission, 2018); and leaders were held responsible for their failings in handling complaints (BBC, 2018). This accountability was achieved through intense and sustained pressure from the media, social media, lobby groups, advocates, activists, parliamentarians and governments. However, these were singular cases and victims/survivors and whistle-blowers reported feeling aggrieved at the lack of redress across the board and being penalized for speaking out (Code Blue, 2018; Kay, 2019).

In the context of the UN's new victim-centred approach, there were renewed calls for mechanisms to give victims a voice in the aid sector (Hilhorst, 2018; Naik, 2018), and the Dutch government funded a study on the feasibility of an international ombudsman for aid (Hilhorst et al, 2018). This study found widespread support among aid workers for a backup appeal function should agency complaints mechanisms fail. However, strong resistance at institutional levels meant that the initiative ultimately ended up being little more than just another piece of research (CHS Alliance, nd), thereby again thwarting calls for independent oversight of responses to sexual misconduct in aid.

There were also some positive developments at the policy and institutional levels, particularly among donors who hitherto had largely left the aid organizations to their own devices. The most important change announced at the 2018 Global Safeguarding Summit was an agreement by 22 donor governments (controlling over 90 per cent of the world's humanitarian aid) to use their financial clout to require aid agencies to adhere to high standards on tackling SEA in exchange for funding (UK Government, 2018). The Organisation for Economic Co-operation and Development (OECD) Development Assistance Committee's Recommendation on Ending Sexual Exploitation, Abuse, and Harassment in Development Co-operation and Humanitarian Assistance was subsequently adopted, setting out the first international standard on how to prevent and respond to sexual exploitation, abuse and harassment. It was intended for governments to apply to national aid agencies and the wider international community, when working with civil society, charities and other bodies delivering humanitarian or aid programs (OECD, 2019). The Multilateral Organisation Performance Assessment Network hosted by the OECD carries out organizational performance assessments of UN agencies and other multilateral institutions, which now also incorporates indicators to assess efforts to address SEA and sexual harassment (see, for example, Multilateral Organisation Performance Assessment Network, 2023).

In practical terms, this meant that some donors integrated enhanced due diligence requirements into their funding agreements. Further efforts have since been made to harmonize the wording of grant requirements, which is important for mainstreaming and streamlining standards across the sector. Likewise, the UN and NGOs have also incorporated requirements into agreements with downstream partners (UN, 2018). The scandals discussed earlier have led to a wider awareness of and engagement with an approach to tackling SEA within the aid sector that includes donors, multilateral development banks and vertical funds, and private sector suppliers, as well as the better institutionalization of legal requirements through partnership contracts.

The scandals have also prompted some organizations to take their own action – for instance, by strengthening investigations and response mechanisms. Some donors, such as the US and the UK, have increased oversight of their own programmes, thus providing channels for complaints and some level of recourse for complainants who otherwise would have nowhere else to turn (USAID, 2023; Foreign, Commonwealth and Development Office, nd).[2] The renewed attention on this issue has led to good practice being developed on an ad hoc basis, with some exploring what the implementation of SEA standards means in practice. Girls' Education Challenge, for example, has an operating model that consists of very hands-on support to partners on the ground, making them aware of standards, building their capacity and helping them with the management and investigation of complaints.[3] This encouraging experience shows that while protection might be possible, it requires serious investment (Cornish-Spencer, 2021).

However, despite these important steps and commitments in response to the Oxfam scandal, there has not been fundamental change, as subsequent revelations of misconduct reveal. *The New Humanitarian*'s exposure of extensive SEA by aid workers from the World Health Organization and other agencies in the Democratic Republic of Congo during the 2018–20 Ebola response proved that all the high-level activity was not directly resulting in real change to how organizations were dealing with allegations of SEA (Flummerfelt and Peyton, 2020). Further, two recent reviews have also found inadequate progress. An IASC external review found that despite standards and guidance being in place, the 'pace of progress has not been steady', with particular gaps relating to accountability to victims and communities. It concluded by calling for investment in and scaling up of actions at the country level (IASC, 2021: 9). The Independent Commission for Aid Impact (ICAI), a UK body which oversees UK aid, was similarly critical of a lack of accountability to affected populations, the 'top-down approach' and the 'imbalance in favour of global, high-level initiatives, with less focus on the grassroots and operational levels' (ICAI, 2021: 18, 32). These are damning conclusions given the widespread commitments – and investments – made in 2018 and since (UK Government, 2018).

A need for accountability

In recent years, there has been much talk of 'survivor-centred' approaches that prioritize survivor choices, wishes, rights, dignity, safety, security and confidentiality. The aid sector has developed solid policies and procedures on how this can be turned into concrete measures – for example, through safe reporting, listening to survivors, providing them with support (including medical, psychosocial and financial), prompt and sensitive investigations, and accountability for perpetrators and others who fail to act (Tinde, 2018). The UN developed a Victims' Rights Statement, followed by further guidelines aimed at helping victims/survivors of abuse and exploitation better understand the redress and support available to them (UN, nd; also see Jane Connors in Chapter 6).

However, few organizations are prepared to confront the reality of what taking a survivor-centred approach means. Being survivor-centred and being accountable as an organization are intrinsically linked; putting survivors first means putting organizations second, allowing complaints to come to the fore irrespective of the cost to an organization's reputation and budget.

The only meaningful way to take a survivor-centred approach is to remove the conflict of interest that lies at the heart of an organization's ability to respond – a lesson already learned by better-regulated sectors around the world – ensuring that cases of misconduct are handled by those without vested interests, meaning ombudsman-type models (Warren, 2023).

Efforts to bring about external sector-wide oversight of responses to SEA through the establishment of an international ombuds office for the aid sector have been met with strong institutional resistance (Hilhorst et al, 2018: 14). The absence of a collective mechanism with sufficient leverage and clout to hold large international organizations accountable to the implementation of the PSEA standards they have agreed to has led to a splintered and inadequate response. It falls on each organization in the aid supply chain to handle cases professionally and exercise oversight on those lower down the delivery chain by providing channels for reporting backed by protection for complainants. Aid organizations have avoided external scrutiny for their internal management of SEA allegations and investigations, and their donors have allowed them to remain unaccountable, because of concerns regarding reputation management, confidentiality, public perceptions of the sector and the clash of legal regimes regarding privacy and employment law (Hilhorst et al, 2018: 14).

Approaches that involved holding organizations to account were disregarded in favour of schemes which diverted attention from organizational responsibility and focused narrowly on the accountability of individual perpetrators. An ecosystem of various initiatives was designed to enable employers to check for past misconduct by prospective employees. This included the Misconduct Disclosure Scheme, allowing participating organizations to share information on misconduct going back five years; the Aid Worker Registration Scheme (or 'humanitarian passports'), which seems to have been dropped after an initial scoping study by the UK; the Soteria project, a £10 million flagship Interpol project to strengthen and digitize criminal record checks and improve information sharing between national law enforcement agencies and aid sector organizations; and the United Nations Misconduct Tracking Scheme and Clear Check (see Naik, 2020, for further details of initiatives).

While strengthening pre-employment checks to prevent perpetrators from being hired is an important part of the response, this first requires perpetrators to be identified. It also needs functioning complaints mechanisms and investigative and disciplinary processes to be in place, and it relies on individuals understanding and feeling confident to report when they are aware of behaviour that constitutes sexual misconduct. This is challenging given the high rates of misunderstanding and disagreement with elements of the zero tolerance policy's prohibition on sexual exploitation (Westendorf, 2023), the significant barriers to reporting, including fear of retaliation

(Westendorf, 2020), and the realities of the contexts in which humanitarian actors tend to operate, which are often characterized by high levels of sexual and gender-based violence and mistrust in authorities. Recent reviews have confirmed the 'inherent limitations' of these approaches (ICAI, 2021: 26; see also IASC, 2021).

Furthermore, aside from doubts as to the efficacy of these approaches, the schemes raise serious questions about adherence to basic principles of fairness, due process and privacy. The storing and sharing of data on individual aid workers without sufficient effort to ensure the quality and veracity of such information is concerning and risks miscarriages of justice. The risk is particularly pronounced for locally recruited aid workers, who tend to have the least protection under national laws. Such databases pose risks to victims as well – see, for example, the 2019 CNN report about a female victim of sexual harassment who found herself the target of retaliation and was the subject of a false claim of sexual assault (Krever, 2019). The sharing of spurious personal data reduces confidence in the system and makes the reporting of complaints even more unlikely.

The sector has pursued other futile and ineffectual paths that have not helped to focus on the SEA of beneficiaries by aid workers, including the conflation of traditional protection programming aimed at addressing external threats with the internal risks posed by organizations and their staff, such as fraud – which has been amplified with the importation of the 'safeguarding' frame to the international aid sphere; the fusion of abuses against beneficiaries with abuses against staff, resulting in a detraction in focus from those most vulnerable and lacking in recourse; the pursuit of criminal justice solutions for behaviours that either do not reach the criminal threshold or do not have a realistic prospect of criminal conviction; and the transference of approaches used in stable Western democracies for tackling child abuse and sexual violence into war-torn contexts without a functioning rule of law.

Conclusion

While there has been some investment in more practical action on the ground – for example, guidance, training and support on safeguarding offered to smaller charities – these efforts have been overshadowed both in budget and attention by the high-level, top-down schemes described in this chapter. Ultimately, however, the guidance has existed for a long time, and the sector knows what to do about SEA. The real challenge is overcoming inadequate implementation, insufficient political will and reluctance on the part of donors and aid agencies alike to move beyond rhetoric and bureaucracy to actually implement meaningful change and address the systemic and structural factors that give rise to SEA, discourage reporting of incidences and hamper effective investigations and accountability mechanisms.

We already know what needs to be done: undertake operational action to raise awareness of rights; enable victims and others to raise concerns through safe and accessible complaints mechanisms; act on this information promptly through high-quality independent investigations; take robust disciplinary action to sanction perpetrators (including sharing misconduct information if this can be done fairly); and refer matters to the police where crimes are involved. This, coupled with stronger donor oversight of aid-receiving organizations – including, for instance, through random spot checks and human rights fact-finding missions to test the reality on the ground – would send a clear signal to those working in the sector and beyond that inaction on sexual exploitation, abuse and harassment by aid workers will not be tolerated.

If the problem of sexual exploitation in aid is to be addressed, it requires aid agencies and donors to turn away from partisan interests and initiatives which miss the mark and be willing to genuinely stand on the side of beneficiaries, provide implementing organizations with the funds they need to take action (rather than simply setting standards for them) and then be ready to hold them to account when they do not act in ways that effectively prevent, investigate and ensure accountability for SEA. The global media spotlight has moved on and is unlikely to visit again until there is a new generation ready to be shocked by the incongruity of aid workers causing harm to those they are supposed to help. Without this, it falls on the aid sector, donors and implementers alike to do what is needed to ensure beneficiaries of aid are protected from those individuals working within aid organizations who take the opportunities presented by their employment in crisis and conflict contexts to abuse and exploit.

References

Bachelor, T. (2018) 'Ex-Save the Children boss Justin Forsyth resigns from Unicef after allegations of inappropriate behaviour', *The Independent*, 22 February. Available from: www.independent.co.uk/news/uk/home-news/save-the-children-unicef-charity-scandal-misconduct-justin-forsyth-resigns-a8223901.html (accessed 13 March 2023).

BBC (2018) 'Save the Children chairman Sir Alan Parker resigns', *BBC*, 19 April. Available from: www.bbc.co.uk/news/uk-43831101 (accessed 21 October 2023).

Bulman, M. (2018) 'Government threatens to cut aid funding for charities accused of sexual exploitation after Oxfam scandal', *The Independent*, 11 February. Available from: www.independent.co.uk/news/uk/home-news/oxfam-sexual-exploitation-charity-aid-funding-government-penny-mordaunt-international-development-a8204896.html (accessed 13 March 2023).

Charity Commission (2018) 'Charity Commission opens statutory inquiry into Oxfam and sets out steps to improve safeguarding in the charity sector', *Gov.uk*, 12 February. Available from: www.gov.uk/government/news/charity-commission-opens-statutory-inquiry-into-oxfam-and-sets-out-steps-to-improve-safeguarding-in-the-charity-sector (accessed 13 March 2023).

CHS Alliance (nd) 'Closing the accountability gap to better protect victims/survivors of SEAH (PSEAH 2.0) – project', *CHS Alliance*. Available from: www.chsalliance.org/get-support/article/closing-the-accountability-gap-to-better-protect-victims-survivors-of-sexual-abuse-project/ (accessed 13 March 2023).

CNN (2002) 'Insight' [transcript], *CNN*. Available from: http://edition.cnn.com/TRANSCRIPTS/0205/08/i_ins.01.html (accessed 13 March 2023).

Code Blue (2018) 'Code Blue exposes UNFPA efforts to prevent Indian police from investigating sexual assault charges against senior official', *Code Blue*, 16 August. Available from: www.codebluecampaign.com/press-releases/2018/8/16 (accessed 13 March 2023).

Cornish-Spencer, D. (2021) *Protection is Possible*, Girls' Education Challenge and UK Aid. Available from: https://girlseducationchallenge.org/media/ftvjxa5u/protection_is_possible_report_final.pdf (accessed 13 March 2023).

Csáky, C. (2008) *No One To Turn To: The Under-Reporting of Child Sexual Exploitation and Abuse by Aid Workers and Peacekeepers*, London: Save the Children. Available from: www.savethechildren.org.uk/content/dam/global/reports/education-and-child-protection/no-one-to-turn-to.pdf (accessed 13 March 2023).

Flummerfelt, R. and Peyton, N. (2020) 'More than 50 women accuse aid workers of sex abuse in Congo Ebola crisis', *The New Humanitarian*, 29 September. Available from: www.thenewhumanitarian.org/2020/09/29/exclusive-more-50-women-accuse-aid-workers-sex-abuse-congo-ebola-crisis (accessed 13 March 2023).

Hilhorst, D. (2018) 'Aid agencies can't police themselves. It's time for a change', *The New Humanitarian*, 22 February. Available from: www.thenewhumanitarian.org/opinion/2018/02/22/aid-agencies-can-t-police-themselves-it-s-time-change (accessed 13 March 2023).

Hilhorst, D., Naik, A. and Cunningham, A. (2018) *International Ombuds for Humanitarian and Development Aid Scoping Study*, The Hague: International Institute for Social Studies.

ICAI (Independent Commission for Aid Impact) (2021) *The UK's Approach to Safeguarding in the Humanitarian Sector: Approach Paper*, London: ICAI. Available from: https://icai.independent.gov.uk/review/the-uks-approach-to-safeguarding-in-the-humanitarian-sector/review/ (accessed 13 March 2023).

IASC (Inter-Agency Standing Committee) (2002) *Plan of Action and Core Principles: Codes of Conduct on Protection from Sexual Abuse and Exploitation in Humanitarian Crises*, New York: IASC.

IASC (Inter-Agency Standing Committee) (2021) *External Review: Global Report on Protection from Sexual Exploitation and Abuse and Sexual Harassment*, New York: IASC.

International Development Committee (2018) 'Sexual exploitation and abuse in the aid sector', *UK Parliament*. Available from: https://publications.parliament.uk/pa/cm201719/cmselect/cmintdev/840/84002.htm (accessed 13 March 2023).

Kay, L. (2019) 'Oxfam whistleblower receives award', *Third Sector*, 23 January. Available from: www.thirdsector.co.uk/oxfam-whistleblower-receives-award/management/article/1523575 (accessed 13 March 2023).

Krever, M. (2019) 'UN worker who accused official of sexual assault has been fired', *CNN*, 17 December. Available from: https://edition.cnn.com/2019/12/16/world/unaids-martina-brostrom-intl/index.html (accessed 23 March 2023).

Multilateral Organisation Performance Assessment Network (2023) *Progress on PSEAH? From Words to Deeds*, Paris: Multilateral Organisation Performance Assessment Network. Available from: https://issuu.com/mopan_network/docs/seah_note (accessed 13 March 2023).

Naik, A. (2002) 'Protecting children from the protectors: lessons from West Africa', *Forced Migration Review*. Available from: www.fmreview.org/displaced-children-and-adolescents/naik (accessed 13 March 2023).

Naik, A. (2003) 'The West Africa sex scandal', *Humanitarian Practice Network*, 31 July. Available from: https://reliefweb.int/report/guinea/west-africa-scandal-points-need-humanitarian-watchdog (accessed 13 March 2023).

Naik, A. (2018) 'Trial by media not the answer to safeguarding concerns', *Civil Society*, 17 May. Available from: www.civilsociety.co.uk/voices/asmita-naik-trial-by-media-not-the-answer-to-safeguarding-concerns.html (accessed 13 March 2023).

Naik, A. (2020) 'Opinion: global aid worker register to prevent abuse risks doing more harm than good', *Devex*, 10 July. Available from: www.devex.com/news/opinion-global-aid-worker-register-to-prevent-abuse-risks-doing-more-harm-than-good-97628 (accessed 13 March 2023).

Newsweek (2018) 'Exclusive: senior U.N. Official Fired, Referred to Criminal Authorities for Alleged Sexual Misconduct', *Newsweek*, 17 September. Available from: www.newsweek.com/senior-un-official-sexual-misconduct-1124719 (accessed 13 March 2023).

OECD (Organisation for Economic Co-operation and Development) (2019) *DAC Recommendation on Ending Sexual Exploitation, Abuse, and Harassment in Development Co-operation and Humanitarian Assistance*, OECD. Available from: https://legalinstruments.oecd.org/en/instruments/OECD-LEGAL-5020 (accessed 13 March 2023).

O'Neill, S. and Haddou, L. (2018) 'Oxfam sex scandal: sacked staff found new aid jobs', *The Times*, 10 February. Available from: www.thetimes.co.uk/article/new-shame-for-oxfam-h5nq8lmfn (accessed 13 March 2023).

Sandvik, K. (2019) '"Safeguarding" as humanitarian buzzword: an initial scoping', *Journal of International Humanitarian Action*, 4: 3. doi: 10.1186/s41018-019-0051-1

Tinde, T. (2018) 'Survivor-centred approach in protection and response to sexual exploitation and abuse (PSEA)', *SlideShare*. Available from: www.slideshare.net/TinaTinde/webinar-psea-survivor-centered-approach (accessed 13 March 2023).

Transparency International (2020) 'Breaking the silence around sextortion: the links between power, sex and corruption', *Transparency International*, 5 March. Available from: www.transparency.org/en/publications/breaking-the-silence-around-sextortion (accessed 13 March 2023).

UK Government (2018) 'Safeguarding Summit 2018', *Gov.uk*. Available from: www.gov.uk/government/topical-events/safeguarding-summit-2018 (accessed 13 March 2023).

UK Government (2020a) *Aid Worker Registration Scheme Legal Review*, London: UK Government.

UK Government (2020b) *Cross-Sector Progress Report on Safeguarding Against Sexual Exploitation, Abuse and Sexual Harassment (SEAH) 2019–2020*, London: UK Government.

UN (United Nations) (2018) *United Nations Protocol on Allegations of Sexual Exploitation and Abuse Involving Implementing Partners*, 21 March. Available from: www.un.org/en/pdfs/UN%20Protocol%20on%20SEA%20Allegations%20involving%20Implementing%20Partners%20-%20English_Final.pdf (accessed 13 March 2023).

UN (United Nations) (nd) 'Victims' rights first', *United Nations*. Available from: www.un.org/en/victims-rights-first (accessed 13 March 2023).

UNGA (United Nations General Assembly) (2003) *Investigation into Sexual Exploitation of Refugees by Aid Workers in West Africa*, UN Doc A/RES/57/306.

UNHCR and Save the Children UK (2001) *Sexual Violence and Exploitation: The Experience of Refugee Children in Liberia, Guinea and Sierra Leone*, UNHCR. Available from: www.parliament.uk/globalassets/documents/commons-committees/international-development/2002-Report-of-sexual-exploitation-and-abuse-Save-the-Children.pdf (accessed 13 March 2023).

UNSG (United Nations Secretary-General) (2003) *Secretary-General's Bulletin: Special Measures for Protection from Sexual Exploitation and Sexual Abuse*, UN Doc ST/SGB/2003/13.

UNSG (United Nations Secretary-General) (2017) *Special Measures for Protection from Sexual Exploitation and Abuse: A New Approach*, UN Doc A/71/818.

van der Vat, D. (2018) 'Ruud Lubbers obituary', *The Guardian*, 19 February. Available from: www.theguardian.com/world/2018/feb/19/ruud-lubbers-obituary (accessed 13 March 2023).

Warren, M. (2023) 'Professional healthcare regulation explained', *Professional Standards Authority for Health and Social Care*, 10 April. Available from: www.professionalstandards.org.uk/news-and-blog/blog/detail/blog/2018/04/10/professional-healthcare-regulation-explained (accessed 13 March 2023).

Westendorf, J. (2020) *Violating Peace: Sex, Aid, and Peacekeeping*, Ithaca, NY: Cornell University Press.

Westendorf, J. (2023) 'A problem of rules: sexual exploitation and UN legitimacy', *International Studies Quarterly*, 67(3): 1–13.

Westendorf, J. and Searle, L. (2017) 'Sexual exploitation and abuse in peace operations: trends, policy responses and future directions', *International Affairs*, 93(2): 365–87.

6

The Imperative of Prioritizing Victims' Rights

Jane Connors

Introduction

For over 20 years, the United Nations (UN) and partner organizations have developed and implemented increasingly comprehensive standards and policies to prevent and respond to sexual exploitation and abuse by UN and related personnel. These include the 2002 six core principles (revised in 2019) adopted by the Interagency Standing Committee (IASC, 2019), the body responsible for coordination of humanitarian action by UN and non-UN partners,[1] and the 2003 UN Secretary-General's Bulletin on 'special measures for protection from sexual exploitation and abuse' (UN Secretariat, 2003). Successive secretaries-general have implemented a 'zero-tolerance' policy requiring action on every allegation, and a plethora of prevention and response policies, mechanisms and tools has been, and continues to be, crafted and implemented.[2] These include efforts to engender accountability of staff, particularly leadership; risk assessment and management tools; mandatory regular training; and the operationalization in 2018 of the screening database 'ClearCheck', a UN system-wide database directed to preventing re-employment of individuals with substantiated allegations of sexual exploitation, sexual abuse or sexual harassment, or who left employment for any reason during a related investigation. Security Council Resolution 2272 confirms the Secretary-General's capacity to repatriate military or formed police units where there is credible evidence of widespread or systemic sexual exploitation or abuse (UN Security Council, 2016). This constitutes a significant sanction, and was used most recently in 2021 and 2023 in relation to Gabonese and Tanzanian contingents, respectively, deployed to the peacekeeping operation in the Central African Republic (see

UN, 2021c, 2023). The Resolution also empowers the Secretary-General to replace all units of a contributing state which has not taken appropriate steps to investigate allegations, hold perpetrators accountable and inform the Secretary-General of progress in these areas with personnel from other countries; the Secretary-General can also determine, based on an assessment of the contributing state's performance, whether it should participate in peacekeeping at all.

Despite these and other measures, allegations – many substantiated – of sexual exploitation and abuse by UN peacekeeping, humanitarian and development personnel continue to surface. Those reported to the UN are made public on its website (see UN, nd-a) in more or less 'real time', and in the Secretary-General's annual reports on special measures for protection from sexual exploitation and abuse.[3] The media and academia also uncover allegations implicating both UN personnel and people working in civil society and other organizations delivering humanitarian and development aid (Lee and Bartels, 2020; Dodds, 2023). Many of the latter implement UN programmes on the ground and are, accordingly, referred to as 'implementing partners'.

To step up progress, in early 2017, UN Secretary-General António Guterres launched a 'new approach' to confront sexual exploitation and abuse, the centrepiece of which was a pledge to elevate the voice of victims themselves and put their rights and dignity at the forefront of UN efforts. Other elements of the approach were to end impunity; build a multistakeholder network of civil society, communities, leaders, experts, organizations and states to support prevention and response; and reorient the UN approach to communications to raise awareness, confront the stigma and discrimination victims may face and promote the UN as a global platform to exchange best practices (UNGA, 2017: 6).

As the first UN Victims' Rights Advocate (VRA) for victims of sexual exploitation or abuse by UN or related personnel (with tenure from 2017–24), I focus in this chapter on the first element of the Secretary-General's new approach – the centring of victims and their rights and dignity – which cuts across the three elements noted in the previous paragraph.

Elevating the rights and dignity of those harmed by sexual exploitation and abuse represents a profound shift in emphasis from previous prevention and response efforts, which predominantly prioritized the reputation of UN organizations, operational effectiveness and the conduct and discipline of perpetrators. Here, I outline the Secretary-General's vision of the approach and how it would be delivered. I describe progress in its implementation in terms of the VRA's global outreach and advocacy, including to clarify the meaning of the victim-centred/victims' rights approach. Drawing on the work of the Senior Victims' Rights Officers (SVROs), whose role mirrors mine on the ground in four countries (Central African Republic,

Democratic Republic of the Congo, Haiti and South Sudan), I examine how the approach has been implemented in the field. Throughout, I point to stumbling blocks in implementing the approach. I conclude by highlighting the challenges confronting full realization of the Secretary-General's vision (also see Connors, 2019).

The rights and dignity of victims at the forefront

In setting out his new approach, the Secretary-General emphasized that, first and foremost, the priority for UN entities in addressing sexual exploitation and abuse must be to strengthen the support it gives to victims. He reflected on the fact that the international community has developed extremely sophisticated ways to confront and respond to suffering, but in doing so, and dealing with the magnitude of pain and deprivation around the world, may have inoculated itself against its worst effects. To mitigate this, he called for the restoration of personal connections with, and empathy towards, victims of sexual exploitation and abuse in meaningful ways, giving visibility to those who have suffered the most. The Secretary-General expressed his intention to provide victims with a 'platform for their voice that the world will not be able ignore', to meet with them and hear from them directly, and to let them know that their protection is the UN's priority and that, going forward, the organization will be at their side to support them through the healing process as they rebuild their lives (UNGA, 2017: 8).

To operationalize the approach, which is directed to ensuring that all victims have adequate protection, appropriate assistance and reliable recourse to justice, the Secretary-General announced his intention to appoint a system-wide VRA. The VRA works, with the support of a small office, across the UN family of organizations at headquarters and in the field[4] to ensure that reliable, gender-sensitive pathways exist for every victim or witness to file complaints, and that assistance is rapidly and sensitively delivered. The VRA was envisaged to work with local authorities, civil society organizations and UN entities to ensure that the rights of each victim are protected through access to appropriate and timely judicial processes. Every victim should receive appropriate personal care, follow-up attention and information on the progress of their case, and their rights should be respected as investigations and accountability processes unfold (UNGA, 2017: 9). The VRA would collaborate with government institutions, civil society and national legal human rights organizations in host countries and countries of alleged perpetrators to build networks of support to assist in harnessing the full effect of local laws, including remedies, and facilitate provision to victims of updated information on judicial and administrative proceedings. The VRA would invite external experts, advocates and leading aid organizations to inform the development of policies and tools to strengthen support for victims (UNGA, 2017: 9; UN, nd-b).

To translate the VRA's global advocacy into practical action to benefit victims on the ground, the Secretary-General instructed his special representatives in the peace operations in the Central African Republic, the Democratic Republic of the Congo, Haiti and South Sudan[5] – the four operations with the greatest number of allegations reported at the time – to designate a mid- to senior-level staff member to perform the role of victims' rights advocate in the field. At the outset, these advocates, who report both to the Secretary-General's special representative in the missions and the VRA, performed this function along with their pre-existing duties. Now dedicated SVRO posts, performing the field advocate role, are formally established in the staffing tables of the missions and, in the case of Haiti, the UN Integrated Office in Haiti. As in the case of the VRA position, their role concerns victims of all UN and related personnel, with their tasks being to maintain direct and regular contact with victims, accompany them as they report, support them in investigations and as they seek assistance and accountability, including through judicial redress, and keep them abreast of their cases.

As sexual exploitation and abuse are not unique to peace operations, the Secretary-General also called for the designation of advocates, with appropriate resources, in humanitarian and development contexts where reported cases of sexual exploitation and abuse suggested that similar special measures might be required (UNGA, 2017: 10). As discussed later, despite the encouragement of the Secretary-General, the VRA and other UN leadership, to date no other dedicated field advocate is operational, due to resource constraints and the humanitarian sector's desire to prioritize deployment of interagency coordinators for protection from sexual exploitation and abuse, whose role includes working on victim/survivor-centred assistance (see IASC, nd-b). As a middle ground, however, Victims' Rights Focal Points – individuals who promote victims' rights and interests, along with other duties – are increasingly being designated in development contexts. Positively, several UN entities have created dedicated senior victims' care specialist roles at their headquarters.

Global advocacy

I began work as the first VRA in mid-September 2017, alongside the double-hatted field victims' rights advocates who started work at the same time. They were progressively replaced as the full-time SVROs were recruited, with the latter all operational from the end of November 2021. These roles were entirely new to the UN – although such functions exist in many Member States, with victims' advocates, commissioners or advisors promoting the rights of victims of crime and other wrongs (for example,

Home Office, 2017). The initial tasks were to establish the contours of the roles and to flesh out the content of an approach placing the rights and dignity of victims of sexual exploitation and abuse at the forefront, and how this was to be achieved. At the outset, I sought to give visibility and a voice to victims, making clear that the priority concern in prevention and response is a woman, girl, man or boy who is hurt, often fearful, and may be subject to retaliation or reprisal, stigma, exclusion or abandonment. In many cases, victims are left with a child as a result of the sexual exploitation and abuse.

Generating an understanding of the system-wide reach of the roles in a context where each UN entity has separate competencies and governance structures required advocacy, engagement and consultation directed to institutionalization of a victim-centred, rights-based approach in all UN activities to prevent and respond to sexual exploitation and abuse. I convened similar UN mandates – such as the Special Representatives of the Secretary-General on children and armed conflict, sexual violence in conflict, and violence against children; special procedures mandate holders of the Human Rights Council; and UN entity representatives – to identify best practices and lessons learned in preventing sexual exploitation and abuse, encouraging reporting of complaints, providing services to victims and facilitating access to justice. Drawing on synergies and complementarities in mandates, this contributed to a growing understanding of the approach.

I maintained close interaction with Member States to raise awareness of the new roles and the Secretary-General's policy of elevating the rights and dignity of victims in relation to protection from sexual exploitation and abuse. Sustained advocacy was also required to secure the establishment of the VRA position, the Office of the Victims' Rights Advocate (OVRA) and the SVROs in the UN budgetary framework in 2018 and 2019 (UNGA, 2018: 6, 2019: 4). Briefings for, and discussions with, intergovernmental and regional organizations, civil society, academia and the media became regular and routine. I partnered with the Global Alliance of National Human Rights Institutions, which, together with the OVRA, produced a guide to encourage national human rights institutions in-country to support victims on the ground (OVRA, 2021). This included strengthening reporting and referral mechanisms; facilitating victims' access to appropriate and quality legal aid; raising awareness of service providers and others of the importance of realizing the rights of victims of sexual exploitation and abuse; and pressing for legislation, such as that establishing extraterritorial jurisdiction.

In October 2017, beginning with the Central African Republic, I initiated the practice of visiting countries with varying UN presences – peace, humanitarian, development or a combination of these – to observe how the Secretary-General's victims' rights approach is implemented on the ground. These visits provided an important opportunity for me to meet with victims at their request, individually and confidentially, to hear their concerns, in particular so that responses can be tailored to their individual needs and, based on their feedback, UN action to prevent and respond to sexual exploitation and abuse can be strengthened. During these visits, UN system actors, civil society, state entities and other stakeholders often come together, allowing for the creation of stronger partnerships, clarification and strengthening of their understanding of the victims' rights approach and identification of areas of synergy and potential overlap. By the end of 2023, I had visited 16 countries (in chronological order, the Central African Republic, South Sudan, Haiti, Colombia, Lebanon, Jordan, the Democratic Republic of the Congo, Kenya, Uruguay, Argentina, Mali, South Africa, Liberia, Thailand, Cambodia and Indonesia) and made follow-up visits to several of them. I also visited some of these countries to facilitate the resolution of outstanding paternity and child maintenance claims, usually with the relevant SVRO and colleagues from the Conduct and Discipline Service of the UN Department of Management Strategy, Policy and Compliance. Although much needs to be done, it is gratifying to see the progress made in implementing the victims' rights approach, particularly through the efforts of the SVROs.

An initial challenge to the implementation of the Secretary-General's policy to centre the rights and dignity of victims was the perception that it, and the work of the VRA and the SVROs, related to victims of peacekeeping personnel only. Beginning with the IASC, this perception changed. In 2018, the IASC launched a 'championship' strategy to address sexual exploitation, abuse and sexual harassment which inter alia focuses on strengthening safe and accessible reporting, improving quality of assistance for victims and enhancing accountability, including through prompt and safe investigations (see IASC, nd-a). The SVROs and I, participating as observers in its Technical Advisory Group, have worked closely with successive champions and the IASC principals to support the creation of robust systems, assistance capacities and follow-up to encourage victims/survivors to come forward (IASC, nd-c). We also participated in the development of the *IASC Definition & Principles of a Victim/Survivor Centered Approach*, released in June 2023 (IASC, 2023) and assisted in the IASC's efforts to improve internal investigations by its members and related entities. I was invited to co-lead a workstream of the UN Chief Executives Board (CEB) Task Force on Addressing Sexual Harassment within the organizations of the UN (UN, 2021a). Where the UN development system is concerned, I support resident coordinators and UN country teams to deliver on their responsibilities to prevent and respond to sexual exploitation and abuse, as outlined in the Management and Accountability Framework, which encourages the coordinators to designate system-wide victims' rights focal points (UN, 2021b: 6–7, 9), and I brief country teams. Notably, resident coordinators have been instrumental in encouraging states which deploy personnel in peacekeeping to secure accountability of perpetrators of sexual exploitation and abuse, and facilitate resolution of paternity claims.

My advocacy on embedding a victims' rights approach to sexual misconduct was not confined to the UN system, but included interaction with other entities, such as the North Atlantic Treaty Organization (NATO) as it developed its policy on preventing and responding to sexual exploitation and abuse, adopted in November 2019 (NATO, 2021), and FIFA in its consultations on the creation of an international safe sport entity (Beutler, 2021). I partnered closely with the Development Assistance Committee of the Organisation for Economic Co-operation and Development (OECD), whose recommendation on ending sexual exploitation, abuse and harassment in development cooperation and humanitarian assistance emphasizes the importance of implementation of a victim/survivor-centred approach (OECD, 2019: 9–10). I participated in its reference group and regular peer learning sessions, including to support its work to develop a toolkit on implementation of the recommendation. Cooperation with Member States continued, notably through taking part in events such as the UK's Safeguarding Summit 2018, the conference of the International Prevention of Sexual Violence in Conflict Initiative hosted by the UK in November 2022, and the UK Foreign, Commonwealth and Development Office's work to lead the creation of a Common Approach to Sexual Exploitation, Abuse and Sexual Harassment.[6]

Clarifying the victim-centred/victims' rights approach

Despite a general endorsement of the Secretary-General's policy from the outset, steps required to implement a victims' rights approach remained unclear. The IASC's external review of protection from sexual exploitation, abuse and sexual harassment, released in late 2021, concluded that there was no shared understanding of the meaning of a victim-centred approach nor what it meant in practice nor its implications for organizational culture, services and resources (IASC, 2021). Similarly, in 2022, the UK's Independent Commission for Aid Impact report on safeguarding in the aid sector indicated that staff and partners of the Foreign, Commonwealth and Development Office understood the approach in principle, but few were able to describe how it was to be delivered (Independent Commission for Aid Impact, 2022: 28). This was echoed by the Multilateral Organisation Performance Assessment Network (2023) in *Progress on PSEAH? From Words to Deeds*.

Inspired by national victims' rights codes, charters and principles,[7] early in my mandate I decided to craft a document drawing on existing UN standards and resolutions (for example, UNGA, 1948, 2005, 2007) and setting out the rights of victims of sexual exploitation and abuse from UN and related personnel. Informed by a 2019 consultation which brought together experts working with victims/survivors of national and international crimes, trafficking, terrorism, child sex tourism and sexual exploitation and abuse and harassment, as well as lengthy, open and inclusive discussions with colleagues across the UN system, a Victims' Rights Statement was concluded by consensus and endorsed by the UN High-level Steering Group on preventing sexual exploitation and abuse in late May 2023 (OVRA, 2023). The statement, which creates no new rights, is designed to empower victims by describing their rights and entitlements in simple terms and underlining the responsibilities of staff and implementing partners. It is underpinned by four principles: prioritization of victims' rights, needs, safety and dignity; the right not to be judged, blamed or held responsible for the harm; the right to assistance to promote well-being and recovery; and the right to non-discrimination on any ground. Ten rights are set out – the right: to be treated with respect; to receive assistance and support; to justice and accountability; to decide how involved to be; to get information; to be heard; to privacy and confidentiality; to be protected; to a remedy; and to complain where these rights are not realized.

It is positive that other entities have introduced policies and guidance clarifying the content of the victim-centred/victims' rights approach. These include the United Nations High Commissioner for Refugees (UNHCR) policy on a victim-centred approach in its response to sexual misconduct (UNHCR, 2020), the CEB's principles on a victim-centred approach to sexual harassment (UN, 2021a), InterAction's Core Standards for Survivor-Centered Support of Sexual Exploitation, Abuse, and Harassment (InterAction, 2023) and the *IASC Definition & Principles of a Victim/Survivor Centered Approach* (IASC, 2023). To guide implementation of the approach, the CHS Alliance, bringing together humanitarian and development organizations committed to improving the quality of aid work, recently launched a foundational paper identifying practical steps forward (CHS Alliance, 2023). Further, in early 2023, the OVRA, with the CEB Task Force on Addressing Sexual Harassment secretariat, the International Organization for Migration and the UNHCR, released a practical, scenario-based training module that articulates the meaning and application of a victim-centred/victims' rights approach to prevention of and response to sexual exploitation, abuse and sexual harassment. The IASC convened an expert panel, supported by an advisory group on which I serve, to embed a victim-centred/victims' rights approach in investigations with a focus on building the trust of victims, communities, staff and partners. I regularly discuss the victims' rights approach with the judges and staff of the UN internal justice system, with full respect for its independence. It is my hope that these initiatives will underline that a victim-centred/victims' rights approach is essential to prevention of, as well as response to, sexual exploitation and abuse by emphasizing that victims and their communities are diverse and risks to their enjoyment of rights and dignity cannot be generalized but must be considered individually, taking account of the particular context.

Implementation on the ground: the SVROs

Now seasoned in their positions, the SVROs have been crucial in translating my global advocacy into practical action benefiting victims on the ground, with their work demonstrating that the presence of a person on the ground tasked with prioritizing victims' rights – someone victims trust and can turn to for assistance, confident that they will advocate on their behalf – makes a real difference to victims.

A detailed description of the work of the SVROs is provided in my article in a special edition of *Humanitarian Exchange* on 'protection from sexual exploitation and abuse and sexual harassment in humanitarian action' (Connors, 2022). They maintain direct, regular contact with victims; accompany them as they report; coordinate medical care and psychosocial support; secure access to legal aid; and support them during internal UN and Member State investigations and judicial processes, including courts martial, and keep them updated on their cases. They also coordinate capacity building to support victims to generate income, as well as educational and other support for children born of sexual exploitation and abuse. Their physical proximity to victims and knowledge of the local context allows them to contribute to strengthening referral pathways to service providers, outreach to communities, community-based complaint mechanisms and practical support for victims. They engender cooperation and coordination with UN entities and local partners, and, informed by the wishes of victims, support the creation of projects, financed by the UN's Trust Fund in Support of Sexual Exploitation and Abuse (see UN, nd-c) and other funding sources, to repair the harm experienced. They facilitate the collection of DNA samples from victims and their children to support resolution of paternity and child maintenance claims; secure pro bono services by lawyers in host countries and countries of jurisdiction to this end; assist in gathering crucial documents, such as birth certificates; facilitate transmission of maintenance payments, including by assisting victims to open bank accounts; and arrange interactions between the children and their fathers and other family members. Notably, SVROs participate in my visits to countries whose contributed personnel have children born of sexual exploitation or abuse, to encourage their authorities to use their good offices to foster amicable resolution of outstanding claims.

Although the SVROs have contributed significantly to prioritizing the rights and dignity of victims on the ground in the countries in which they operate, they face challenges. Their functions are new and not well known within, let alone outside, the UN. As in the case of the VRA, it is important to understand that they support victims of all UN personnel, not just those in peace operations. They are human- and financial-resource poor and operate alone, although some have ad hoc or surge support provided by the relevant mission or the OVRA. They usually work in vast countries with many victims, who are often located in remote and insecure areas that are difficult to reach. They also have the complex task of managing victims' expectations in a landscape where support and assistance are frequently unavailable or, as in the case of capacity building for income generation, not fit for purpose in markets in poor and unstable contexts.

The Secretary-General continues to call for more resources for existing SVROs and the deployment of others in contexts where the risk of sexual misconduct by UN personnel is high. Unfortunately, boosting the capacity of the SVROs in three countries through the addition of very modest human resources has proven difficult given that the UN budgetary bodies which approve such requests wish to see synergy of efforts and delineation of roles to avoid duplication of functions, and encourage streamlining of coordination and harmonization in the implementation of the Secretary-General's strategy (UNGA, 2023d: 3). Moreover, they consider that victims' rights and dignity can be secured through the collaboration of staff recruited to deliver other functions (UNGA, 2023a: 12, 2023b: 7, 2023c: 9). Disappointingly, no other SVRO post has been created, although the implementation of the policy is supported by victims' rights focal points designated in over seven countries. While it is positive that the focal points promote victims' rights and dignity while undertaking other duties, they are unable to provide the level of care and support to a multiplicity of victims that is delivered by SVROs dedicated to this task. It is pleasing that victim care, specialist support and anti-harassment coordinator positions exist in the UNHCR, the World Bank (for victims of sexual harassment), the UN Office for Project Services and the International Organization for Migration, and that the World Health Organization intends to have such a position. Notably, victims' rights professionals are essential in contexts where UN operations are winding down or withdrawing, as reports of sexual misconduct often come forward at this time and thereafter, and support must be sustained.

Conclusion

It is undeniable that there has been progress in focusing the UN's gaze on those harmed by its personnel and related personnel, but much more is required. For example, the notion of accountability must encompass not only accountability of the perpetrator but also accountability to the victim. Support and assistance are crucial. The General Assembly's 2007 Comprehensive Strategy on Assistance and Support for Victims of Sexual Exploitation and Abuse promises a lifeline to victims (UNGA, 2007), but is premised on the understanding that support should be delivered through existing services. While it envisages that gaps should be filled by UN programmes, it does not provide for their funding. Where individual accountability is concerned, it focuses on the individual perpetrator of the wrong.

This policy has resulted in a patchwork of ad hoc responses, with victims directed to the programming for victims of sexual and gender-based violence. This is chronically underfunded, often non-existent in crisis and remote areas, and of variable quality. Service providers may fail to understand the specific requirements and needs of victims of UN personnel. The Victims' Assistance Tracking System, operational since 2019, follows the trajectory of victims of personnel in peace operations and special political missions, but there is no comprehensive mechanism for tracking the assistance victims receive and their feedback, including on its quality and efficacy. In addition to compromising realization of the rights and dignity of victims, this precludes identification of risks and trends, essential for prevention.

Where the accountability of perpetrators is concerned, UN entities as employers use administrative and disciplinary mechanisms to sanction personnel who engage in misconduct, including sexual exploitation and abuse. The UN refers credible allegations of what may amount to crimes to national authorities and, irrespective of whether it made the initial referral, cooperates with national investigations and prosecutions to facilitate the proper administration of justice. Between 1 July 2016 and 30 June 2022, 26 credible allegations of sexual exploitation and abuse against UN officials were referred to their states of nationality, with information on the status being provided in an annual report on the criminal accountability of UN officials and experts on mission (UNGA, 2023e: 13).[8] Troop-contributing countries retain authority to investigate allegations implicating their own personnel, with individual accountability depending on the national laws and procedures that apply to the conduct concerned (UNGA, 2023d: 13). While all acts of sexual exploitation and abuse violate the standards of conduct of the UN, they may not amount to crimes in national jurisdictions. Even where they do, evidentiary and procedural requirements may pose difficulties. The resolution of paternity and child support claims related to children born of sexual exploitation and abuse are also dependent on the legal framework of the state which has jurisdiction over the matter, although the UN is required to facilitate pursuit of resolution (UNGA, 2007). Although some progress has been made, contributed to by the commitment of some states and supported by their use of DNA testing, there are many outstanding claims, and more continue to be received.

The framework of accountability of perpetrators is confusing and dispiriting for victims and children born of sexual misconduct.[9] The victims I meet are patient and resilient, but require immediate, sustained and uninterrupted support so they can rebuild their lives. Centring their rights and dignity requires recognizing the harm they have experienced and providing independent advice and assistance, including legal support and follow-up information. Notably, our policies, programmes and projects should be crafted and delivered on the basis of their views.

Acknowledgements

I thank Mia Wick, doctoral student in the School of Law, the University of Reading, UK, for her assistance in preparing this chapter.

References

Beutler, I. (2021) *Final Report of the Consultation Process to Consider the Creation of an International Safe Sport Entity*, Zürich: FIFA.

CHS Alliance (2023) *Taking a Victim/Survivor-Centred Approach to Protection from Sexual Abuse, Exploitation and Harassment in the Aid Sector*, Geneva: CHS Alliance.

Connors, J. (2019) 'A victims' rights approach to the prevention of, and response to, sexual exploitation and abuse by United Nations personnel', *Australian Journal of Human Rights*, 25(3): 498–510.

Connors, J. (2022) 'Advocating for the rights of victims of sexual exploitation and abuse', *Humanitarian Exchange*, Issue on Protection from Sexual Exploitation and Abuse and Sexual Harassment in Humanitarian Action, 81, 16 June. Available from: https://odihpn.org/magazine/protection-from-sexual-exploitation-and-abuse-and-sexual-harassment-in-humanitarian-action/ (accessed 29 February 2024).

Dodds, P. (2023) 'More UN sex abuse allegations in CAR; 60 peacekeepers to be sent home', *The New Humanitarian*, 9 June. Available from: www.thenewhumanitarian.org/news/2023/06/09/UN-sex-abuse-allegations-Central-African-Republic-peacekeepers (accessed 24 October 2023).

European Commission (nd) 'Victims' rights in the EU', *European Commission*. Available from: https://commission.europa.eu/strategy-and-policy/policies/justice-and-fundamental-rights/criminal-justice/protecting-victims-rights/victims-rights-eu_en#victims-rights-in-the-eu (accessed 29 February 2024).

Home Office (2017) *The Role of the Independent Sexual Violence Adviser: Essential Elements*, London: Home Office.

Hu, C. (nd) 'Dozens of children were left behind by UN personnel in Haiti. Their mothers want justice', *CNN*. Available from: www.cnn.com/2023/09/15/americas/haiti-un-peacekeepers-trust-fund-sexual-abuse-as-equals-intl-cmd/index.html (accessed 29 February 2024).

IASC (Inter-Agency Standing Committee) (2019) 'IASC six core principles relating to sexual exploitation and abuse', *IASC*. Available from: https://interagencystandingcommittee.org/inter-agency-standing-committee/iasc-six-core-principles-relating-sexual-exploitation-and-abuse (accessed 24 October 2023).

IASC (Inter-Agency Standing Committee) (2021) *Global Report on Protection from Sexual Exploitation and Abuse and Sexual Harassment*, Geneva: IASC.

IASC (Inter-Agency Standing Committee) (2023) *IASC Definition & Principles of a Victim/Survivor Centered Approach*, IASC. Available from: https://interagencystandingcommittee.org/iasc-champion-protection-sexual-exploitation-and-abuse-and-sexual-harassment/iasc-definition-principles-victims-urvivor-centered-approach (accessed 24 October 2023).

IASC (Inter-Agency Standing Committee) (nd-a) 'IASC Champion on Protection from Sexual Exploitation and Abuse and Sexual Harassment', *IASC*. Available from: https://interagencystandingcommittee.org/iasc-champion-on-protection-from-sexual-exploitation-and-abuse-and-sexual-harassment (accessed 24 October).

IASC (Inter-Agency Standing Committee) (nd-b) 'IASC PSEA coordinators', *IASC*. Available from: https://psea.interagencystandingcommittee.org/iasc-psea-coordinators (accessed 29 February 2024).

IASC (Inter-Agency Standing Committee) (nd-c) 'The Technical Advisory Group', *IASC*. Available from: https://psea.interagencystandingcommittee.org/technical-advisory-group (accessed 24 October 2023).

Independent Commission for Aid Impact (2022) *The UK's Approach to Safeguarding in the Humanitarian Sector*, London: Independent Commission for Aid Impact.

InterAction (2023) *Core Standards for Survivor-Centered Support of Sexual Exploitation, Abuse, and Harassment*, Washington, DC: InterAction. Available from: www.interaction.org/blog/core-standards-for-survivor-centered-support-of-sexual-exploitation-abuse-and-harassment/ (accessed 24 October 2023).

Lee, S. and Bartels, S. (2020) '"They put a few coins in your hand to drop a baby in you": a study of peacekeeper-fathered children in Haiti', *International Peacekeeping*, 27(2): 177–209.

Multilateral Organisation Performance Assessment Network (2023) *Progress on PSEAH? From Words to Deeds*, Paris: Multilateral Organisation Performance Assessment Network.

NATO (North Atlantic Treaty Organization) (2021) 'The NATO policy on preventing and responding to sexual exploitation and abuse', *NATO*, updated 21 April. Available from: www.nato.int/cps/en/natohq/official_texts_173038.htm (accessed 24 October 2023).

OECD (2019) *DAC Recommendation on Ending Sexual Exploitation, Abuse and Harassment in Development Co-Operation and Humanitarian Assistance: Key Pillars of Prevention and Response*, OECD. Available from: https://legal instruments.oecd.org/en/instruments/OECD-LEGAL-5020 (accessed 24 February 2024).

OVRA (Office of the Victims' Rights Advocate) (2021) *Guide for National Human Rights Institutions*, United Nations: New York.

OVRA (Office of the Victims' Rights Advocate) (2023) *Your Rights as a Victim of Sexual Exploitation or Abuse Committed by United Nations Staff or Related Personnel*, United Nations: New York.

UN (United Nations) (2021a) *Advancing a Common Understanding of a Victim-Centred Approach to Sexual Harassment*, United Nations: New York.

UN (United Nations) (2021b) *Management and Accountability Framework of the UN Development and Resident Coordinator System*, United Nations: New York.

UN (United Nations) (2021c) 'UN sends Gabon peacekeepers home from Central African Republic, following abuse allegations', *United Nations News*, 15 September. Available from: https://news.un.org/en/story/2021/09/1100032 (accessed 29 February 2024).

UN (United Nations) (2023) 'Central African Republic: Tanzanian peacekeepers to be repatriated following abuse allegations', *United Nations*, 9 June. Available from: https://news.un.org/en/story/2023/06/1137527 (accessed 29 February 2024).

UN (United Nations) (nd-a) 'Conduct in UN field missions', *United Nations*. Available from: https://conduct.unmissions.org/ (accessed 29 February 2024).

UN (United Nations) (nd-b) *Terms of Reference: Victims' Rights Advocate*, United Nations. Available from: www.un.org/sg/sites/www.un.org.sg/files/files/other-vacancies/VRA_TOR.pdf (accessed 29 February 2024).

UN (United Nations) (nd-c) 'Trust Fund in Support of Sexual Exploitation and Abuse', *United Nations*. Available from: www.un.org/preventing-sexual-exploitation-and-abuse/content/trust-fund (accessed 29 February 2024).

UN (United Nations) (nd-d) 'UN system', *United Nations*. Available from: www.un.org/en/about-us/un-system (accessed 29 February 2024).

UNGA (United Nations General Assembly) (1948) *Universal Declaration of Human Rights*, UN Doc A/RES/40/3.

UNGA (United Nations General Assembly) (1991) *Strengthening of the Coordination of Humanitarian Emergency Assistance of the United Nations*, UN Doc A/RES/46/182.

UNGA (United Nations General Assembly) (2005) *Basic Principles of Justice for Victims of Crime and Abuse of Power*, UN Doc A/RES/60/147.

UNGA (United Nations General Assembly) (2007) *United Nations Comprehensive Strategy on Assistance and Support to Victims of Sexual Exploitation and Abuse by United Nations Staff and Related Personnel*, UN Doc A/RES/62/214.

UNGA (United Nations General Assembly) (2017) *Special Measures for Protection from Sexual Exploitation and Abuse: A New Approach*, UN Doc A/71/818.

UNGA (United Nations General Assembly) (2018) *Special Subjects Relating to the Proposed Programme Budget for the Biennium 2018–2019*, UN Doc A/RES/72/262.

UNGA (United Nations General Assembly) (2019) *Special Subjects Relating to the Programme Budget for the Biennium 2018–2019*, UN Doc A/RES/73/279.

UNGA (United Nations General Assembly) (2023a) *Report of the Advisory Committee on Administrative and Budgetary Questions for MINUSCA*, UN Doc A/77/767/Add. 13.

UNGA (United Nations General Assembly) (2023b) *Report of the Advisory Committee on Administrative and Budgetary Questions for MONUSCO*, UN Doc A/77/767/Add. 8.

UNGA (United Nations General Assembly) (2023c) *Report of the Advisory Committee on Administrative and Budgetary Questions for UNMISS*, UN Doc A/77/767/Add. 11.

UNGA (United Nations General Assembly) (2023d) *Special Measures for Protection from Sexual Exploitation and Abuse*, UN Doc A/77/748.

UNGA (United Nations General Assembly) (2023e) *Special Measures for Protection from Sexual Exploitation and Abuse*, UN Doc A/77/831.

UNHCR (United Nations High Commissioner for Refugees) (2020) *Policy on a Victim-Centred Approach to UNHCR's Response to Sexual Misconduct*, United Nations: New York.

United Nations Secretariat (2003) *Special Measures for Protection from Sexual Exploitation and Sexual Abuse*, UN Doc ST/SGB/2003/13.

United Nations Security Council (2016) *Resolution 2272 (2016)*, UN DOC S/RES/2272 (2016).

United States Mission to the United Nations (2022) 'Statement by Ambassador Chris Lu, U.S. Representative for UN Management and Reform, following the sentencing of Karim Elkorany', *United States Mission to the United Nations*, 8 November. Available from: https://usun.usmission.gov/statement-by-ambassador-chris-lu-u-s-representative-for-un-management-and-reform-following-the-sentencing-of-karim-elkorany/ (accessed 29 February 2024).

6A

United Nations Victims' Rights Statement

The United Nations (UN) Victims' Rights Statement is a landmark document designed to inform victims and survivors of sexual exploitation and abuse by UN and related personnel – including contributed uniformed personnel, UN experts, consultants, interns and staff of partners who implement UN programmes on the ground – of their rights. It also seeks to make UN and related personnel aware of these rights and how they should behave in their interaction with individuals and communities in which they work.

The Victims' Rights Statement was crafted through a lengthy and inclusive consultative process with staff across the UN system, civil society (including national human rights institutions and victims' rights groups and advocates), scholars and activists. Its development was led by the UN's Victims' Rights Advocate, Jane Connors (author of Chapter 6), and it was endorsed in May 2023 by the UN High-level Steering Group on Preventing Sexual Exploitation and Abuse. The Statement is based on UN instruments, including the Universal Declaration of Human Rights, human rights treaties and other declarations; it creates no new rights, but brings together existing norms and standards. It is available in all UN official languages, as well as in German. Translations in other languages, including Haitian Creole, Khmer, Polish, Swahili and Ukrainian, have been and continue to be made at the local level. In addition, child-friendly and accessible versions are under preparation. In the few months since its endorsement, the Statement has encouraged and empowered victims/survivors to claim their rights and has provided inspiration for those who support them.

To showcase the groundbreaking nature of this Statement and the way the UN now frames the rights of victims and survivors of sexual exploitation and abuse by UN and related personnel, we reprint the Statement here in full.[1]

UNITED NATIONS VICTIMS' RIGHTS STATEMENT

YOUR RIGHTS

As a victim of sexual exploitation or abuse committed by United Nations staff or related personnel

You have the right to seek assistance and support from the United Nations if you are a victim of sexual exploitation or abuse committed by any United Nations staff or related personnel.

You suffered sexual abuse if you engaged in a sexual act because you were threatened, or were forced to do so, or agreed to engage in a sexual act under unequal conditions, for example because you were unable to decide freely, or felt fearful of the consequences of refusing to participate in such an act. Under United Nations rules, you suffered sexual abuse if you engaged in, or were subjected to, a sexual act when you were under 18 years of age. You are also a victim of sexual abuse if any of these wrongs were attempted.

You suffered sexual exploitation if you were promised or given money, food or any other benefit, like housing or a job, in return for engaging in a sexual act with United Nations staff or related personnel.

If you have experienced sexual exploitation or abuse, the United Nations will help you obtain medical care and other assistance you may need and wish to receive. It will also help you explore available legal remedies, if you wish to do so.

Sexual exploitation and abuse are prohibited for all United Nations staff and related personnel. Such acts are unacceptable, whatever the circumstances. The United Nations will refer complaints of sexual exploitation or abuse for investigation. The United Nations will use its best efforts to hold the offender accountable. This could involve internal disciplinary action or cooperation with Member States.

This document describes your rights, and how the United Nations will assist you.

The United Nations' guiding principles:

Your rights, needs, safety and dignity are priorities.

You have the right not to be judged, blamed or held responsible for the harm you suffered from sexual exploitation or abuse.

You will be offered assistance to promote your well-being and to support you to recover.

You will not be discriminated against because of your race, ethnicity, nationality, class, caste, religion, belief, sex, language, sexual orientation, gender identity, age, health, disability, residence status or any other ground.

Your rights as a victim of sexual exploitation or abuse:

1. **The right to be treated with respect**
    a. You will be treated with courtesy, compassion, professionalism and fairness.
    b. Your culture, values and views will be respected. Your individual needs and informed choices will be considered as a central priority.
2. **The right to receive assistance and support**
    a. You have the right to receive assistance and support in accordance with your individual needs.
    b. Your access to assistance and support does not depend on whether, or how, you cooperate with any investigation or accountability process.
    c. If you need and want it, the United Nations will help you seek and obtain emergency assistance, such as medical care, including on sexual and reproductive health; psychological support; livelihood and basic material assistance, such as food, clothing, transportation and safe shelter.
    d. If you need and want it, the United Nations will help you seek and obtain longer-term assistance, such as comprehensive health care, psychological support, access to legal assistance, livelihood support, skills training.
    e. For your emotional support, and in keeping with your wishes and best interests, you have the right to be accompanied by a person whom you trust when choosing or accessing assistance and support.
    f. If you are under 18 years of age, any assistance or services provided to you will take account of your age and individual needs, including, for example, school reintegration.
    g. You have the right to refuse any form of assistance or support at any time, including after you have begun to receive it. Such a decision will not prevent you from requesting and receiving it at a later stage.
3. **The right to justice and accountability**
    a. You have the right to submit a complaint of sexual exploitation or abuse by United Nations staff or related personnel to the United Nations, which has the responsibility to refer your complaint for investigation.
    b. You have the right to seek justice and accountability for the harm you suffered through criminal and civil processes as well as administrative, disciplinary and non-judicial mechanisms that may be available to you.
    c. If you wish, the United Nations will help you obtain information on how to access legal assistance and how best to seek justice and accountability, including in national proceedings.
    d. If you had a child born of sexual exploitation or abuse, the United Nations will seek to assist you to get information and legal help to establish paternity and related claims, if you so wish.

UNITED NATIONS VICTIMS' RIGHTS STATEMENT

4. **The right to decide how involved to be in United Nations processes**
   a. You have the right to decide whether to participate or cooperate in any United Nations processes and proceedings, including those resulting from the fact that you are a victim of sexual exploitation or abuse.
   b. If you decide not to participate or cooperate at any point, this choice may affect the outcome of the investigation, including whether the offender is held accountable.
5. **The right to get information**
   a. You have the right to be informed, as early as possible, about the processes and procedures involved in reporting incidents of sexual exploitation or abuse.
   b. You have the right to receive information about all the services available to help you. If you have a child born as a result of sexual exploitation or abuse, this will include information on ways to establish paternity, claim child support and other rights for your child.
   c. You have the right to be informed about the status of the investigative process and any other proceedings. You also have the right to be informed about your role and the choices you have in participation in the investigation and any other proceedings. The United Nations will help you obtain and fully understand this information.
   d. You have the right to request that information is provided to you in a language that you understand, and in a way that is clear and accessible to you, taking into account your personal circumstances, such as any hearing, visual or intellectual disability. If you are under 18 years of age, you have the right to receive the information in a way that takes account of your age.
6. **The right to be heard**
   a. You are entitled to express your views on any issue relating to these rights, and be listened to and heard. You are also entitled to advocate on your own behalf and to identify your needs. What you have to say will be taken into account in any decisions or actions made by the United Nations that may impact on your safety, dignity or well-being or that of those who are close to you.
   b. For your emotional and practical support and in keeping with your wishes and best interests, you have the right to be accompanied by a person you trust, in any investigative procedures, interviews and meetings. You may be accompanied by a legal representative in some circumstances.
   c. You have the right to have your individual needs and personal circumstances that may affect your ability to exercise effectively your right to be heard taken into account. If you are under 18 years of age, you have the right to have any investigative procedures, interviews or meetings conducted in a manner that takes account of your age. You

have the right to choose to be accompanied by a person you trust, or not, during any of these procedures, interviews or meetings.

  d. You are entitled to associate and organize with other victims if you and they wish to do so.

7. **The right to privacy and confidentiality**

  a. You are entitled to decide what information to provide about your situation to the United Nations. You may not wish to provide any information, or you may wish to stop providing information. This may impact or affect the scope and/or outcome of the investigation.

  b. You are entitled to confidentiality, although if you provide any information that may identify you to a United Nations staff member this may be transmitted to those within the United Nations who need to know it to ensure that the offender is held accountable. You have the right to request that any information that may identify you personally is not released to actors outside of the United Nations.

  c. You are entitled to be told of the intended use of any information you decide to provide, including to whom this information may be disclosed. You should be informed that any choice to keep information confidential may limit the scope of the investigation, including the possibility of holding the offender accountable. Your decision not to provide information will not affect your right to receive assistance and support.

  d. You are entitled to be informed by the United Nations about its assessment of any potential implications of your complaint for your safety and that of those close to you.

8. **The right to be protected**

  a. Keeping you safe is of utmost importance to the United Nations. Any harassment, intimidation, and retaliation for reporting what happened to you, faced by you or those close to you, or any witnesses on your behalf, are unacceptable. If you report such acts to the United Nations, it will take action to protect your physical safety and you from further trauma or additional victimization, in accordance with your wishes, by working with State authorities or non-governmental organizations.

  b. The United Nations will do everything possible to protect you from any contact with the alleged offender during any process or proceedings conducted by the United Nations.

  c. The United Nations will cooperate with Member States to seek that protection measures are available in any national proceedings.

9. **The right to a remedy**

  a. Offenders are individually responsible for acts of sexual exploitation and abuse. You have the right to seek remedies from them that acknowledge the harm you have suffered and help to repair it. The remedies you are entitled to will depend on the law of the country

where your case is investigated or heard and could consist of financial compensation; physical and psychological rehabilitation and material support; an apology; or measures to ensure that there is no repetition of the wrong.
  b. If paternity of a child born as the result of sexual exploitation or abuse has been established, you are entitled to bring proceedings against the father to require him to accept his parental responsibility, including by obliging him to provide child support in line with the applicable national law of the country where your case is determined. Your child may be able to claim further rights, such as to the father's nationality or citizenship. The United Nations will help you with these processes and work with the relevant State to facilitate a fair and just resolution of these claims.

10. **The right to complain of the treatment you have received**
  a. If you consider that the rights in this document have not been respected by the United Nations, you have the right to complain to the Office of the Victims' Rights Advocate. In line with your wishes, your complaint will be considered and you will be informed of the status of any action taken in response.
  b. You will be protected against reprisals from the United Nations if you complain.

Contact the Office of the Victims' Rights Advocate at: ovra@un.org.

7

Accountability Advocates: Representing Victims

Sabrina White

Introduction

The United Nations Secretary-General's (UNSG's) 2017 announcement of a 'new' approach to dealing with sexual exploitation and abuse (SEA) signals a shift in thinking on how United Nations (UN) institutional actors address accountability for SEA perpetrated by UN personnel. At the core of the new approach is the intention to place the rights and dignity of victims first (UNSG, 2017b: section III), based on what has become known as the victim-centred approach (UNSG, 2018: para 11). The victim-centred approach in part seeks to ensure that victims' voices are heard (UNSG, 2017b: para 13(a)) on a 'platform ... that the world will not be able to ignore' (para 21). This platform centres on the newly established Office of the Victims' Rights Advocate (OVRA), which has a mandate to promote the protection of victims' rights through a dual role of supporting coordination of assistance for victims and creating space for victims' voices in UN policy and strategy development. The purpose of this chapter is to reflect on the constitution of the political space within which UN advocacy on SEA emerged from 2004 to 2021 in the new victim-centred approach.

I argue, first, that advocating on behalf of victims/survivors and paternity claimants is restricted conceptually and practically by the limited political will evidenced by underprioritization of resourcing for and access to complaints mechanisms and support, and, second, that the UN's new advocacy efforts are both necessary for advancing political will and a problematic filter through which the voices of victims, survivors, children fathered by peacekeepers and the mothers of those children are heard. As discussions are taking place regarding what a victim-centred approach entails (see United Nations

Security Council, 2019; CHS Alliance, 2022), this chapter contributes critical reflections on the political meanings embedded in claims to represent victims/survivors of SEA and the nature of the platforms meant to share their voices.

In the chapter, I first set out the concepts of victim-centred and advocacy as they connect to a notion of the politics of representation that guides the analysis that follows. I then analyse the representation of victims in official policy from 2004 to 2021 to situate the discursive context within which the new approach emerged. Following this, I explore the status of the practice of a victim-centred approach through the early OVRA initiatives, identifying problems of both resourcing and bypassing that affect representation of victims.

The politics of representation

Advocacy can be understood as a process of representing the views of a particular person, or a group, to bring about some change in policy and/or practice. It has a political purpose and constitutes a form of public accountability connected to integrity in decision-making (Dewatripont and Tirole, 1999). The notion of an advocate comes from legal practice, whereby a lawyer advocates on behalf of their client through the instrument of the law. Individuals can also advocate on behalf of themselves or form alliances to represent the voices of a broad community with shared concerns. Advocates in the global and public policy space largely serve to speak on behalf of a set community in specific issue areas. Advocacy is often built in circumstances where the represented are disempowered in some way (Rick and Mike, 2001), and the advocate has a responsibility for their position of power in this relationship (Jordan and Tuijl, 2002).

The problem of how to represent victims has been a core point of contention in nascent scholarship on victim-centred approaches. Victim-centred approaches derive from legal practices that sought to provide greater protection for victims' participation in formal judicial processes (Goodey, 2005), but are increasingly popular in transitional justice practice as restorative measures, which seek to 'repair' harm done to victims (Burgess et al, 2009). The transitional justice scholarship is critical of the production of victims in victim-centred approaches, suggesting that they can be co-opted and instrumentalized in ways that silence some victims' voices (McEvoy and McGregor, 2008; Madlingozi, 2010; Gready and Robins, 2014; Robins, 2017; Lawther, 2021). Victims can be produced in problematic ways through the state, bureaucracies and researchers, who all play a role in how victimhood can be defined, understood and studied (Krystalli, 2021). The exercise of voice is an aspect of agency (Gammage et al, 2016), and survivor-centred approaches are offered as an alternative that acknowledge the resistance, coping strategies and agency of those who have been victimized (Kelly, 1998; hooks, 2000). Yet this voice is also about being heard. The extent to which heterogeneous subaltern and marginalized voices can be heard is limited by how they are constructed as subjects and by whom (Spivak, 1988), and by who is listening, why and how (Griffiths, 2018). Work in this area suggests that production of victims and relationships constituted with victims are critical areas of inquiry that help reveal the motives and effectiveness of victim-centred approaches. Critically, it also emphasizes that representation of victims and survivors is not apolitical.

Advocacy is inherently connected to the political space within which accountability relationships are constituted and how subjects of those relationships are represented. The politics of representation is a political matter of justice that, for Nancy Fraser, constitutes the political space within which social relationships among accountability subjects are constituted, as well as how the subjects themselves are produced (see Fraser, 2010). Just representation entails that subjects are appropriately recognized as equal rights bearers, they have the requisite resources to draw on to participate in accountability deliberations and they are represented in terms of agency (Fraser, 2009). The politics of representation is a useful notion for exploring representation of victims in the discourse and practice of the 'UN as advocate' within the new victim-centred approach.

Discursive representation of victims

The discursive representation of victims in official policy has implications for how survivors' agency, rights and dignity constitute their status within accountability relationships. The UNSG has released annual reports on SEA since 2004, offering an update to Member States, the UN system and wider global publics on the status of UN action to address the problem. The discourses regarding victims in these reports have undergone significant change since 2017 (see Figure 7.1). Prior to 2017, there were very few references to the rights and needs of victims, and only two references to justice for victims were made between 2004 and 2012. The fallout from the internal release of a document on the poor status of UN action in four missions (Awori et al, 2013) and the crisis in the Central African Republic involving allegations of sexual abuse of boys by French forces (Deschamps et al, 2015) accompanied a shift in discourse on victims' rights, including justice rights, from 2013 to 2016, and a shift in action on paternity claims, with acceleration in the response to this issue from 2017 to 2021. Post 2017, new areas of concern emerged – though they had been identified by others as issues years earlier (Csáky, 2008) – including protection from retaliation for allegations and providing feedback to victims on the status of their case.

ACCOUNTABILITY ADVOCATES

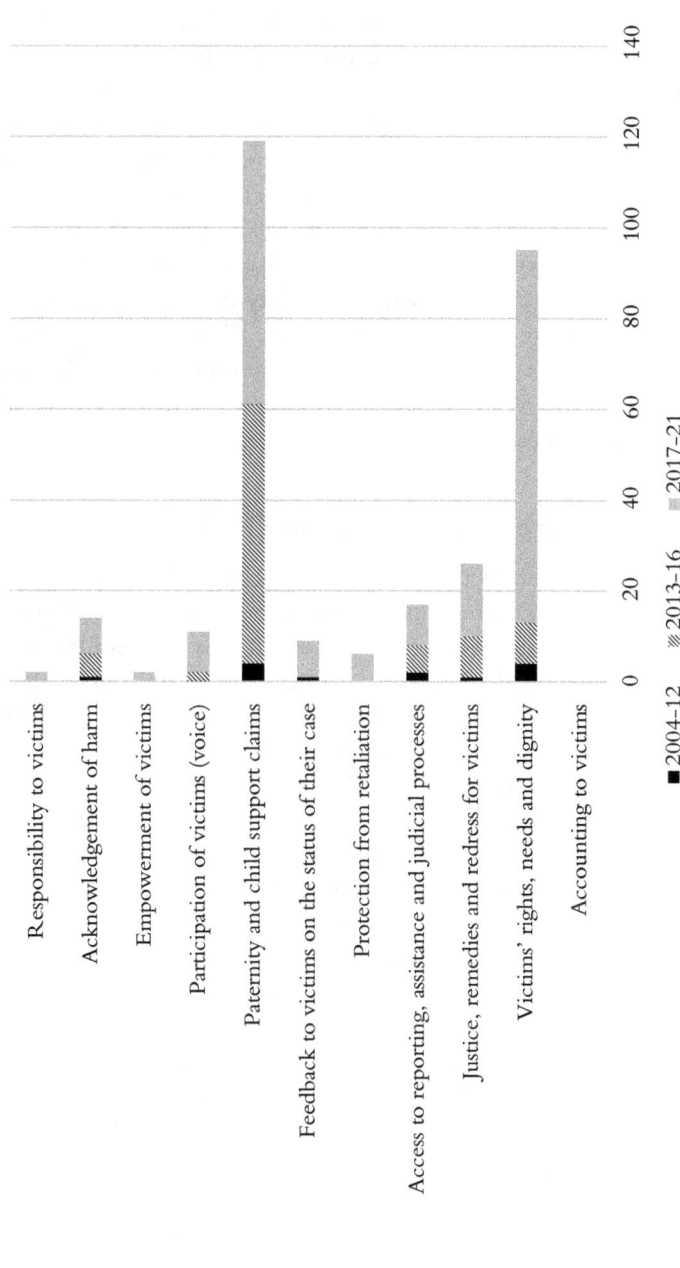

Figure 7.1: References to victims in the United Nations Secretary-General's annual reports on 'special measures for protection from sexual exploitation and abuse', 2004–21

Discursively, the reports of the UNSG indicate a shift in thinking about 'who counts' in accountability arrangements in the SEA policy agenda, moving from a focus on prevention of SEA and punishment of perpetrators towards a focus on victims. However, there is no direct acknowledgement that SEA accountability action should involve being accountable *to* victims, signifying a limited perspective of victims' agency and representation in accountability relationships. Accountability of perpetrators, for instance, implies a relationship between perpetrators and the authority holding them to specific standards which have been violated. Perpetrators must answer to that authority. Being accountable to victims implies that victims are also recognized as subjects in accountability relationships who are due an answer for the violation of standards leading to harm against them.

The next section analyses accountability practices in the victim-centred approach associated with the work of the OVRA to support and provide assistance to victims. It identifies the achievements of the office and explores how limitations with respect to resourcing and trust have affected its representative capacity.

Victim-centred practices: the OVRA

The adoption of the victim-centred approach in 2017 led to the establishment of the OVRA and the appointment of the first Victims' Rights Advocate (VRA), Jane Connors, and four Senior Victims' Rights Officers (SVROs – positions which had been referred to as field victim rights advocates from 2017 to 2019). The SVROs were located in the four mission countries with the largest number of allegations: the Central African Republic, the Democratic Republic of Congo (DRC), Haiti and South Sudan. The VRA was to 'be supported by a small staff ... to ensure that reliable, gender-sensitive pathways exist for every victim or witness' (UNSG, 2017b, para 27), and the SVROs support this work (OVRA, 2021: 4). The work involves collating best practices on approaches to promoting victims' rights, ensuring the availability of services system-wide, improving work on facilitating paternity claims, coordinating assistance and support, developing a methodology to seek feedback from victims, conducting gap analysis and coordinating with existing gender-based violence responses (UNSG, 2018, 2019, 2020, 2021). They also work with local authorities and civil society organizations to promote victims' access to judicial processes, appropriate care, and follow-up on their case, and to develop tools and networks to support victims, including in access to remedies (UNSG, 2017b: paras 27–9). For a detailed description of the work of the OVRA since its establishment, see Jane Connors contribution to this volume in Chapter 6.

By 2021, the OVRA included a team of eight: one global advocate, three members of support staff and four SVROs. This small team receives rather a lot of attention in the annual reports of the UNSG as proof of a victim-centred approach. Much of the work of the OVRA centres on implementation of UNSG resolution 62/214 (2007), known as the Victim Assistance Mechanism, which sets out obligations to ensure that appropriate assistance and support is available to victims. This includes emergency assistance, such as medical care and safe shelter, and medium- to long-term legal, psychological and other support, as well as assistance for children fathered by UN personnel (United Nations General Assembly, 2007: paras 6–8). However, the Victim Assistance Mechanism has never had a dedicated budget. The advocates did find their way into the permanent budget, but resourcing only covers personnel, not project costs, meaning the resources they have to work with on the ground are limited.

One of the key achievements of the OVRA is the adoption of the 2019 UN Protocol on the Provision of Assistance to Victims of Sexual Exploitation and Abuse (UN, 2019a), which is meant to clarify what victims should expect from safeguarding and the response to SEA. This protocol is a non-binding internal document meant to support implementation of the Victim Assistance Mechanism. Evaluations of the mechanism in 2015 and 2021 found that very few victims of SEA had received any form of assistance (Office of Internal Oversight Services, 2015, 2021), and there remains a 'lack of adequate and sustainable funding and resourcing to provide for the assistance and support to victims' (OVRA, 2020: 3). At the 'Strengthening the United Nations' victim-centred response to sexual exploitation and abuse' online event in 2021, Christine Besong, SVRO in the DRC, admitted that 'at times, we don't have all the different services that victims do need. At times we are able to bridge the gap with the little resources we have' (Besong, 2021). One area of assistance that is 'largely unavailable' is legal aid that supports the accountability of perpetrators, including for paternity claims (UNSG, 2021: para 34). Structural and systemic underprioritization of victims' access to assistance and support grossly undermines their ability to exercise their rights to pursue justice, redress and remedies for the harms perpetrated against them.

One of the ways the UN has sought to fill this resourcing gap is through the Trust Fund in Support of Sexual Exploitation and Abuse, established in 2016. It is funded by contributions from 24 Member States (UN, nd) and the pay withheld from UN personnel implicated in substantiated allegations – recommendations made more than a decade earlier in the Zeid Report (United Nations General Assembly, 2005). The UNSG emphasizes that money withheld from perpetrators 'will amount to a limited, but symbolic, source of funding' (UNSG, 2016: para 76). In 2021, contributions to the Trust Fund stood at US$4.3 million (UN, 2022), and this money can be used for a wide array of activities to support victims, but not as a form of direct payment to victims nor for compensation. The Trust Fund is designed to be a mechanism for providing 'seed funds to address gaps or provide additional support to victims' and to create 'projects in partnership with humanitarian and development actors' (UN, 2020: 31). Funds are allocated centrally by UN headquarters to fill resource gaps in the implementation of the Victim Assistance Mechanism and to run community projects.

The Trust Fund has quite far to stretch in both fulfilling basic responsibilities to victims needs and resourcing empowerment projects, as it provides support for intitiatives to help victims of SEA perpetrated by UN personnel across the *entire* UN system, including UN staff (UN, 2019b: 2). Evidently, this US$4.3 million will not go very far, given the number of victims across the entire UN system. Moreover, it does not offer support for the victims in allegations recorded across 33 peace operations since 2007.

The underfunding of victim assistance is compounded by under-resourcing of complaints reception mechanisms and other posts that support victims, such as SEA focal points, who are meant to coordinate support on receiving complaints and establish Victim Assistance Mechanisms in field missions (Nduka-Agwu, 2009; Reddick, 2010; IASC Task Force, 2012; Independent Commission for Aid Impact, 2020). Poor access to support for pursuing claims and receiving safeguarding and other essential assistance significantly weakens victims' rights and their ability to participate in accountability and justice processes.

Under-resourcing and lack of trust in the complaints mechanisms and UN institutional actors had implications for the response to public allegations implicating UN agency staff and aid workers in perpetrating SEA, including sex-for-jobs schemes, in the Ebola response in the DRC in 2020 (Flummerfelt and Peyton, 2020). Many victims came forward to reporters but not to UN officials through formal complaints mechanisms (Flummerfelt and Peyton, 2020), despite there being 64 complaints mechanisms in the area (Emergency Director's Group, 2020: 12–13). Indeed, the DRC established its first national protection from SEA network in 2018 (Emergency Director's Group, 2020: 9), and by 2020 there were 43 complaints networks supported by over a thousand community volunteers (OVRA, 2020). Yet in the Ebola response, while the community and many staff were reportedly well aware that SEA was widespread – international aid workers allegedly referred colloquially to local people, especially women, as 'appetisers' (Dodds, 2020) – national staff and NGOs feared that if they reported abuse there would be retribution from UN agencies, including losing jobs or access to essential funding (Emergency Director's Group, 2020: 14).

After the scandal broke, the SVRO in the DRC went to the areas linked to SEA in the Ebola response, to reach out to victims. But 'despite the reports and corroboration of local community members that such misconduct had taken place', no victims came forward (OVRA, 2020: 4). The individual meant to represent victims' rights was not trusted, nor were formal complaints mechanisms.

This lack of trust in complaint procedures occurred despite a few years of identified progress in the country. The DRC was the only peacekeeping mission that had referred all victims to some form of assistance by 2015 (Office of Internal Oversight Services, 2015: para 59), and from 2016 an increase in community consultations on the design of complaints mechanism efforts to secure feedback, and assessment from communities on their functionality, led to improvements (IASC, 2016: 19). Community-based complaints mechanisms were piloted in a few regions to collect information on what did and did not work, in one case finding that nearly half of SEA victims using one mechanism were children and that women and children in particular did not have sufficient access to or understanding of the complaints mechanism (IASC, 2016: 125). The community-based complaints mechanism then enhanced efforts to reach out to women and girls in the community, and the pilot sites saw a marked increase in allegations, some of which dated back several years. This increase was seen as a positive sign of the functionality and gender-sensitivity of the mechanism (IASC, 2016: 126).

However, in 2017 the UNSG failed to make the connection in the DRC case between the effectiveness of complaints mechanisms and the number of allegations, stating: 'The community-based complaint networks implemented over the past six months have proven effective, *with no new allegations received by the networks* in their areas of operation' (UNSG, 2017a: para 52; emphasis added). The fact that there were no new allegations may mean no cases, but it may also indicate a lack of trust and poor accessibility to complaint mechanisms. The lack of allegations should lead to questions regarding how the distribution of power, as in the Ebola response, might affect willingness to complain.

There is very little evidence on the status of complaints mechanisms after 2017, but all peace operations should have had 'formal or informal' community-based complaints mechanisms since 2016 (UNSG, 2018: 40). One review on SEA coordination described telephone hotlines as the new black box of reporting mechanisms (Reddick, 2021). Hotlines were established widely, often without consultation with communities about whether they were appropriate or indeed whether people had access to working telephones (Reddick, 2021: 32). SEA responses faced unfunded networks and struggled to fund UN volunteers in coordinator posts for conducting risk assessments with communities and establishing sustainable networks to prevent and respond to SEA (Reddick, 2021: 50).

In the DRC and elsewhere, it is widely understood that there is a gross under-reporting of allegations (Kent, 2007; Ndulo, 2009; UNSG, 2019: para 71). Victims may face multiple potential harms when making a complaint. In Haiti, a boy was abducted by peacekeepers to prevent him from participating in an investigation (Dodds, 2017) and a woman pursuing a paternity claim was threatened with death if she did not get an abortion (Zabludovsky, 2021). In Somalia, victims faced stigma, family alienation and retaliation from perpetrators, police and insurgent groups (Human Rights Watch, 2014: 28). One UN agency found that because of threats of retaliation or 'offers of money', a third of sexual harassment victims did not pursue further action (IASC and CEB, 2019: 3). Even internally, within the UN system, there is evidence of a lack of confidence, especially among female peacekeepers, in processes for reporting sexual harassment and abuse (IASC, 2019; Donnelly et al, 2022).

Advocates outside the UN system have also faced challenges supporting victims. Various advocates have been publicly expressing concerns and advocating for potential solutions regarding the sexual behaviours of UN personnel since at least 1992 (The Phnom Penh Post, 1992), but they have been met with little support and even pushback from the UN (Nduka-Agwu, 2009; Smith, 2017; Bureau des Avocats Internationaux and Institute for Justice and Democracy in Haiti, 2021). Despite the active engagement of women's organizations in raising concerns on SEA and promoting support for legal redress for survivors during the 13-year mission in Timor-Leste, advocates were often unaware of outcomes of investigations and efforts to seek redress for victims were largely unsuccessful (Smith, 2017). This was also evidenced in Liberia (Martin, 2005). In general, engagement with advocates has been quite limited, and the outcomes of this engagement for victims were frequently a mystery, including to the victims themselves (Delva, 2012; Odello and Burke, 2016; REDRESS, 2017). More recently, in Haiti, a legal organization representing ten clients pursuing paternity claims against UN personnel claimed their clients' legal counsel was circumvented in communications on both paternity claims and the Trust Fund-led distribution of school fees and lunch boxes for children fathered by peacekeepers (Joseph and Concannon, 2019: 4). Official legal advocates representing victims were allegedly bypassed.

In the DRC, victims and survivors may have decided that the cost of claiming rights by participating in accountability processes outweighed the anticipated benefits. Whether it is the moral and material costs of claiming rights (Choo, 2013) or the belief that nothing will be done, the incentives for claiming rights may not add up. The lack of incentives for claiming rights constitutes silencing of victims. Building trust with communities across a complex and enormous crisis context, especially with scarce resources, is a huge challenge, but perceptions that complaining to those attached to the UN is undesirable or too risky further undermine the response to SEA and the content and meaning of the victim-centred approach.

Conclusion

Representing victims/survivors and paternity claimants in advocacy is restricted by how representation of victims is conceptualized and done. In representing voices, especially marginalized and subaltern voices, there is always a process of filtering bound up in the politics of representation itself. This filtering process is more pronounced where approaches to representation of victims excludes their agency as participants in accountability relationships, processes and deliberations. The discursive shift in recognition of victims as rights bearers is a promising step, but it has yet to materialize into robust human, material and financial measures to actually support victims' agential representation. Further, the OVRA as a platform for victims' voices is limited by UN approaches to accountability, which have consistently prioritized accountability as a set of administrative procedures over concerns with participation of, and outcomes for, victims, survivors and affected populations.

Yet the UN's new advocacy efforts have a role to play, with some caveats. The work of the OVRA is necessary to generate attention, resourcing and political will to meet basic obligations to support victims' and survivor's rights – but the OVRA is still part of the UN. The barrier of distrust between affected communities and UN institutional actors is a significant mountain to climb. The small office of the OVRA is not enough to ensure meaningful representation of victims and survivors.

What remains a key challenge is ensuring that the cost to victims of claiming rights does not outweigh the risks they encounter by not claiming rights. Accountability responses need to answer to victims rather than viewing them largely as just part of a process, and victims themselves need access to the political space to exercise their voice and agency in accountability deliberations and be heard.

References

Awori, T., Lutz, C. and Thapa, P.J. (2013) *Final Report: Expert Mission to Evaluate the Risks to SEA Prevention Efforts in MINUSTAH, UNMIL, MONUSCO, and UNMISS, United Nations.* Available from: https://www.codebluecampaign.com/press-releases/2015/03/16 (accessed 1 October 2022).

Besong, C. (2021) 'Strengthening the United Nations' victim-centred response to sexual exploitation and abuse', *GANHRI*, 28 October. Available from: https://ganhri.org/event/ovra-ganhri-event/#:~:text=The%20United%20Nations%20Office%20of%20the%20Victims%E2%80%99%20Rights,the%2076%20th%20session%20of%20the%20General%20Assembly (accessed 28 October 2021).

Bureau des Avocats Internationaux and Institute for Justice and Democracy in Haiti (2021) 'IJDH statement: internal evaluation of the UN's response to peacekeeper sexual exploitation and abuse, BAI/IJDH', *Bureau des Avocats Internationaux and Institute for Justice and Democracy in Haiti.* Available from: www.ijdh.org/press_release/ijdh-statement-internal-evaluation-of-the-uns-response-to-peacekeeper-sexual-exploitation-and-abuse/ (accessed 23 September 2022).

Burgess, A., Regehr, C. and Roberts, A. (2009) *Victimology: Theories and Applications*, Sudbury, MA: Jones & Bartlett.

Choo, H. (2013) 'The cost of rights: migrant women, feminist advocacy, and gendered morality in South Korea', *Gender & Society*, 27(4): 445–68.

CHS Alliance (2022) *Humanitarian Accountability Report 2022: Accountability Is Non-Negotiable*, Geneva: CHS Alliance.

Csáky, C. (2008) *No One To Turn To: The Under-Reporting of Child Sexual Exploitation and Abuse by Aid Workers and Peacekeepers*, London: Save the Children. Available from: https://resourcecentre.savethechildren.net/document/no-one-turn-under-reporting-child-sexual-exploitation-and-abuse-aid-workers-and-peacekeepers/ (accessed 1 October 2017).

Delva, J. (2012) 'Pakistani U.N. peacekeepers sentenced in Haiti rape case', *Reuters*, 13 March. Available from: www.reuters.com/article/us-haiti-un-idUSBRE82C06C20120313 (accessed 11 March 2023).

Deschamps, M., Jallow, H. and Sooka, Y. (2015) *Taking Action on Sexual Exploitation and Abuse by Peacekeepers*. Available from: https://whistleblower.org/wp-content/uploads/2018/05/Independent-Review-Report.pdf (accessed 29 February 2024).

Dewatripont, M. and Tirole, J. (1999) 'Advocates', *Journal of Political Economy*, 107(1): 1–39.

Dodds, P. (2017). 'AP Exclusive: UN child sex ring left victims but no arrests', *Associated Press*, 12 April. Available from: https://apnews.com/e6ebc331460345c5abd4f57d77f535c1 (accessed 27 July 2021).

Dodds, P. (2020) 'How we broke the Ebola sexual abuse scandal', *The New Humanitarian*, 5 October. Available from: www.thenewhumanitarian.org/opinion/2020/10/05/Ebola-sexual-abuse-scandal-investigation (accessed 4 November 2020).

Donnelly, P., Mazurana, D. and Papworth, E. (2022) *Blue on Blue: Investigating Sexual Abuse of Peacekeepers*, New York and Bahrain: International Peace Institute. Available from: www.ipinst.org/2022/04/blue-on-blue-investigating-sexual-abuse-of-peacekeepers (accessed 1 May 2022).

Emergency Director's Group (2020) *Senior PSEA Technical Support Mission to the Democratic Republic of the Congo*, IASC. Available from: https://psea.interagencystandingcommittee.org/resources/iasc-psea-support-mission-18-dec-2020 (accessed 1 May 2022).

Flummerfelt, R. and Peyton, N. (2020) 'Exclusive: more than 50 women accuse aid workers of sex abuse in Congo Ebola crisis', *The New Humanitarian*, 29 September. Available from: www.thenewhumanitarian.org/2020/09/29/exclusive-more-50-women-accuse-aid-workers-sex-abuse-congo-ebola-crisis (accessed 25 August 2021).

Fraser, N. (2009) 'Social justice in the age of identity politics', in G. Henderson and M. Waverstone (eds) *Geographic Thought: A Praxis Perspective*, Abingdon: Routledge, pp 72–91.

Fraser, N. (2010) 'Who counts? Dilemmas of justice in a post-Westphalian world', *Antipode*, 41(suppl 1): 281–97.

Gammage, S., Kabeer, N. and Van der Meulen Rodgers, Y. (2016) 'Voice and agency: where are we now?', *Feminist Economics*, 22(1): 1–29.

Goodey, J. (2005) *Victims and Victimology: Research, Policy and Practice*, Harlow: Pearson Education.

Gready, P. and Robins, S. (2014) 'From transitional to transformative justice: a new agenda for practice', *International Journal of Transitional Justice*, 8(3): 339–61.

Griffiths, M. (2018) 'For speaking against silence: Spivak's subaltern ethics in the field', *Transactions of the Institute of British Geographers*, 43(2): 299–311.

hooks, b. (2000) *Feminist Theory: From Margin to Center* (2nd edn), London: Pluto Press.

Human Rights Watch (2014) '"The power these men have over us": sexual exploitation and abuse by African Union forces in Somalia', *Human Rights Watch*, 8 September. Available from: www.hrw.org/report/2014/09/08/power-these-men-have-over-us/sexual-exploitation-and-abuse-african-union-forces (accessed 1 April 2022).

IASC (Inter-Agency Standing Committee) (2016) *Guideline: Inter-Agency Community-Based Complaint Mechanisms, Protection against Sexual Exploitation and Abuse*, Geneva: International Organization for Migration. Available from: https://interagencystandingcommittee.org/system/files/best_practice_guide_inter_agency_community_based_complaint_mechanisms_1.pdf (accessed 15 July 2021).

IASC (Inter-Agency Standing Committee) (2019) *Summary of IASC Good Practices: Preventing Sexual Exploitation and Abuse and Sexual Harassment and Abuse of Aid Workers*, IASC. Available from: https://interagencystandingcommittee.org/inter-agency-standing-committee/summary-iasc-good-practices-preventing-sexual-exploitation-and-abuse-and-sexual-harassment-and-abuse (accessed 11 October 2019).

IASC (Inter-Agency Standing Committee) and CEB (United Nations Chief Executives Board) (2019) *Inter-Agency Standing Committee and United Nations Chief Executives Board Task Force on Addressing Sexual Harassment in the Organizations of the UN System: Second Meeting of Investigatory Bodies on Protection from Sexual Exploitation, Abuse and Sexual Harassment*. Available from: https://psea.interagencystandingcommittee.org/sites/default/files/2020-06/SummaryRecord_IASCCEB%20investigatory%20bodies%20on%20%20PSEAH%20Nov2019.pdf (accessed 23 November 2022).

IASC (Inter-Agency Standing Committee) Task Force (2012) *Protection from Sexual Exploitation and Abuse: Compendium of Practices on Community-Based Complaints Mechanisms*, IASC Task Force. Available from: https://interagencystandingcommittee.org/system/files/9_protection_from_sexual_exploitation_and_abuse_-_compendium_of_practices_on_community-based_complaints_mechanisms_0.pdf (accessed 30 June 2020).

Independent Commission for Aid Impact (2020) *Sexual Exploitation and Abuse by International Peacekeepers: An Accompanying Report to the ICAI Review of the Preventing Sexual Violence in Conflict Initiative*. Available from: https://reliefweb.int/report/world/sexual-exploitation-and-abuse-international-peacekeepers-accompanying-report-icai (accessed 30 March 2022).

Jordan, L. and Tuijl, P. (2002) 'Political responsibility in transnational NGO advocacy', *World Development*, 28(2): 2051–65.

Joseph, M. and Concannon, B. (2019) 'Open letter to UN Victims' Rights Advocate Jane Connors', 14 January. Available from: www.ijdh.org/wp-content/uploads/2019/01/EN-BAI-IJDH-Demand-UN-Accountability-for-SEA-Victims-in-Open-Letter-REDACTED.pdf (accessed 13 March 2023).

Kelly, L. (1998) *Surviving Sexual Violence*, Cambridge: Polity Press.

Kent, V. (2007) 'Protecting civilians from UN peacekeepers and humanitarian workers: sexual exploitation and abuse', in C. Aoi, C. de Coning and R. Thakur (eds) *Unintended Consequences of Peacekeeping Operations*, New York: United Nations University, pp 44–66.

Krystalli, R.C. (2021) 'Narrating victimhood: dilemmas and (in)dignities', *International Feminist Journal of Politics*, 23(1): 125–46.

Lawther, C. (2021) '"Let me tell you": transitional justice, victimhood and dealing with a contested past', *Social & Legal Studies*, 30(6): 890–912.

Madlingozi, T. (2010) 'On transitional justice entrepreneurs and the production of victims', *Journal of Human Rights Practice*, 2(2): 208–28.

Martin, S. (2005) *Must Boys Be Boys? Ending Sexual Exploitation and Abuse in UN Peacekeeping Missions*, Washington, DC: Refugees International.

McEvoy, K. and McGregor, L. (eds) (2008) *Transitional Justice from Below: Grassroots Activism and the Struggle for Change*, Oxford: Hart.

Nduka-Agwu, A. (2009) '"Doing gender" after the war: dealing with gender mainstreaming and sexual exploitation and abuse in UN peace support operations in Liberia and Sierra Leone', *Civil Wars*, 11(2): 179–99.

Ndulo, M. (2009) 'The United Nations responses to the sexual abuse and exploitation of women and girls by peacekeepers during peacekeeping missions', *Cornell Law Faculty Publications*, 27(59): 127–61.

Odello, M. and Burke, R. (2016) 'Between immunity and impunity: peacekeeping and sexual abuses and violence', *The International Journal of Human Rights*, 20(6): 839–53.

Office of Internal Oversight Services (2015) *Evaluation of the Enforcement and Remedial Assistance Efforts for Sexual Exploitation and Abuse by the United Nations and Related Personnel in Peacekeeping Operations*, Office of Internal Oversight Services. Available from: www.un.org/en/ga/sixth/70/docs/oios_report.pdf (accessed 1 October 2022).

Office of Internal Oversight Services (2021) *Evaluation of the Prevention, Response and Victim Support Efforts against Sexual Exploitation and Abuse by United Nations Secretariat Staff and Related Personnel*, UN Doc A/75/820.

OVRA (Office of the Victims' Rights Advocate) (2020) *'Voices from the Field': Briefing by United Nations Field Victims' Rights Advocates and Dedicated Protection from Sexual Exploitation and Abuse Coordinators*, Summary of online event, 28 October. Available from: www.un.org/preventing-sexual-exploitation-and-abuse/content/events (accessed 1 July 2021).

OVRA (Office of the Victims' Rights Advocate) (2021) *Frequently Asked Questions on the Work of the Victims' Rights Advocate and Senior Victims' Rights Officers*, New York: OVRA. Available from: www.un.org/preventing-sexual-exploitation-and-abuse/content/frequently-asked-questions-faqs (accessed 22 July 2021).

Reddick, M. (2010) *Global Synthesis Report: IASC Review of Protection from Sexual Exploitation and Abuse by UN, NGO, IOM and IFRC Personnel*. Available from: www.unocha.org/sites/unocha/files/dms/Documents/PSEA_Synthesis_Report_-_submitted_to_IASC_WG_Jul10_mtg_-_FINAL.pdf (accessed 17 July 2021).

Reddick, M. (2021) *Global Report on Protection from Sexual Exploitation and Abuse and Sexual Harassment*, Geneva: IASC. Available from: https://psea.interagencystandingcommittee.org/sites/default/files/2022-01/IASCExternalReview_GlobalReportPSEAH_2021.pdf (accessed 20 February 2023).

REDRESS (2017) *Sexual Exploitation and Abuse in Peacekeeping Operations: Improving Victims' Access to Reparation, Support and Assistance*, London and The Hague: REDRESS. Available from: www.refworld.org/pdfid/59c383034.pdf (accessed 1 October 2018).

Rick, H. and Mike, P. (2001) *A Right Result? Advocacy, Justice and Empowerment*, Bristol: Policy Press.

Robins, S. (2017) 'Failing victims: the limits of transitional justice in addressing the needs of victims of violations', *Human Rights & International Legal Discourse*, 11: 41–58.

Smith, S. (2017) 'Accountability and sexual exploitation and abuse in peace operations', *Australian Journal of International Affairs*, 71(4): 405–22.

Spivak, G. (1988) 'Can the subaltern speak?', in C. Nelson and L. Grossberg (eds) *Marxism and the Interpretation of Culture*, Chicago: University of Illinois Press, pp 271–316.

The Phnom Penh Post (1992) 'An open letter to Yasushi Akashi', *Phnom Penh Post*, 11 October. Available from: www.phnompenhpost.com/national/open-letter-yasushi-akashi (accessed 5 February 2021).

UN (United Nations) (2019a) *United Nations Protocol on the Provision of Assistance to Victims of Sexual Exploitation and Abuse*, 12 December. Available from: www.un.org/en/pdfs/UN%20Victim%20Assistance%20Protocol_English_Final.pdf (accessed 7 June 2023).

UN (United Nations) (2019b) *2017 and 2018 Report: Trust Fund in Support of Victims of Sexual Exploitation and Abuse*, New York: United Nations. Available from: www.un.org/preventing-sexual-exploitation-and-abuse/sites/www.un.org.preventing-sexual-exploitation-and-abuse/files/tf_annual_report_june_2019_vf.pdf (accessed 3 March 2023).

UN (United Nations) (2020) *2019 Annual Report: Trust Fund in Support of Victims of Sexual Exploitation and Abuse*, New York: United Nations. Available from: www.un.org/preventing-sexual-exploitation-and-abuse/content/projects-and-reports (accessed 30 June 2020).

UN (United Nations) (2022) *Fourth Annual Report of the Trust Fund in Support of Victims of Sexual Exploitation and Abuse 2021*, New York: United Nations. Available from: www.un.org/en/content/psea-trust-fund-report-2022/ (accessed 7 April 2021).

UN (United Nations) (nd) 'Contribute to the Trust Fund', *United Nations*. Available from: www.un.org/preventing-sexual-exploitation-and-abuse/content/donate-trust-fund (accessed 15 September 2023).

United Nations General Assembly (2005) *A Comprehensive Strategy to Eliminate Future Sexual Exploitation and Abuse in United Nations Peacekeeping Operations*, UN Doc A/59/710.

United Nations General Assembly (2007) *United Nations Comprehensive Strategy on Assistance and Support to Victims of Sexual Exploitation and Abuse by United Nations Staff and Related Personnel*, UN Doc A/RES/62/214.

United Nations Security Council (2019) *Resolution 2467 (2019)*, UN Doc S/RES/2467.

UNSG (United Nations Secrtary-General) (2016) *Special Measures for Protection from Sexual Exploitation and Abuse*, UN Doc A/70/729.

UNSG (United Nations Secrtary-General) (2017a) *Report of the Secretary-General on the United Nations Organization Stabilization Mission in the Democratic Republic of the Congo*, UN Doc S/2017/206.

UNSG (United Nations Secrtary-General) (2017b) *Special Measures for Protection from Sexual Exploitation and Abuse: A New Approach*, UN Doc A/71/818.

UNSG (United Nations Secrtary-General) (2018) *Special Measures for Protection from Sexual Exploitation and Abuse*, UN Doc A/72/751.

UNSG (United Nations Secrtary-General) (2019) *Special Measures for Protection from Sexual Exploitation and Abuse*, UN Doc A/73/744.

UNSG (United Nations Secrtary-General) (2020) *Special Measures for Protection from Sexual Exploitation and Abuse*, UN Doc A/74/705.

UNSG (United Nations Secrtary-General) (2021) *Special Measures for Protection from Sexual Exploitation and Abuse*, UN Doc A/75/754.

Zabludovsky, K. (2021) 'UN peacekeepers fathered dozens of children in Haiti. The women they exploited are trying to get child support', *BuzzFeed News*, 30 August. Available from: www.buzzfeednews.com/article/karla zabludovsky/haiti-earthquake-un-peacekeepers-sexual-abuse (accessed 22 September 2021).

8

Masculinities and Institutional Blind Spots

Jasmine-Kim Westendorf

Introduction

That masculinities are central to the phenomenon of sexual exploitation and abuse (SEA) is taken as a given in the United Nations (UN) and humanitarian worlds. In organizational policy responses as well as discussions I have had with policy makers and practitioners, masculinities are often implicitly positioned at the heart of 'causes' of sexual misconduct by peacekeepers and humanitarian workers. Policy responses tend to treat masculinities as inevitable and inherent personnel traits that must be accommodated to prevent those embodying them – men – from perpetrating SEA, rather than addressing how they are produced in patriarchal systems of power and how they intersect with other systems of power, such as race and capital. In this chapter, I explore how institutions and policy makers have made sense of the causes of SEA. Drawing on interviews with policy makers and practitioners globally, I show how the 'masculinity' analysis produces both a clear narrative and a straightforward policy path, but fails to adequately capture the dynamics at play in peacekeeper and humanitarian SEA. I argue that the dominant narratives that centre masculinity as the cause of SEA are shaped by institutional imperatives in ways that, perhaps inadvertently, render invisible the intersecting local, international, normative and systemic factors that create the conditions in which some personnel choose to perpetrate SEA against local people. Consequently, policy efforts have too often focused on individualized compliance based on a 'bad apple' model of understanding perpetrators, rather than on addressing the structural, normative and contextual factors that together give rise to SEA. I argue that addressing these – in part through more proactively grappling with the multiple sets of power relations that define the relationship between peacekeepers and the peacekept – would more effectively prevent local individuals and communities from becoming vulnerable to exploitation and abuse in the first place.

The chapter begins with an exploration of institutional narratives that centre masculinities as a primary cause of SEA. I explore how institutions have taken up the 'masculinities' narrative in ways that divorce it from the rich critical scholarship that produced the concept and which provides the grounding for a structural analysis of how masculinities are produced and sit within multiple, intersecting systems of power. The next section considers the limitations these dominant narratives present in terms of understanding, preventing and responding to sexual misconduct in peacekeeping and humanitarian contexts. The section that follows considers the structural, normative and contextual factors – among which masculinities is one – which create the conditions in which SEA is perpetrated, and the policy implications of this broader explanation, which demand a greater focus on prevention rather than accountability mechanisms.

Boys will be boys: a problem of masculinity?

Sexual exploitation and abuse perpetrated by peacekeepers first garnered international attention during the UN Transitional Authority in Cambodia. The arrival of UN peacekeepers in 1993 resulted in the growth of the number of prostitutes in the country from six thousand to twenty-five thousand within a year (Whitworth, 2004: 67). Uniformed peacekeepers were highly implicated in this sexual exploitation, which involved violence against women working as sex workers and the sexual abuse of girls (Whitworth, 2004: 68). A UNAIDS survey found that 45 per cent of Dutch navy and marine personnel deployed to the UN Transitional Authority in Cambodia had sexual contact with members of the local population during their five-month deployment and that they did not use condoms consistently (UNAIDS, 1998: 2). The UN's response at the time was threefold: the head of mission, Yasushi Akashi, dismissed the significance of the issue, declaring that 'boys will be boys'; mission leadership advised peacekeepers not to wear uniforms when visiting brothels or park UN vehicles directly outside; and an additional 800,000 condoms were shipped to the country to prevent the spread of HIV/AIDS among UN personnel (Ledgerwood, 1994; Simić, 2012: 41). This early response to peacekeeper misconduct effectively framed SEA as an 'unintended consequence' of peacekeeping and as an activity that is largely carried out by male soldiers, putting masculinity at the heart of the explanation: *boys will be boys, but please be discrete*. It also frames the consequences of such masculinity as inevitable, but with some edges that can be softened: *boys will be boys, but please use protection*. The UN's response in Cambodia notably did not attempt to address the patterns or dynamics of masculinity that contribute to men choosing (or encouraging one another) to perpetrate sexual exploitation or abuse with varying levels of violence, nor address the structural and economic conditions that meant many women were seeking income through transactional sex.

The critical step in centring men and masculinities in institutional discourse about SEA is to put the focus on men to the exclusion of others. This institutional response conceals both the victim and the structures of power that were leveraged in their abuse or exploitation – such as gender, patriarchy, race and poverty – all of which are critical to understanding both individual acts of SEA and the phenomena across contexts. The refrain that not a single allegation of sexual misconduct has been made against a woman was often one of the first things that policy makers explaining SEA would say to me; it served to emphasize that men and their masculinity are at the heart of the problem.[1] While it is true that very few, if any, substantiated allegations of SEA have been made against women, when narratives focus so heavily on the fact that men are the perpetrators of SEA, attention is diverted from the gendered systems and structures of power that create the contexts in which those men choose to perpetrate sexual exploitation and abuse. This centring of men – rather than gender structures – is also reinforced in policy material. For example, in a discussion of the benefits women peacekeepers bring to mission success, the global study on the women, peace and security agenda highlighted that 'not a single female peacekeeper has ever been accused of sexual exploitation and abuse on mission' (Coomaraswamy, 2015: 141). By focusing on the sex binary in this way, the gender orders and other power structures are made invisible in favour of a narrower assumption that masculinity inevitably produces certain types of behaviours, because *that's just how men are*.

As a result, many suggested responses to SEA focus on mitigating the consequences of men's excesses and their problematic masculinities, rather than tackling the multiple, intersecting power structures that produce those masculinities and create the conditions in SEA occurs. For instance, a senior UN Women expert on SEA told me that he had observed a strong view in the UN that SEA is the product of male peacekeepers being away from their families, and soliciting sex work as a result, despite the fact that data shows that a significant portion of cases involve egregious crimes such as sex with minors, rape and child rape.[2] He suggested that people often excused SEA by reference to masculine tropes (*they are far from home, in stressful situations and working conditions, and they need to let off steam*) rather than considering broader structural explanations for these behaviours. Paula Donovan, CEO of Aids-Free World – which runs the high-profile Code Blue campaign against peacekeeper SEA and has a long history of working on issues of SEA in the UN – recalled that the attitude of many people within the UN that she had interacted with, including those officially working on SEA specifically, was that "boys will be boys", and therefore that the UN should address what those "boys" need – for example, providing ping-pong tables and pool tables for entertainment – to prevent them from "getting bored" and perpetrating SEA.[3] Paul Higate has documented how peacekeepers themselves (both women and men) in the Democratic Republic of Congo (DRC) and Sierra Leone emphasized that 'the male sex drive [reflected] an integral component of deep masculinity' and that they had to access sex to 'satisfy' their sex drives which 'have a mind of [their] own' (Higate, 2007: 106).

A typical operationalizable thought, once men and masculinity are centred, is to link the problem to the conditions of their work (another masculine trope). For example, a senior diplomat involved in issues of peacekeeper SEA linked higher rates of sexual misconduct among African peacekeepers to the unequal standards of accommodation and infrastructure, deployment lengths and rest and recuperation provisions for African peacekeepers as compared to European peacekeepers in Mali.[4] While acknowledging the challenges of the Global North/Global South dynamics in the practice of peacekeeping, he nonetheless suggested that the poorer living standards created an impetus for those peacekeepers to find ways to de-stress, including through sex which might be exploitative or abusive (Westendorf, 2020: 117–23). Congruently, a legal advisor in the UN's Department of Peacekeeping Operations noted the stress caused to some peacekeeping contingents in West Africa because of terrible living conditions, low pay and poor food supplies. They suggested that improving these and ensuring better leave arrangements, including visits home to family, could relieve such stress and prevent peacekeepers seeking "release" by visiting brothels.[5] Noting the link between masculinized preconceptions and the institutional need to address them, another senior UN humanitarian expert on gender-based violence noted that peacekeepers deployed in Kosovo had been "encouraged" to go to Moldova for their rest and recuperation leave and to access prostitution there in order to "let off steam" while off duty and out of country.[6]

Modern management techniques, whether in the civilian or military field, rest on the traditions of patriarchal authority and draw on its resources in response to behaviour that conflicts with identified goals. Moreover, institutions take up ideas in ways that can be easily implemented – together this creates momentum for particular types of response that deal with measurable, fixable things (such as rest and recuperation arrangements and standing order modifications) rather than responses that more ambitiously attempt to dismantle the systems of power which produce the conditions for some personnel to perpetrate SEA (Westendorf and Searle, 2017). The notion that *boys will be boys but their excesses can be curbed* is reflected in the fact that standing orders relating to fraternization, alcohol consumption and curfews – or, more recently, increasing the proportion of women deployed to peace operations – are presented as ways to limit SEA (Coomaraswamy, 2015: 141; United Nations Secretary-General, 2017). One senior military official who had led contingents of his country's peacekeepers in numerous operations emphasized to me the importance of preventing large groups of soldiers from being off duty at the same time and able to go drinking together. He told me how he would ensure that his troops were rostered off as little as possible after the time when drinking alcohol was permitted, and he would also roster them sequentially rather than in groups to prevent large groups from "knocking off" at the same time.[7]

These examples illuminate the assumption that SEA is an undesirable but essentially unavoidable consequence of deploying men into stressful peacekeeping contexts. In fact, some senior staff dealing with sexual violence and SEA at a major humanitarian organization argued that we all must accept that (as one of them put it) "soldiers misbehave. They are kids, and a commander should know it", and that the enforcement of strong discipline is the only way to prevent sexual misconduct.[8] These examples also reflect the institutional appeal of a straightforward narrative of sexual misconduct and its solutions: men break the rules because they need to let off steam and because they do not believe they will be caught. On this view, the way you keep the problematic masculinities that cause SEA in check is by appeasing or distracting them through contextual interventions, or by increasing the credibility of threats of punishment to deter perpetration. As the UN Women expert I interviewed observed, this narrative "manages to both demonize and take male peacekeepers off the hook" by construing SEA as something they will inevitably perpetrate because of their inherent masculinity, which is beyond their control. Moreover, this framing takes SEA out of the context of other forms of abuse, misconduct or human rights and accountability issues that manifest in peacekeeping – for instance, peacekeepers' abandonment of their protection mandate at Srebrenica resulting in the genocide of over 8,000 Bosniak men and boys, or the involvement of peacekeepers in weapons trafficking in Bosnia (Andreas, 2011).

Consequently, the dominant narrative of peacekeeper SEA frames it as essentially an issue of individual bad behaviour by a small number of men – a few bad apples – and has resulted in a train-and-punish model of dealing with sexual misconduct that is primarily an administrative exercise focusing on the training and enforcement of codes of conduct (Westendorf and Searle, 2017). The dominant narrative, however, also undermines accountability measures to enforce codes of conduct, because it belies the more complex set of behaviours and contributing factors that characterize SEA in practice. These must be recognized and grappled with in order for people to report suspected misconduct and for investigations and their findings to fairly reflect the realities of abuses of power that manifest as SEA (Westendorf, 2023a, 2023b). Simić (2010) has furthermore suggested that the reality that many peacekeepers have never faced accountability for their engagement in sex trafficking suggests the general acceptance of this practice as part of a 'boys will be boys' mentality.

Importantly, the focus on military peacekeepers and the way that peacekeeper misconduct scandals have unfolded in the media have not only reinforced the 'masculinity' narrative but also sharpened it into one about 'military masculinities'. Several prominent misconduct scandals have involved military peacekeepers and reporting has tended to focus on cases involving soldiers (see, for example, Wax, 2005); this has contributed to linking the issue of peacekeeper SEA with soldiers in the public imaginary. For example, in 2015 a whistle-blower revealed that military peacekeepers from Chad, Equatorial Guinea and France had regularly raped homeless and starving boys in refugee camps in the Central African Republic, and that a French military commander had raped four girls with a dog, after which one of the girls died (Aids-Free World, 2015; Deschamps et al, 2015). Shocking, gruesome cases like this have been more likely to dominate global headlines than, for example, revelations of civilian staff engaging in transactional sex with adults, although this has perhaps shifted since the 2018 Oxfam scandal. The assumption that soldiers are primarily responsible for peacekeeper sexual exploitation is bolstered by the fact that soldiers make up most peacekeeping personnel and are therefore responsible for the largest number of allegations of misconduct of any personnel group, although civilian personnel are disproportionately responsible for allegations when measured per capita (Conduct in UN Field Missions Unit, nd). The assumption has also been reinforced by the growing public awareness of conflict-related sexual violence perpetrated by soldiers and militias, and also of the well-documented prevalence of sexual violence in military training schools and institutions, particularly in Global North countries (Associated Press, 2011; BBC, 2017; Arbour, 2022). It has also been bolstered by the public and institutional focus on violent sexual abuse and child abuse, which in peacekeeping and humanitarian contexts is more likely to be perpetrated by military than civilian personnel; the latter are consistently implicated in non-criminal acts of sexual exploitation, which are much harder to address and even investigate in the first place, based on my interviews.[9] Karen Engle (2020) has written insightfully about the 'grip of sexual violence' on the imaginations and programmatic focus of those working in international criminal courts. I have observed a similar focus in relation to SEA, particularly by those who oversee organizations and their accountability processes. These factors together created a powerful convergence around the notion that militarized masculinities were at the heart of the problem of peacekeeper SEA. The problem was, and remains, that this is only a limited part of the picture: the causes of SEA are much broader.

Masculinity: a limiting analysis

Masculinity is clearly part of the problem of SEA. However, common institutional narratives around SEA collapse masculinity into a set of inherent characteristics, rather than seeing it as the product of multiple, intersecting systems of power. This has a limiting effect on how those institutions understand and respond to SEA. The way such organizations construct ideas and narratives of problems and responses creates powerful structures of thought that shape (and limit) how they engage with the people they work with and for, and can obscure their view of the broader systems of power that shape the way those people experience being peacekept. Others have also noted this trend. Myrttinen et al have argued, based on their work in and with organizations dealing with 'masculinities', that

> much of the debate in NGOs', national governments', and international agencies' circles on peacebuilding seems at times trapped in discourses that either revolve around essentialist arguments highlighting men's 'innate' propensity to violence or focus on simplistic uses of frameworks such as hegemonic, military/militarized, or 'hyper'-masculinities. Problematically, these discourses have also often been reinforced and reproduced without relating them to their respective historical, political, and socio-economic contexts. (2017: 104)

Marysia Zalewski has similarly argued that the concept of 'military masculinities' has been 'easy' for hegemonic governance institutions to take on in their work, and, building on the work of Kathy Davis, suggested this is because it is a concept 'appealing to both generalists and specialists, particularly [as it appears] to be readily understandable and (relatively) easily applied' (2017: 201). Higate has noted the 'analytical allure' of the concept of military masculinities – partly because of the dominance of military men in peacekeeping – but argues that it 'can distract ... from the social-structural contexts in which ... peacekeepers find themselves' and prompts us instead to consider SEA in the context of (oppressive) social masculinities which are produced by gendered practices (2007: 100, 112–13). However, as Kirby (2013) had shown, attributing causal responsibility for the perpetration of SEA to gender orders and structures, such as masculinity or patriarchy, may inadvertently mask both individual and collective moral responsibility: individual men make choices about their sexual behaviours, and groups can act as bystanders, facilitators and beneficiaries of those behaviours. It is imperative we look beyond masculinity as an explanation to understand the broader range of factors that supplement and intersect with gender orders to explain the phenomenon of SEA.

The essentialist framings of men and masculinity that are prominent in the way the UN has dealt with SEA are a clear departure from the critical literature on masculinities that provided the intellectual and analytical foundations for how many people make sense of men's violence and abuses. That literature draws attention not simply to the outcomes of masculinities, but to the structural conditions and systems of power that produce it. For example, Cynthia Enloe (2000) has focused on processes of militarization, rather than simply the ideology and practice of militarism, and how they go hand in hand with processes of socialization in militarized settings that produce a particular set of gendered roles and identities, which, in turn, shape how individuals perform gender – including through the perpetration of SEA. Raewyn Connell's (1995) foundational work on masculinities showed the importance of understanding the gender orders and regimes in which they function, seeing them as products of structures and systems of power. Marsha Henry has shown the importance of situating analyses of men and masculinities firmly within the Black feminist project of intersectionality – as originally defined by Kimberlé Crenshaw (1989), not as a way of capturing gender differences and their effects, but rather to be attentive to intersecting systems of oppression – while also grounding structural analyses and challenging the patriarchal relations that persist (Henry, 2017). Crenshaw described intersectionality as like 'traffic in an intersection, coming and going in all four directions. … If an accident happens at an intersection, it can be caused by cars travelling from any number of directions and, sometimes, from all of them' (1989: 139). It is only by understanding these multiple, intersecting structures that we can make sense of the particular harms, violence or inequalities they cause – often at their points of intersection.

At the intersections of masculinity and SEA

The way organizations have made sense of 'masculinity' as a primary cause of SEA is an illustrative case of Habermas' instrumental rationality – where particular choices about means are made in order to achieve a specific goal, which then produces bureaucracies that revolve around commodified knowledge and action. As I have shown, in UN peacekeeping this has manifested as an emphasis on codes of conduct and their enforcement: prevention work revolves around training on what the rules are, and enforcement focuses on ensuring reporting mechanisms and investigations procedures are in place, along with policies determining appropriate punishments. Organizations, by taking up the 'masculinities' explanation but untethering it from its critical underpinnings, have created a way of knowing and responding to SEA that fundamentally fails to recognize – let alone respond to – the multiple, intersecting systems of power that give rise to its perpetration and which colour the way individuals and communities experience such misconduct (Westendorf and Searle, 2017). These include, but go far beyond, patriarchy and its product, masculinity. An intersectional view, responding to Crenshaw's invitation to focus on intersecting structures and systems of power and inequality, therefore draws into sight patriarchy as a system of power – rather than just masculinity as one of its products – as well as racism, coloniality and global capitalism as systems of power that create the conditions in which individual peacekeepers choose to perpetrate SEA, and in which local individuals are drawn into the economies of abuse and exploitation with which peacekeepers interact (for more on this, see Nof Nasser-Eddin in Chapter 13).

Take, for example, the case of 13-year-old Faela in the DRC, who became pregnant after repeated wartime rapes by soldiers, and whose father refused to support her because of the shame of her being an unmarried mother (Holt and Hughes, 2004). She walked to an internally displaced persons camp in Bunia, eastern DRC, which was located next to UN peacekeeping headquarters in the area. In the camp, Faela and her baby faced starvation, so every night she – along with other girls in the same situation – climbed through the fence into the compound where Uruguayan and Moroccan peacekeepers were based. She told reporters:

> 'If I go and see the [United Nations Organization Mission in the Democratic Republic of Congo (MONUC)] soldiers at night and sleep with them, then they sometimes give me food, maybe a banana or a cake,' she says, looking down at her son. 'I have to do it with them because there is nobody to care, nobody else to protect Joseph except me. He is all I have and I must look after him. ... Going over to the camp is OK because the soldiers are kind to me and don't point their guns at me like the other soldiers did.' (In Holt and Hughes, 2004)

The SEA perpetrated by peacekeepers in this case cannot be explained by masculinity alone; in fact, their motivations are secondary in Faela's story to her own motivations for her and her child's survival. The context of conflict-related sexual violence, social stigma, extreme poverty and the presence of peacekeepers creates the conditions for survival sex economies to emerge and flourish – a pattern that has been seen in many peacekeeping contexts globally (Westendorf, 2020: 33–4). These structural and contextual factors are at least equally as important in understanding Faela's story of SEA than the motivations of peacekeepers or humanitarians who engage in transactional sex, and who sometimes construe these encounters in terms of generosity to the civilians who seek them out, rather than insatiable masculine sexuality (Higate and Henry, 2004: 491; Higate, 2007: 100). As one UN worker in Sierra Leone who visits sex workers told *The New Humanitarian*, 'Yes, we've been given the lectures about power imbalances and everything – and

I understand that – but if we don't pay women for this type of thing, then realistically that means they or their children may not eat for the day. It's as simple as that' (in Jones and Cole, 2023).

Racism and coloniality are also at play in economies of transactional sex, which are prevalent in peacekeeping and humanitarian contexts. A former MONUC employee told reporters that 'the Belgians [in MONUC] won't touch anything over fourteen' (Spencer, 2005: 167), and peacekeepers interviewed by Higate suggested a fetishization of sex with children, arguing both that soldiers wanted to see if sex with children 'is different' and that in fact 'having sex with [young girls] was "respectful" of "local culture" where age of consent norms are different' (2007: 107). The relevance of colonialism is underlined by the explanation given by the French civilian peacekeeper with MONUC who admitted having sex with 24 under-age girls in 2004 – he said, 'over there the colonial spirit persists. The white man gets what he wants' (UN, 2004).

These examples highlight the complexity of factors that intersect to create the conditions in which some peacekeepers and humanitarians perpetrate SEA against the civilian populations they have been sent to protect and support, and in which some of those civilians seek out such encounters to meet the basic needs of their and their families' survival. The masculinities narrative that I have shown in this chapter to be dominant in institutional contexts responding to SEA fails to capture these complexities and, moreover, sets policy on a course to interventions that are unable to respond to the intersections of contextual, structural and normative factors that fuel SEA in different ways in different contexts. Critically, the masculinities narrative results in an individualized understanding of SEA which masks the diverse range of factors that create circumstances in which individuals choose to exploit or abuse. It masks the challenges posed by officials who refuse to deal with allegations or are simply too occupied with 'hard security' issues to take 'gender issues' seriously (Westendorf, 2013: 468). It puts a heavy emphasis on prevention through individualized training and enforcement of codes of conduct as well as contextual interventions that mollify the troublesome masculinities understood to cause SEA, which this chapter has demonstrated do not address the root causes of SEA. Moreover, this compliance-based approach assumes that robust accountability mechanisms will deter breaches of rules – a logic for which there is little evidence in relation to male-perpetrated conflict-related sexual violence (Kirby, 2015: 464). It is further undermined by the low rates of criminal charges or material punishments for perpetrators of SEA, particularly in relation to transactional sex, which is both the most common form of SEA alleged and the most challenging to investigate and punish (Westendorf, 2023a). Finally, the individualization of responsibility for SEA reflects a broader trend in dealing with 'gender issues' at international levels, namely that technocratic 'fixes' – such as training and end point accountability mechanisms – take precedence over efforts to address the underlying causes of gendered inequality and violence. The logic of response that stems from the masculinity narrative relies on the assumption that technocratic fixes are appropriate responses to what are essentially complex social, political and economic issues.

Conclusion

In this chapter, I argued that institutions and policy makers have made sense of SEA in ways that centre notions of masculinity, which are used to both explain and excuse the perpetration of SEA as an inevitable, unintended consequence of international interventions into crisis- and conflict-affected contexts. These narratives produce an individualized understanding of SEA – one in which individual 'bad apples' break rules to perpetrate harm against vulnerable local people – and result in policies that are primarily technocratic exercises to mitigate or prevent SEA through contextual and procedural mechanisms. These are hampered in practice by the limiting narratives of masculinity and individual responsibility. While well-intended, these interventions and the narratives that underpin them fail to respond to multiple, overlapping factors that cause SEA – including not only contextual factors, but also normative factors (such as sexism, racism and coloniality) and structural ones (such as poverty, material inequality and differential access to economic participation). To prevent and respond to SEA, there needs to be a more proactive grappling with the multiple sets of power relations that define the relationship between peacekeepers and the peacekept to more effectively prevent local individuals and communities from becoming vulnerable to exploitation and abuse in the first place.

References

Aids-Free World (2015) *The UN's Dirty Secret: The Untold Story of Child Sexual Abuse in the Central African Republic and Anders Kompass*, New York: Aids-Free World.

Andreas, P. (2011) *Blue Helmets and Black Markets: The Business of Survival in the Siege of Sarajevo*, Ithaca, NY: Cornell University Press.

Arbour, L. (2022) 'Key points from the Arbour report', *CDA Institute*, 30 May. Available from: https://cdainstitute.ca/key-points-from-the-arbour-report/ (accessed 8 June 2022).

Associated Press (2011) 'Two Australian military cadets in court over sex scandal', *The Guardian*, 29 April. Available from: www.theguardian.com/world/2011/apr/29/australian-military-cadets-sex-scandal (accessed 8 June 2022).

BBC (2017) 'Cadets sex abuse scandal was "hidden in full sight"', *BBC*, 4 July. Available from: www.bbc.com/news/uk-england-birmingham-40446666 (accessed 8 June 2022).

Conduct in UN Field Missions Unit (nd) 'Sexual exploitation and abuse', *United Nations*. Available at: https://conduct.unmissions.org/sea-data-introduction (accessed 8 June 2022).

Connell, R. (1995) *Masculinities*, Berkeley: University of California Press.

Coomaraswamy, R. (2015) *Preventing Conflict, Transforming Justice, Securing the Peace: A Global Study on the Implementation of United Nations Security Council Resolution 1325*, New York: United Nations.

Crenshaw, K. (1989) 'Demarginalizing the intersection of race and sex: a Black feminist critique of antidiscrimination doctrine, feminist theory and antiracist politics', *University of Chicago Legal Forum*, 1989(1): 139–67.

Deschamps, M., Jallow, H.B. and Sooka, Y. (2015) *Taking Action on Sexual Exploitation and Abuse by Peacekeepers: Report of an Independent Review on Sexual Exploitation and Abuse by International Peacekeeping Forces in the Central African Republic*, New York: United Nations External Independent Panel.

Engle, K. (2020) *The Grip of Sexual Violence in Conflict*, Stanford, CA: Stanford University Press.

Enloe, C. (2000) *Maneuvers: The International Politics of Militarizing Women's Lives*, Berkeley: University of California Press.

Henry, M. (2017) 'Problematizing military masculinity, intersectionality and male vulnerability in feminist critical military studies', *Critical Military Studies*, 3(2): 182–99.

Higate, P. (2007) 'Peacekeepers, masculinities, and sexual exploitation', *Men and Masculinities*, 10(1): 99–119.

Higate, P. and Henry, M. (2004) 'Engendering (in)security in peace support operations', *Security Dialogue*, 35(4): 481–98.

Holt, K. and Hughes, S. (2004) 'Sex and death in the heart of Africa', *The Independent*, 25 May. Available from: www.independent.co.uk/news/world/africa/sex-and-death-in-the-heart-of-africa-564563.html (accessed 29 June 2016).

Jones, S. and Cole, N.M. (2023) 'Business as usual for Sierra Leone sex workers despite aid sector bans', *The New Humanitarian*, 19 April. Available from: www.thenewhumanitarian.org/news-feature/2023/04/19/aid-industry-sex-workers-sierra-leone (accessed 10 October 2023).

Kirby, P. (2013) 'Refusing to be a man? Men's responsibility for war rape and the problem of social structures in feminist and gender theory', *Men and Masculinities*, 16(1): 93–114.

Kirby, P. (2015) 'Ending sexual violence in conflict: the Preventing Sexual Violence Initiative and its critics', *International Affairs*, 91(3), 457–72.

Ledgerwood, J. (1994) *UN Peacekeeping Missions: Analysis from the East-West Center 11*, Honolulu, HI: East-West Center.

Myrttinen, H., Khattab, L. and Naujoks, J. (2017) 'Re-thinking hegemonic masculinities in conflict-affected contexts', *Critical Military Studies*, 3(2): 103–19.

Simić, O. (2010) '"Boys will be boys": human trafficking and UN peacekeeping in Bosnia and Kosovo', in L. Holmes (ed) *Trafficking and Human Rights*, Cheltenham: Edward Elgar Publishing, pp 79–94.

Simić, O. (2012) *Regulation of Sexual Conduct in UN Peacekeeping Operations*, Berlin: Springer Science and Business Media.

Spencer, S. (2005) 'Making peace: preventing and responding to sexual exploitation by United Nations peacekeepers', *Journal of Public and International Affairs*, 16: 167–81.

UN (United Nations) (2004) 'UN civilian worker in DR of Congo accused of child molestation', *UN News*, 1 November. Available from: https://news.un.org/en/story/2004/11/119742 (accessed 29 October 2023).

UNAIDS (1998) *AIDS and the Military: UNAIDS Best Practices Collection*, Geneva: UNAIDS.

United Nations Secretary-General (2017) *Special Measures for Protection from Sexual Exploitation and Abuse: A New Approach*, UN Doc A/71/818.

Wax, E. (2005) 'Congo's desperate "one-dollar U.N. girls"', *The Washington Post*, 21 March. Available from: www.washingtonpost.com/wp-dyn/articles/A52333-2005Mar20.html (accessed 29 June 2016).

Westendorf, J.-K. (2013) '"Add women and stir": the Regional Assistance Mission to Solomon Islands and Australia's implementation of United Nations Security Council Resolution 1325', *Australian Journal of International Affairs*, 67(4): 456–74.

Westendorf, J.-K. (2020) *Violating Peace: Sex, Aid, and Peacekeeping*, Ithaca, NY: Cornell University Press.

Westendorf, J.-K. (2023a) 'A problem of rules: sexual exploitation and UN legitimacy', *International Studies Quarterly*, 67(3): 1–13.

Westendorf, J.-K. (2023b) 'Sex on mission: care, control and coloniality in peacekeeping and humanitarian operations', *International Affairs*, 99(4): 1653–72.

Westendorf, J.-K. and Searle, L. (2017) 'Sexual exploitation and abuse in peace operations: trends, policy responses and future directions', *International Affairs*, 93(2): 365–87.

Whitworth, S. (2004) *Men, Militarism, and UN Peacekeeping: A Gendered Analysis*, Boulder, CO: Lynne Rienner Publishers.

Zalewski, M. (2017) 'What's the problem with the concept of military masculinities?', *Critical Military Studies*, 3(2): 200–5.

9

Power, Consent and Peacekeeping Economies

Kathleen M. Jennings

Introduction

The United Nations' (UN's) zero-tolerance policy (ZTP) against sexual exploitation and abuse (SEA) targets three broad types of sexual interaction or relationships involving peacekeepers: sex with minors under the age of 18 (section 3.2(b)); transactional sex, defined in the policy as the 'exchange of money, employment, goods or services for sex, including sexual favours or other forms of humiliating, degrading or exploitative behaviour' as well as 'any exchange of assistance that is due to beneficiaries of assistance' (section 3.2(c)); and non-transactional sexual relationships between UN staff and 'beneficiaries of assistance' (section 3.2(d)). The policy invokes a blanket prohibition on both sex with minors and transactional sex; sexual relationships with beneficiaries of assistance are not banned, but instead 'strongly discouraged' on the grounds that 'they are based on inherently unequal power dynamics' and 'undermine the credibility and integrity of the work of the United Nations' (United Nations Secretary-General, 2003: 2). Enforcement of the policy is largely dependent on reporting by the victim/accuser or people in their circle, or by the peacekeepers' colleagues, acquaintances, or witnesses to the act or relationship. The breadth of the policy, its lack of precision and the essentially arbitrary nature of its enforcement have come under scrutiny almost since the moment of its passage. Critiques have focused on both the difficulties of enforcing the ZTP and the assumptions underpinning it (Jennings, 2008, 2010; Otto, 2009; Simić, 2012; Henry, 2013, McGill, 2014; Westendorf, 2023a, 2023b).

This chapter is in the latter tradition. It problematizes how the ZTP represents the notion of consent by both peacekeepers and beneficiaries of assistance. I argue that the ZTP writes into regulation narrow understandings of sexual intimacy against puritanical and contested conditions for consent, in contexts characterized by complex power relations between interveners and residents. The ZTP places power in sexual interactions and relationships always in the person of the (presumed male) peacekeeper. In terms of 'strongly discouraged' sexual relationships, the ZTP implies both that the peacekeeper will be the most (economically) powerful partner *and* that economic power determines whether consent is genuine or even possible. It thus homogenizes our understanding of 'the local', as embodied in the sexualized (presumed female), raced body, while disregarding the local person's capacity for agency. Yet, I argue, this assumption of where power lies and how it operates does not always map onto peacekeepers' and local residents' experiences and interactions. Cumulatively, the restrictiveness of the ZTP's conceptualizations of sexual relations and consent, and the way the policy flattens power relations between peacekeepers and locals – often counter to their lived experiences – undermines the policy's legitimacy and complicates its implementation.

In the following, I problematize understandings of power and consent as assumed in the ZTP, and their implications. I focus on three aspects that are particularly significant in relation to consent, power and the ZTP: meaningful consent and the conditions under which it is 'allowed'; how power and consent in sexual relationships are understood and gendered in and by the ZTP; and the policy's homogenization of the local and the peacekeeper, in contrast to many people's lived experiences in peacekeeping economies.

A note on terminology: in this chapter, I use gender-neutral language as much as possible ('people transacting sex' rather than 'women transacting sex') to counter the gendered and heteronormative assumptions I am otherwise unpicking. While it is true that most reported cases of SEA involve women alleging instances of exploitation or abuse against men, and while I have in previous publications used 'woman' as shorthand for the local person and 'man' for the peacekeeper (Jennings, 2008, 2010, 2014), in this chapter I wish to get away from reinforcing this default. Further, rather than 'prostitution', I refer to 'sex work' or 'transacting sex'; the latter is meant to encompass those who do not identify as sex workers, but who (situationally or sporadically) exchange sex for money, goods, services or other benefits. I also refer to 'sexual relationships' rather than 'romantic relationships', both to reflect the language of the ZTP and to avoid assuming or assigning specific connotations to these relationships. While I hold out transactional sex/sex work and sexual relationships as distinct categories, in line with the ZTP's categorization, it should be emphasized that the line between the two can be blurry (Jennings, 2010; Westendorf, 2023a). I use 'sexual partner(s)' to recognize that sexual interactions may involve more than two people. Finally, I use 'locals' or some variation (local people or residents) as an imperfect proxy for beneficiaries of assistance, in line with the UN's own guidance (United Nations, 2017), and I use 'peacekeeper' to encompass both civilian and uniformed peacekeepers; while the ZTP technically applies to both local and international UN staff, I restrict my analysis to international peacekeepers.

When is consent meaningful and when is it 'allowed'?

As a starting point, and to knock down a potential straw man before it arises: few people within or outside the UN – be they activists, practitioners or scholars, including myself – wish to imply that the UN should not have *any* rules relating to what could be deemed 'problematic', much less abusive and/or illegal, sexual activity by peacekeepers. When it comes to uniformed peacekeepers, having an entirely hands-off approach to sexual interactions with local residents smacks of the 'boys will be boys' permissiveness of days past (Whitworth, 2004; Martin, 2005); when it comes to civilians, of the stereotypical colonialist menacing of house girls (or boys).

The issue is that what is legal or illegal varies over space and time; and what is considered 'problematic' is even more individualized and subjective, however much people may be influenced by the cultural norms and legal regimes that surround them. The question then becomes where to draw the line for permissible sexual activity by peacekeepers. There is little controversy around the prohibition against sexually *abusive* behaviour by peacekeepers; the challenge lies in the notion and operationalization of *exploitation*.

In an early policy report on the subject (Jennings, 2008), I argued that the differing ways that the ZTP was operationalized in the missions in Haiti and Liberia, especially with respect to sexual exploitation, reflected this confusion. The mission in Haiti adopted a minimalist, low-key, internally focused approach to implementing the ZTP, with the primary aim of protecting the mission's reputation. The mission in Liberia, conversely, took a maximalist, externally oriented approach, including public outreach campaigns and messaging that focused on Liberians' rights to not experience SEA. Where the referent of protection in Haiti was the mission, the referent of protection in Liberia was the local population. This argument was useful insofar as it put forth the idea, then relatively novel, that the ZTP potentially has multiple subjects of protection (see also Kanetake, 2010). Yet what it obscured is that the ZTP, in the way it regulates the sexual activity of peacekeepers – prohibiting or strongly discouraging sexual encounters or relationships with locals – is a policy with fundamentally maximalist aims. When it comes to how exploitation is defined, the clear message contained in the ZTP is that it is better to err on the side of caution. It is extending the humanitarian principle of 'do no harm' to peacekeepers' sexual interaction with locals.

Yet applying 'do no harm' to sex in such a sweeping manner assumes that *any* sex between peacekeepers and locals is de facto damaging. As Otto points out, this indicates that 'the "problem" is sex itself, rather than sexual harm' (2009: 34). Thus, if sex (with a member of a specified group) is the problem, prohibition (against sex with a member of that group) is the obvious solution. This is why most jurisdictions in the world have a legal age of consent. But the point of an age of consent is that any person under that age is considered legally unable to consent to sex, regardless of whether they themselves perceive the sex as desired: their presumed physical and emotional immaturity signifies that any consent given is not meaningful. Applying this reasoning to a population of adults, however, is a more problematic proposition. Although the ZTP does not prohibit *all* sex with *all* local adults, the breadth of what is either outright banned or 'strongly discouraged' is so expansive that most sexual interactions between peacekeepers and locals would fall under the purview of the ZTP. This signals that any sex between peacekeepers and local adults is suspect, because the situation locals are in vis-à-vis peacekeepers makes locals' ability to meaningfully consent questionable.

Meaningful consent entails that all parties understand and are in a position to give consent, without any form of coercion. Of course, adults (in transactional or non-transactional contexts) may be unable to meaningfully consent to sex for manifold reasons, including impairment from drugs or alcohol, being asleep or unconscious, involvement in a physically or emotionally abusive relationship, and – controversially – intellectual disabilities. Only the latter involves a distinct population (adults with certain disabilities) as opposed to an individual, transitory state of being. In contrast to being intoxicated or asleep, 'being poor' does not nullify one's ability to meaningfully consent. Nor does having lower social status than one's partner(s). The ability to consent is similarly unaffected by being of a different nationality or race than your sexual partner(s), or otherwise marginalized. Nor does being a sex worker (or someone transacting sex) nullify consent, although abolitionists and their political allies who believe that all sex work is abuse might contest this position (Rossoni, 2021).

In the introduction, I referred to the ZTP's puritanical and contested conditions for consent. By this, I mean the conditions under which consent is given that make it meaningful, not to the individuals involved, but under the terms of the ZTP: the conditions under which, according to the policy, consent is 'allowed' to count, and the conditions under which it is effectively void. By prohibiting transactional sex with locals, the ZTP makes consent given by the adult transacting sex – regardless of the (il)legality of sex work in the host country – immaterial, as the simple existence of a transaction cancels the meaningfulness of the consent. As others (Otto, 2009; Henry,

2013; McGill, 2014; Bys, 2022) note, this stance aligns with that of anti-sex work abolitionists, who characterize all sex work as exploitative, harmful and coercive. Such an argument identifies all sex work as necessarily coerced, by which it follows that consent given under coercion can never be meaningful. This may be a logical chain of thought, but it is also one that denies agency to anyone transacting sex, regardless of their motives, experiences and autonomy. While the decision to sell or trade sex – as one's primary source of income, or sporadically and situationally, or for survival – may not be people's preferred choice were there other, easier ways of earning money or goods, this fact does not justify ignoring the validity of people's decisions and actions. Positing that the simple fact of transacting sex empties consent of meaning removes that person's ability to make autonomous decisions in that context. This in turn effectively eliminates people's ability to articulate distinctions between experiences of sexual abuse, rape and mutually consensual sexual transactions – because if none of these involve meaningful consent, it is a distinction without a difference.

For people transacting sex who do not experience it as automatically non-consensual, this approach to consent is gaslighting-by-policy. As Otto incisively notes, it has 'the effect of reducing women's (and men's) sexual agency to a "privilege" that is able to be enjoyed only by those who engage in sexual conduct that is officially sanctioned' (2009: 41). Moreover, the nullification of consent is not merely a function of the sex being, from an institutional standpoint, against the rules and therefore unacceptable. There is a shaming dimension. Because the ZTP discursively equates 'transaction' with 'exploitation', the implication is that a local who consensually transacts sex with a peacekeeper is consenting to their own exploitation, connoting complicity in one's own degradation. Conversely, peacekeepers are not just breaking administrative rules when they transact sex with local adults: they are having sex with someone whose consent is not deemed meaningful, which in most jurisdictions is considered sexual assault. The ZTP does not have the power of law, but by voiding the meaningfulness of consent in most sexual interactions between peacekeepers and locals, it conceptually blurs the line between exploitation and abuse – even if none of the parties experience the encounter as either of these.

While this section has focused primarily on section 3.2(c) of the ZTP, relating to transactional sex, there are also issues with how consent is conceptualized in 'strongly discouraged' sexual relationships between peacekeepers and locals (section 3.2(d)). Unlike transactional sex, these relationships are not always defined as exploitative by the ZTP, but there is a *presumption* of exploitation that forms the basis on which these relationships are intended to be understood. This takes us to the next point: how power in sexual relationships is represented and gendered in the ZTP.

How the ZTP represents and genders power

For a policy so broad in scope, the ZTP reflects a narrow understanding of sexual relations, including with respect to relationships that fall into the 'strongly discouraged' category. Specifically, the premise of 'inherently unequal power dynamics' in relationships between peacekeepers and locals demonstrates that 'power' in (sexual) relationships is conceptualized by the ZTP primarily in terms of economic power. This conceptualization is doing two interlocking things: eliding the complexity of power in intimate relationships, making it into a zero-sum game, and investing the default male peacekeeper with more power and agency than the default female local. In this section, I first examine my conceptual qualms with the ZTP's representation of power, then turn to empirically based objections.

Strongly discouraging consensual sexual relationships on the presumption of an inherent inequality between partners begs the obvious question: what is the basis of these 'inherently unequal power dynamics'?[1] The least generous read of this formulation is that the UN assumes some fundamental difference between peacekeepers and locals, whether that be of race, ethnicity, social class or otherwise, that prohibits their being perceived as equals. This interpretation certainly adds credence to critiques of UN peacekeeping as colonialist interventions (Tudor, 2023). Stepping away from this unflattering reading, and in line with the emphasis on transaction in other parts of the policy, another alternative is to understand 'inherently unequal power dynamics' as referring to the local partner's economic status compared to the peacekeeper. The assumed inequality is that the local partner is poor(er); the peacekeeper, relatively wealthy.

Economic status, both absolute and relative to one's partner(s), is undoubtedly important in sexual relationships. There is a reason that increasing women's economic independence has been a cornerstone of the feminist project since its beginnings (Federici, 2012): lessening women's economic dependence on husbands or families enables their flourishing and attainment of their rights, and can be crucial in enabling women and their children to leave failed or abusive marriages or relationships. Cultural tropes like 'gold-digger' or 'sugar daddy' indicate that the tendency to reduce sexual relationships to economics is not exclusive to the ZTP.

Yet injecting into policy the assumption that one category of person, the local, will necessarily be poorer than the other category of person, the peacekeeper, and that this difference creates an *inherent* inequality between the parties testifies to a transactional view of relationships. Gone is any notion of intimacy, mutual affection or companionship that is not driven by dollars. More practically, the recognition that there are other sources of power in relationships is also done away with: the reality that – abusive relationships aside – there is rarely one side with all the power and the other side with none. Attractiveness is a source of power in relationships, as is youth, intelligence, and social connections.

The association of the ZTP's 'inherently unequal power dynamics' with economic status matters because the corollary of equating 'money' with power is equating a lack of it with powerlessness: a simplifying move that, however well-intentioned, strips away agency and dignity and likens the lack of financial resources to incapacity. Further leaps contained in the ZTP – conflating 'poor', 'local' and 'exploited' together – have the effect of denying people agency and autonomy under the guise of protecting them. It posits that the purportedly 'weaker' person in the relationship does not know their own interests or desires and is somehow being manipulated.

Here, the link between the ZTP's conceptualizations of power and consent in terms of sexual relationships, not just sexual transactions, becomes clear. The underlying logic of the ZTP means that transactional sexual encounters are necessarily exploitative, thus coercive, and so even if consent exists, it cannot be meaningful. If sexual *relationships* are also essentially transactional, thus presumptively exploitative, then the same applies – regardless of how the parties themselves experience the relationship, or the fact that 'power' in an ongoing relationship is rarely zero-sum or solely economic in nature, or indeed the fact that such a restrictive understanding of consent between adults has no plausible legal basis (see also Simić, 2012).

The 'strongly discouraged' clause is not an outright prohibition, thus leaving the possibility for some peacekeeper–local relationships to be deemed permitted under the policy. In practice, this categorizes sexual relationships between peacekeepers and locals according to a conservative, heteronormative binary. Sexual relationships are either essentially transactional and exploitative, or they are 'love' relationships – despite the 'inherent' inequality between the parties – and thus, according to the ZTP, acceptable. This dichotomized view of relationships, between two relative extremes, ignores the vast area between where most mutually enjoyable, beneficial sexual relationships exist. Getting back to Otto's (2009) argument about sexual puritanism in the ZTP, the implicit idea being communicated is that sex should only be validated in the context of a lasting, romantic, heterosexual relationship.[2] In the absence of such, sex is represented to embody exploitation and harm. This resembles the Christian evangelical movement of purity culture on an institutional scale (Thwaites, 2022). It signals an attitude towards sex that does not align with the lived experiences, convictions or desires of many who are subject to the ZTP, which, in turn, is potentially detrimental to its credibility and implementation (Westendorf, 2023a).

The ZTP's conceptualization of (sexual) power and consent is particularly salient in light of how the policy is gendered and raced. The ZTP is nominally gender-neutral – although it is noted in section 2.2 that UN forces have 'a particular duty of care towards women and children', and in section 3.2

that the regulations are laid down to 'further protect the most vulnerable populations, especially women and children'. As noted earlier, the prevalence of SEA is heavily gendered: most of the accused peacekeepers, whether uniformed or civilian, are men, while most accusers are women. This is why, as stated in the introduction to this chapter, 'man' is often defaulted for peacekeeper, 'woman' for the local person. There are also racialized dimensions and colonialist overtones to the peacekeeper–local encounter; that many uniformed peacekeepers are from the Global South complicates, but does not erase, these dimensions (Henry, 2013).

The gendered and racialized oppositions the ZTP depicts in its attempt at mitigation are thus familiar: man–powerful/woman–powerless; man–aggressor/woman–victim; man–active/woman–passive; peacekeeper (man)–enlightened/local (woman)–backwards; peacekeeper (man)–in control/local (woman)–desperate. Prima facie problematic, these oppositions also obscure the possibility that women can be victimized by women and that men can be victimized by women or other men,[3] and that since victimization is associated with womanhood, it can emasculate male victims of SEA. More fundamentally, the oppositions set up by the ZTP presumptively limit the possibility of sexual interactions, including transactions, where there are no aggressors or victims at all – and, in fact, impose victimhood on people who actively reject that label and end up feeling aggrieved by their relationships being outlawed.

There are two further points I wish to raise here. First, associating 'power' with the economic and fixing it to the person of the (male) peacekeeper always sets the local (woman) up to be the poorer, weaker party – a gendered assumption that likely mirrors and reinforces perceived or existing economic inequalities in the host society. This is particularly ironic in the case of transactional sex or relationships, where sex with peacekeepers is a means of securing financial or other benefits. A woman transacting sex or seeking economic benefits in a relationship could, in fact, have opportunities for, and levels of, income and other benefits unavailable to most men, upending gendered roles and expectations in their own lives and communities (Oldenburg, 2015) in ways counter to the assumptions of the ZTP. Second, the gendering of the ZTP maps onto its conceptualization of (meaningful) consent in a way that, so to speak, disenfranchises – removes the agency of – women more than men. Again, in the guise of protection, the woman is always set up to lose – in this case, losing validation of her ability to make decisions about her own interests, even if these decisions are constrained by circumstance. That said, the ZTP's interconnected gendering and notions of power and consent hardly flatter the presumed male peacekeeper, who is assigned the role of exploiter and aggressor in sexual interactions with locals.

If the UN really wishes to decrease the incidence of sexual transactions and relationships between peacekeepers and locals, which given the longevity of the ZTP is a reasonable assumption, it might make more sense to couch its terms in less normative language. Changing the policy itself has long met resistance – the fear is that opening the ZTP up for change will lead to its being watered down and possibly jettisoned – but implementation guidance for and training in the ZTP are more flexible. Banning peacekeepers from engaging in transactional sex is a policy that can be justified multiple ways without bringing sexual morality into it – most obviously, in places where sex work is criminalized, as a way of ensuring peacekeepers do not run foul of local laws, or as an element of the mission's internal security rules that peacekeepers must adhere to. The application of the 'strongly discouraged' clause could also be clarified as applying to, for example, relationships where there is a clear and potentially coercive economic relationship existing between the parties – such as when the peacekeeper works alongside, employs or lives in a compound that employs the local – rather than to all sexual relationships between peacekeepers and locals.

Finally, it is worth noting that the assumptions reflected in the ZTP's conceptualization of consent and power may not always be empirically supported. This is clearly the case with respect to the aforementioned assumption that peacekeepers are men and affected locals are women. Moreover, the ZTP also assumes that peacekeepers are wealthier and have access to more resources than locals, and that since economic status is aligned with power, peacekeepers are therefore the more powerful actor.[4]

The blanket assumption that peacekeepers have more money and power than locals oversimplifies the complex realities of peacekeeping economies on both sides of the equation. Taking peacekeepers first: while it is true that both uniformed and civilian peacekeepers make a good salary, both compared to the local context and to what they might be making in their home country, it is not a given that this income is disposable or readily available. Uniformed peacekeepers I interviewed in the Democratic Republic of the Congo and Liberia received only a fraction of their salary in-mission, the rest being automatically deposited in their home bank account (Jennings, 2015); this was a standard condition organized by their home military, not something they opted into. Civilian peacekeeper sources related similar voluntary arrangements, sending a set amount of their pay cheque straight into their home bank account and leaving a smaller sum locally to cover rent and living costs. Many peacekeepers also send remittances home (Agence France-Presse, 2012). This is not to imply that peacekeepers are not well compensated or relatively well off. Rather, it provides nuance to the depiction of peacekeepers, who can be economically constrained even though they are well remunerated; which is to say that the economic gap between peacekeepers and locals may not be as wide or unequal as assumed.

Locals, meanwhile, are represented by the ZTP as not just poorer than peacekeepers, but in a position where economic desperation drives them to (allow themselves to) be exploited. Again, this is an oversimplified generalization. First, this privileges an understanding of transactional sex that equates it primarily with survival sex rather than situational or professional sex work.[5] There is undoubtedly survival sex in peacekeeping economies, but the assumption that survival sex predominates among types of sexual transactions is empirically shaky (Beber et al, 2017). While the ZTP's implicit association of transactional sex with survival comports with the anti-sex work ideology the policy is aligned with, it paints a picture of poverty and desperation that colours all beneficiaries of assistance.

Further, by situating locals as 'inherently unequal' to peacekeepers, the ZTP erases socioeconomic diversity among the host population. Even if one brackets the normative dimensions of 'inherently unequal' and allows that poor locals may have a lower economic standing than (most) peacekeepers, not all locals are poor. The existence of a local middle class and elite is ignored by the ZTP. Are there still 'inherently unequal power dynamics' if the local party is the richer one? If not, is the relationship no longer 'strongly discouraged'? But if so, does this give credence to the reading of the ZTP that the 'inherent' unequalness between the parties is based in something other than economic status? Finally, the ZTP seems particularly oriented towards a specific idea of what a peacekeeping host country will look like – low income and poorly functioning – that does not necessarily comport with legacy operations such as the one in Cyprus.

If we expand the ZTP's conceptualization of power beyond the economic and recognize the complexity of power relations in sexual transactions and relationships, the presumed power of the peacekeeper in relation to the local may be on even more tenuous ground. I have argued elsewhere (Jennings, 2014, 2019) that everyday interactions in peacekeeping economies reveal that locals may have certain advantages – superior connections, knowledge of the 'rules of the game' and willingness to take advantage of opportunities that present themselves – that complicate framings of the peacekeeper as always having the upper hand. Moreover, peacekeepers can experience these advantages as sources of threat and vulnerability. This does not stop peacekeepers from transacting sex or having sexual relationships with locals, but it does imply that the peacekeeper–local dynamic is not as straightforward or lopsided as represented in the ZTP – and that locals have more power and agency than the policy allows them.

Conclusion

Over the past two decades, the ZTP has become institutionalized in UN peacekeeping, and real strides have been made on the problem of peacekeeper SEA. There is greater awareness around the problem among both peacekeepers and locals; more transparency about who is committing

SEA, how allegations are followed up and what punishments are levied if the allegations are substantiated; and mechanisms in place to assist survivors. The ZTP, and the apparatus developed to implement it, has been instrumental in setting these changes in motion.

But this does not mean that the flaws of the ZTP should be ignored, especially when those flaws are written into the policy and, thus, compromise its implementation. Many of the arguments made here – that the ZTP's conceptualization of exploitation is based on a contested understanding of consent, reinforces a puritanical view of sex, and denies local people agency while reinforcing gendered and racialized oppositions – were raised in various forms by feminist scholars in the years immediately succeeding the ZTP's adoption. While much of the policy and research focus has since moved on to questions surrounding the ZTP's implementation, as well as how anti-SEA policies have been adapted to related sectors, this chapter resurrects these early debates. This is important because the way the ZTP is written, and the assumptions and ideas it builds on, have significant – and, I argue, deleterious – implications for its implementation. But beyond the implementation effects are the ZTP's signalling effects: what it assumes about local people, about peacekeepers and about consent, power and intimacy, and how harmful these assumptions can be.

References

Agence France-Presse (2012) 'Bangladesh peacekeepers send home $1 billion in three years', *NDTV*, 26 April. Available from: www.ndtv.com/world-news/bangladesh-peacekeepers-send-home-1-billion-in-three-years-478 778 (accessed 22 May 2023).

Beber, B., Gilligan, M., Guardado, J. and Karim, S. (2017) 'Peacekeeping, compliance with international norms, and transactional sex in Monrovia, Liberia', *International Organization*, 71(1): 1–30.

Bys, C. (2022) 'What kind of feminism is behind efforts to address sexual exploitation and abuse?', *Humanitarian Exchange Magazine*, 17 June. Available from: https://odihpn.org/publication/what-kind-of-feminism-is-behind-efforts-to-address-sexual-exploitation-and-abuse/ (accessed 24 August 2023).

Federici, S. (2012) *Revolution at Point Zero: Housework, Reproduction, and Feminist Struggle*, Oakland, CA: PM Press.

Henry, M. (2013) 'Sexual exploitation and abuse in UN peacekeeping missions: problematising current responses', in S. Madhok, A. Phillips, and K. Wilson (eds) *Gender, Agency, and Coercion. Thinking Gender in Transnational Times*, London: Palgrave Macmillan, pp 122–42.

Jennings, K.M. (2008) *Protecting Whom? Approaches to Sexual Exploitation and Abuse in UN Peacekeeping Operations*, Oslo: Fafo.

Jennings, K.M. (2010) 'Unintended consequences of intimacy: political economies of peacekeeping and sex tourism', *International Peacekeeping*, 17(2): 229–43.

Jennings, K.M. (2014) 'Service, sex, and security: gendered peacekeeping economies in Liberia and the Democratic Republic of the Congo', *Security Dialogue*, 45(4): 313–30.

Jennings, K.M. (2015) 'Life in a "peace-kept" city: encounters with the peacekeeping economy', *Journal of Intervention and Statebuilding*, 9(3): 296–315.

Jennings, K.M. (2019) 'Conditional protection? sex, gender, and discourse in UN peacekeeping', *International Studies Quarterly*, 63(1): 30–42.

Kanetake, M. (2010) 'Whose zero tolerance counts? Reassessing a zero tolerance policy against sexual exploitation and abuse by UN peacekeepers', *International Peacekeeping*, 17(2): 200–14.

Martin, S. (2005) *Must Boys Be Boys? Ending Sexual Exploitation & Abuse in UN Peacekeeping Missions*, Washington, DC: Refugees International.

McGill, J. (2014) 'Survival sex in peacekeeping economies: re-reading the zero tolerance approach to sexual exploitation and sexual abuse in United Nations peace support operations', *Journal of International Peacekeeping*, 18(1–2): 1–44.

Oldenburg, S. (2015) 'The politics of love and intimacy in Goma, Eastern DR Congo: perspectives on the market of intervention as contact zone', *Journal of Intervention and Statebuilding*, 9(3): 316–333.

Otto, D. (2009) 'The sexual tensions of UN peace support operations: a plea for "sexual positivity"', *Finnish Yearbook of International Law*, 18: 33–57.

Rossoni, I. (2021) 'Not just semantics: sex work, trafficking and abolitionist discourse in Malta', *Border Criminologies*, 23 June. Available from: https://blogs.law.ox.ac.uk/research-subject-groups/centre-criminology/centreborder-criminologies/blog/2021/06/not-just (accessed 24 August 2023).

Simić, O. (2012) *Regulation of Sexual Conduct in UN Peacekeeping Operations*, Berlin: Springer.

Thwaites, E. (2022) 'The impact of Christian purity culture is still being felt – including in Britain', *The Conversation*, 28 June. Available from: http://theconversation.com/the-impact-of-christian-purity-culture-is-still-being-felt-including-in-britain-182907 (accessed 25 August 2023).

Tudor, M. (2023) *Blue Helmet Bureaucrats: United Nations Peacekeeping and the Reinvention of Colonialism, 1945–1971*, New York: Cambridge University Press.

United Nations (2017) *Glossary on Sexual Exploitation and Abuse.* Available from: https://hr.un.org/sites/hr.un.org/files/SEA%20Glossary%20%20%5BSecond%20Edition%20-%202017%5D%20-%20English_0.pdf (accessed 15 March 2023).

United Nations Secretary-General (2003) *Secretary-General's Bulletin: Special Measures for Protection from Sexual Exploitation and Sexual Abuse*, UN Doc ST/SGB/2003/13.

Westendorf, J.-K. (2023a) 'A problem of rules: sexual exploitation and UN legitimacy', *International Studies Quarterly*, 67(3): 1–13.

Westendorf, J.-K. (2023b) 'Sex on mission: care, control and coloniality in peacekeeping and humanitarian operations', *International Affairs*, 99(4): 1653–72.

Whitworth, S. (2004) *Men, Militarism, and UN Peacekeeping: A Gendered Analysis*, Boulder, CO: Lynne Rienner.

10

Gender, Race, Sexuality and PSEA

Junru Bian, Megan Daigle, Sarah Martin and Henri Myrttinen

Introduction

In 2015, Martina Broström, a former staffer with the Joint United Nations Programme on HIV/AIDS (UNAIDS), lodged a sexual harassment complaint against Luiz Loures, former Deputy Executive Director of UNAIDS. The organization then began to restructure her out of her job, eventually firing her and alleging that she had herself committed sexual and financial misconduct. After Broström went public, a series of internal, independent and legal investigations lasting more than seven years revealed the hidden system of impunity within UNAIDS (Farge, 2021). At the same time, Dr Maurizio Barbeschi, a senior World Health Organization official, was finally fired in 2023 for sexual conduct (after initially only being suspended) when allegations were made against him – some stretching back 20 years came – out in the media. Former colleagues and World Health Organization consultants described the culture within Dr Barbeschi's team as a 'misogynistic pissing circle', with his inappropriate behaviour long being an open secret (Newey and Lovett, 2023).

These stories are, unfortunately, not rare or confined to the United Nations. Sexual exploitation and abuse (SEA) are not new in the humanitarian sector: while the 2018 Oxfam Haiti SEA scandal drew vast international attention, known incidents and scandals predate it. That same year, revelations of sexual harassment inside Save the Children sparked the #AidToo movement, highlighting the widespread problem of sexual harassment, abuse and violence perpetrated against aid workers by their own colleagues (Gayle, 2018). In response, donors increased their scrutiny and agencies implemented a suite of safeguarding measures (as discussed by Sarah Martin in Chapter 1 and Asmita Naik and Jasmine-Kim Westendorf in Chapter 5 of this volume). Despite this flurry of activity, the widespread and systematic SEA perpetrated by humanitarian personnel during the 2018–20 Ebola outbreaks in the Democratic Republic of Congo showed that there is still a long way to go (Mukundi and Flummerfelt, 2023). In this chapter, we examine the issue of SEA by aid workers both 'externally' (for example, against members of the population they purport to serve) and 'internally' (against their colleagues), which tend to be understood as entirely separate concerns. We use this as an entry point to address broader debates around the gendered and racialized nature of the humanitarian sector. While the dynamics surrounding coloniality, race, gender and SEA in the humanitarian sector are not dissimilar to SEA by peacekeeping forces (see, for example, Jennings, 2014; Henry, 2015; Westendorf, 2020), SEA by humanitarian aid workers has, to date, been researched far less. This chapter intends to fill this gap, demonstrating that the dominant self-image of the humanitarian sector and its formal and informal institutional cultures stand in the way of seriously preventing SEA committed by humanitarians, be it against intended beneficiaries or their own colleagues.

Despite the acknowledgement of SEA within the aid sector, the cases that emerge are still being framed as unfortunate individual incidences rather than a structural problem. Misconceptions prevail. Responses continue to focus on safeguarding organizations from criticism instead of systematically exploring preventative practices and policy making.[1] Our central arguments are that the aid sector still assumes that the source of harm against aid workers resides outside the physical confines of aid organizations. This assumption is inherently racialized, gendered and sexualized; it discursively produces a 'standard' aid worker imaginary that is inherently White, expatriate, cis-hetero and masculine – effectively invisibilizing those who do not fit these descriptions in the eyes of aid organizations. It renders them minorities within the aid worker collective. Consequently, violence – including SEA – that may primarily impact this perceived minority remains outside the mainstream security policy considerations in the sector.

In this chapter, we explore discussions around protection from sexual exploitation and abuse (PSEA) for aid workers. Particularly, we reflect on a set of questions still underexamined in the humanitarian policy and scholarly literature: Whose security matters? Who gets to define SEA? Who gets to benefit from this protection? This chapter draws on anonymized interviews with past and current aid workers, as well as a review of humanitarian manuals and policies, social media and blogs, and the authors' observations while conducting research and working in the humanitarian sector.[2] We begin by exploring the experiences and self-protection strategies of aid workers with diverse gender, racial and sexual identity profiles that do not fit the conventional, White, male, heterosexual aid worker imaginary. Then, we reflect on the aid security policy discourse and practice to date. We then explore how existing security practices are founded on the idea of 'stranger danger'. Lastly, we reflect on what a more inclusive response to SEA that accounts for the sector's colonial and patriarchal root causes might look like.

Who is an aid worker?

The experience of SEA is neither gender-neutral nor race-neutral. Women aid workers may face sexual harassment from both the local population and their colleagues. They may also be subject to additional constraints and security risks due to societal norms within and outside their organizations. Non-White women (local and expatriate) and those of diverse sexual orientation, gender identity and expression, and sex characteristics (SOGIESC)[3] can experience heightened risks shaped by the intersections of their racial and gender–sexual identities. For White women aid workers, their Whiteness may sometimes allow them to occupy a 'third gender' status, exempting them from conforming to local gender conventions – a privilege that may not be extended to their non-White counterparts (Partis-Jennings, 2019). Instead, some local women aid workers or expatriate women aid workers of colour may resort to using their physical resemblance to the local population to be less visible, as a means of risk mitigation. However, this has contributed to the existing assumption that they are somewhat less vulnerable than their White women aid worker counterparts, who have long been framed as being particularly vulnerable to sexual abuse because of their Whiteness (Conlin and Davie, 2015; Wekker, 2016; Stoddard, 2020; Cornish-Spencer, 2022). A similar logic also underscores the security experiences of aid workers of colour and those with diverse SOGIESC, who are unaccounted for in organizational security frameworks that ignore both racialized and sexualized aspects of risk.

In our interviews, women aid workers and those with diverse SOGIESC reported that they lack security information relevant to their identity-specific needs (Daigle et al, 2020). They perceive their employing organizations as male-dominated and heteronormative. In response, they engage in self-censoring identity management practices to suppress personal characteristics that may be perceived as outside of accepted gender norms, to reduce security risks both within and outside their organizations (Korff et al, 2015; Tatum et al, 2017). Women aid workers may resort to self-censorship, such as remaining silent when experiencing or witnessing misogynistic remarks and sexual harassment or violence. Many women aid workers are concerned that reporting workplace SEA will make them appear at fault for not preventing or negotiating such situations, which jeopardizes their career prospects and professional recognition (Leach and Laville, 2015; Paton et al, 2000). Mazurana and Donnelly (both in their 2017 publication and in Chapter 4 of this volume) found that survivors of gender-based violence (GBV) or SEA in the aid sector (and arguably in any professional sector) are almost always first questioned by others about their competency in self-protection. This takes precedence over questioning the alleged perpetrator about their actions, thereby serving to normalize workspace SEA and encourage a systemic culture of silence and victim blaming (see also Hearn and Parkin, 1995; Hearn et al, 2005; Gaul et al, 2006; Stoddard et al, 2019).

In conservative contexts, particularly those where homosexuality is criminalized, perpetrators often exploit coercive 'sexual identity blackmailing' strategies to victimize aid workers of diverse SOGIESC, like threatening to expose their sexual identity to their homophobic colleagues or the public (Mazurana and Donnelly, 2017; Cornish-Spencer, 2022; Michelis and Kisa, 2022). For aid workers of diverse SOGIESC, self-censorship for risk management may include claiming that their partners are of the opposite sex or refraining from discussing their marital status, dating preferences or having children (Kumar, 2017; Global Interagency Security Forum, 2018). They may also modify privacy settings and remove photos with their partners from their devices or social media before deployment (Ragins and Cornwell, 2001; Rengers et al, 2019).

Within today's aid sector, there is a persistent normative assumption that aid workers are expected to be 'naturally resilient', which lingers in lived institutional culture despite policy shifts. This assumption feeds into existing organizational security frameworks and risk reduction training – and tacitly implies that these frameworks prepare aid workers adequately for a career replete with risks, some of which are acknowledged and mitigated, while others are simply absorbed. In gendered terms, workplace SEA is framed as an issue for women and aid workers with diverse SOGIESC to cope with rather than to confront, as giving this issue attention may detract organizations from their core, self-evidently important mission of humanitarian response. Any negative emotional reaction to harms experienced is therefore due to a lack of humanitarian professionalism, indicating that staff are simply not cut out for the work. Requests for the organization to change in consideration of staff, rather than staff assimilating to fit within such structures, are discursively framed as diverting already scarce organizational resources from the bigger crisis at hand – the humanitarian one (Paton et al, 2000).

In addition, reporting an incident of SEA inside an organization tends to run up against a fundamental assumption in the sector: that aid workers cannot do harm (and especially cannot do harm to each other). Internal SEA challenges completely dismantle this assumption – yet for managers of aid organizations, maintaining this assumption is very often seen as a crucial requisite for aid workers to work together and maintain the support of donors, governments and the general public. Therefore, managers often try to mitigate risks (real or potential) of reputational damage to the organization by: urging would-be complainants to drop their reports; underplaying the seriousness of the incidents; chalking up malfeasance to generational or cultural rifts, or to failures of 'political correctness'; or emphasizing the importance of the perpetrator to the organization and its mission. As a result, victim blaming in the sector is rampant (see Sarah Martin in Chapter 1 of this volume).

In turn – and as a direct result of such workplace norms – women and aid workers of diverse SOGIESC often refrain from speaking out about workplace discrimination and violence that they witness and experience, fearing being perceived as disruptive to an otherwise cohesive atmosphere among colleagues. Cohesion, which is frequently misunderstood as necessarily entailing socializing and drinking alcohol together outside of work, is seen as paramount to agencies' ability to respond to humanitarian crises (Martin, 2017).

Whose security?

Security measures aimed at protecting aid workers are part of the wider securitization of aid described by Smirl (2008), Duffield (2012) and Autesserre (2014), including the privatization and professionalization of aid security actors (Beerli and Weissman, 2016; Chisholm, 2017). Fundamentally, conceptualizations of security in the sector draw on a binary opposition that positions 'the field' and 'the other' – that is, the mostly non-White 'host communities' and 'beneficiaries' of international humanitarian assistance – as risky and potential threats, while the 'non-field' or 'home' is figured as safe, familiar and welcoming. This security perspective is inherently colonial, and it does not fully consider the risks and challenges faced by women and aid workers of colour or of diverse SOGIESC, particularly those risks and challenges related to workplace sexual discrimination and violence (Mears, 2009; Global Interagency Security Forum, 2018; Stoddard et al, 2019; Stoddard, 2020). This is evident in the way that international aid organizations pursue their duty of care through a proliferation of security trainings and manuals (Daigle et al, 2020). Save the Children's *Safety First* (2010; first published 1995) and the International Committee of the Red Cross's *Staying Alive* (2006; first published in 1995) are early examples of the codification of aid security into manuals, which led to the Humanitarian Practice Network's industry standard guidelines, *Good Practice Review 8: Operational Security Management in Violent Environments* (Humanitarian Practice Network, 2010).[4]

In tandem, the sector has seen the proliferation of hostile environment awareness trainings: residential courses provided by private companies, often led by ex-military facilitators, which focus on preparing participants for high-impact, low-likelihood 'hard' threats, such as bombings, shootings or ambushes (Daigle et al, 2020). Such manuals and trainings produce and reproduce a purportedly authoritative body of knowledge about the threats facing aid workers, and one that paints deployment to 'the field', and indeed 'the field' itself, as the cause of danger – with the implication that the mostly racialized people living in crisis-affected contexts where humanitarian action occurs are the agents of that danger. By defining security and designing its implementation according to an us-versus-them binary, this body of knowledge mostly excludes and obscures the dangers that characterize the non-field, which encompasses the office, the staff guest house and the compound while on deployment. Thus, the very people that international aid workers are ostensibly deployed to support are painted as threats to their own safety and security.

As a result, long-standing dichotomies between aid workers and 'beneficiaries' – us/them, local/expat, White/non-White – are perpetuated as imperative in the pursuit of security. This brings with it two main consequences. First, power is largely erased from the conversation on aid worker security and differences among the aid worker cadre are flattened. In line with humanitarianism's colonial roots, the archetypal aid worker is figured in the imaginary of the public, and of the sector, as White, able-bodied, cis-gender, heterosexual men who travel to far-flung crises to 'help' (Smirl, 2008; Autesserre, 2014; Chisholm, 2017). The ways in which this identity-based power inequality complicates risks for aid workers at the intersections of gender, sexuality, race and 'international'/'local' status is not often discussed in aid security. Furthermore, the kind of 'soft' skills of negotiation and cultural awareness that are central to acceptance by populations in crisis (Fast et al, 2013) and that might help aid workers avoid 'hard' threats entirely by understanding and engaging appropriately in the settings where they work, are not emphasized.

Second, threats to aid workers' safety that emanate from within the sector – including from colleagues – are often swept aside by this security discourse, even as they have so effectively destabilized the notion of a safe 'non-field' space. Patriarchy, violent masculinities, colonialism and other elements of humanitarians' own culture are rarely examined as determinants of gendered or other harms (Daigle, 2022). Furthermore, the idea that aid workers themselves may be a source of danger has been left unspoken. Particularly when it comes to risks of sexual violence, the discourse of aid security inscribes non-White men as the violent and libidinous source of potential harm against expatriate (White women) aid workers (Wekker, 2016, Westendorf, 2023). White men, by contrast, have been figured as explorers and colonizers, and later as humanitarians whose altruism masks any harm they perpetrate, whether against their own 'expatriate' or 'local' colleagues or the populations that they purport to serve (McClintock, 1995; Stoler, 2010). Aid workers of diverse SOGIESC, those living with disabilities and those who are non-White and 'local' take up significantly less space in the discursive world of modern-day humanitarianism. This approach to defining and enacting aid security belies deep-seated ideas that humanitarian aid itself is a White, heteronormative, 'international' project that universalizes Western patriarchal identities, experiences and perspectives, even if the sector is progressively more diverse and includes ever-increasing numbers of locally hired (as opposed to expatriate) staff. Ultimately, it also speaks to the self-interest of aid agencies whose 'duty of care' is revealed to be more about reputational risk, legal jeopardy and satisfying donors than it is about engaging with the lived, everyday risks faced by a diverse cadre of aid workers.

'Stranger danger'

This prevailing security discourse prevents the sector from understanding itself as it is genuinely experienced by many aid workers – that is, as a space of pervasive and multifarious harms that depend on unequal power relations and proximity in spaces like residences and workplaces. Importantly, there is also a notable lack of focus on GBV of all kinds in the aid security space and, especially, of SEA within the sector and among aid workers. When discussed, aid security discourse tends to broach sexual violence in terms of expatriate White women aid workers threatened by armed actors or other local men. Stoddard describes sexual violence as 'the most challenging category to capture and reflect accurately in the global data', and she discusses it in detail only in relation to the high-profile 2016 attack on the Terrain hotel compound in South Sudan, where five expatriate women aid workers were repeatedly raped by armed actors (2020: 7). Likewise, the Humanitarian Practice Network's (2010) *Good Practice Review 8* positions sexual violence within conversations about cultural difference that are seen to exacerbate risks. The Global Interagency Security Forum (2018) notes that risk assessments in the humanitarian sector often inadequately assess internal threats, especially with respect to gender. Nonetheless, an indicative survey of women aid workers conducted by the Humanitarian Women's Network found that 22 per cent of respondents reported unwanted touching, 20 per cent identified threats of physical aggression, 9 per cent disclosed being touched in a sexual way and 4 per cent admitted to being forced to have sexual intercourse. Of those who disclosed experiences of sexual assault in the survey, 69 per cent said that they had not reported them in their organizations (Stoddard et al, 2019: 10). The organization Report the Abuse (2017) found that out of the 1,000 plus aid worker respondents, 72 per cent were survivors of sexual violence, and in 64 per cent of the reported cases, the perpetrator was a colleague. As this chapter has shown, aid workers of diverse SOGIESC, as well as those with disabilities, tend to be more concerned about internal rather than external security threats.

In our own research (Daigle et al, 2020), we found little evidence that aid security manuals or trainings engage with the nuances of SEA *within* aid agencies, instead focusing heavily on 'stranger danger' – that is, external risk. Our interviews showed that some providers of hostile environment awareness trainings have begun to tackle the prospect of sexual violence, and a few even acknowledged that women aid workers are far more likely to experience harassment or assault at the hands of colleagues than outsiders. However, the specific forms that SEA can take place in the context of humanitarian workplaces, the power relations at play and any relevant reporting mechanisms or mitigation strategies all remain largely written outside the scope of security. A continued blind spot in the humanitarian security imaginary and response is in addressing the security concerns faced by local staff, who tend to be more at risk but have the most to lose if they report other staff members. Other individuals, such as interns, volunteers and other 'non-staff', who are more at risk of abuse due to their precarious positions are also far less likely to report (Stoddard et al., 2019). Furthermore, the two surveys on SEA experienced by women aid workers discussed in this chapter almost exclusively reflected the experiences of international staff, with only 4 per cent of respondents in one study and 17 per cent in the other being local staff (Stoddard et al., 2019).

Conclusion

In today's aid sector, the dichotomy between internal and external SEA is at best unhelpful and at worst obfuscating, feeding the largely unspoken assumption that SEA against aid workers is somehow separate from gendered and racialized power imbalances that underpin the entire sector. The construction of humanitarian response as altruistic and selfless also acts as a brake on meaningful engagement, because SEA against aid workers – particularly harassment – is framed as less important than 'hard' security concerns and seen as diverting attention and resources from the core humanitarian mission. The dynamics of internal SEA deserve far more attention from the sector than they currently receive, but they are also illustrative of foundational power relations, structural problems and gaps in commitment when it comes to SEA perpetrated against the so-called 'beneficiaries' of humanitarian aid. Approaches centred on reputational risk and isolating SEA from its enabling environment mean that PSEA 'reveal[s] a good deal of self-interest on the part of aid organisations' (Naik, 2022: 23).

Perhaps unsurprisingly, then, current approaches to PSEA reveal the unwillingness – or even inability – of institutions and decision makers to account for power dynamics directly or confront the root causes of abuses. Following a typical modus operandi for the sector (which has not shown much effectiveness but is replicated due to the lack of other options), aid workers have leaned on technical responses, including mandatory e-learnings, checklists and guidance notes, with an accompanying proliferation of (predominantly women) PSEA and safeguarding 'experts', to meet funding and compliance requirements.[5] The result has been a tokenistic, check box approach that does not touch power structures and can be overwhelming for smaller, place-based organizations. For example, in the Ukraine refugee response, the Resource and Support Hub Eastern Europe found that small civil society organizations were unable to keep up with required trainings on SEA, with one agency trained four times as a condition of funding from four different partners (Martin, 2023). PSEA 'experts' are deployed for weeks and then replaced with others, and few speak the language of the country where they work or have experience in the context.

Risk reduction aimed at internal SEA remains marginal, often amounting to informal 'whisper networks' warning colleagues of known perpetrators. However, our interviewees recounted that some aid workers of diverse SOGIESC who have seniority or feel sufficiently protected have chosen to be open about their sexual orientation to signal their willingness to provide support to others. While these stories of solidarity are encouraging, they do not represent systematic change – only coping mechanisms – and do not change the fact that the humanitarian sector remains one that selectively shields the perpetrators from accountability, as we described at the outset of this chapter. Ultimately, if, for the perpetrator to be disciplined, organizational policy requires self-reporting by survivors of SEA, whether they are aid workers or affected people, then the policy is already ineffective, regardless of what it promises to do once the organization receives the self-report (Mazurana and Donnelly, 2017; see also Sarah Martin, Chapter 1 of this volume).

Meaningful change, if it is to be achieved, will mean bringing together responses to internal and external SEA. Where PSEA has been the purview of human resource departments or accountability programming, and shaped by concern for reputational risk, humanitarians must come to grips with understanding it – like the much wider field of GBV response – as a question of protection and the risks facing marginalized groups inside and outside the sector, including women, racialized people and those with diverse SOGIESC. Perhaps most notably, hostile environment awareness trainings and security manuals currently lack in-depth discussion of aid workers' own potential to do harm, both against their colleagues and against the people they purport to serve – a major oversight if SEA in all its forms is ever to be meaningfully addressed. Humanitarians must come to understand their own position within matrices of power relative to their colleagues and crisis-affected populations, including how their presence and actions are felt by others and how they can do harm, alongside and even despite their ostensibly 'good' intentions.

What is needed is a response that is unashamedly political, rather than technocratic, recognizing power relations embedded in the humanitarian system and its institutional culture. PSEA should not be siloed or treated as solely a human resources issue. Rather it should be addressed in dialogue with system reform agendas on localization and feminism, such as The Grand Bargain and the Compact on Women Peace and Security and Humanitarian Action, as well as pledges for decolonization called for by anti-racist and pro-inclusivity activists and organizations, such as Adeso, Decolonise MSF and the Start Network. The humanitarian sector is beset by imaginaries, practices and mindsets that either echo or reinforce patriarchal, Eurocentrist and, at times, sexist, ableist, heteronormative and neocolonial norms (Loftsdóttir, 2009; Redfield, 2012; Autesserre, 2014; Kagumire, 2018; Rutazibwa, 2019; Daigle et al, 2020). These norms shape understandings of aid security and threats that face aid workers, and they also inform how the sector responds to SEA, in relation to both colleagues and crisis-affected people. The dominant security paradigm, with its underlying assumptions that power dynamics within are unproblematic and security threats emanate from without, fails to fully consider risks facing everyone in the orbit of humanitarian response. A structural reimagining of how SEA should be approached is necessary for the well-being of aid workers and, by extension, the people they purport to serve.

References

Autesserre, S. (2014) *Peaceland: Conflict Resolution and the Everyday Politics of International Intervention*, Cambridge: Cambridge University Press.

Beerli, M. and Weissman, F. (2016) 'Humanitarian security manuals: neutralising the human factor in humanitarian action', in M. Neuman and F. Weissman (eds) *Saving Lives and Staying Alive: Humanitarian Security in the Age of Risk Management*, London: C. Hurst & Co, pp 71–82.

Chisholm, A. (2017) 'Clients, contractors, and everyday masculinities in global private security', *Critical Military Studies*, 3(2): 120–41.

Clare, H. and Bys, C. (2022) 'Post-#aidtoo: are we setting ourselves up to fail?', *Humanitarian Exchange*, 81: 28–34.

Conlin, L. and Davie, W.R. (2015) 'Missing White woman syndrome: how media framing affects viewers' emotions', *Electronic News*, 9(1): 36–50.

Cornish-Spencer, D. (2022) '"We will find some other reason": A personal reflection on queerphobia within women's rights work and the Official Development Assistance (ODA) sector', *Social Development Direct*, 19 July. Available from: www.sddirect.org.uk/blog-article/we-will-find-some-other-reason-personal-reflection-queerphobia-within-womens-rights (accessed 30 October 2023).

Daigle, M. (2022) *Gender, Power and Principles in Humanitarian Action*, London: Overseas Development Institute.

Daigle, M., Martin, S. and Myrttinen, H. (2020) '"Stranger danger" and the gendered/racialised construction of threats in humanitarianism', *Journal of Humanitarian Affairs*, 2(3): 4–13.

Duffield, M. (2012) 'Risk management and the bunkering of the aid industry', *Development Dialogue*, 58: 21–36.

Farge, E. (2021) 'Exclusive: U.N. staffer who complained of sexual assault loses dismissal case – documents', *Reuters*, 23 March. Available from: www.reuters.com/article/un-dismissal-appeal-exclusive-int-idUSKBN2BF0JA (accessed 30 October 2023).

Fast, L., Freeman, F., O'Neill, M. and Rowley, E. (2013) 'In acceptance we trust? Conceptualising acceptance as a viable approach to NGO security management', *Disasters*, 37(2): 222–43.

Gaul, A., Keegan, M., Lawrence, M. and Ramos, M. (2006) *NGO Security: Does Gender Matter?* Fairfield: Save the Children.

Gayle, D. (2018) 'Timeline: Oxfam sexual exploitation scandal in Haiti', *The Guardian*, 15 June. Available from: www.theguardian.com/world/2018/jun/15/timeline-oxfam-sexual-exploitation-scandal-in-haiti (accessed 30 October 2023).

Global Interagency Security Forum (2018) *Managing the Security of Aid Workers with Diverse Profiles*, Manchester: Global Interagency Security Forum.

Harrington, C. (2010) *Politicization of Sexual Violence: From Abolition to Peacekeeping*, London: Routledge.

Hearn, J. and Parkin, W. (1995) *Sex at Work: The Power and Paradox of Organisation Sexuality* (revised edn), New York: St Martin's Press.

Hearn, J., Parkin, W. and Collier, R. (2005) 'Gender, sexuality and violence in organizations', *Gender, Work and Organization*, 12(6): 593–5.

Henry, M. (2015) 'Parades, parties and pests: contradictions of everyday life in peacekeeping economies', *Journal of Intervention and Statebuilding*, 9(3): 372–90.

Humanitarian Practice Network (2010) *Good Practice Review 8: Operational Security Management in Violent Environments*, London: Overseas Development Institute.

International Committee of the Red Cross (2006) *Staying Alive: Safety and Security Guidelines for Humanitarian Volunteers in Conflict Areas*, Geneva: International Committee of the Red Cross.

Jennings, K. (2014) 'Service, sex, and security: gendered peacekeeping economies in Liberia and the Democratic Republic of the Congo', *Security Dialogue*, 45(4): 313–30.

Kagumire, R. (2018) 'Being Black working in a White male-dominated aid industry', *African Feminism*, 8 June. Available from: https://africanfeminism.com/being-black-and-working-in-a-white-male-dominated-aid-industry-byrosebell-kagumire/ (accessed 30 October 2023).

Korff, V.P., Balbo, N., Mills, M., Heyse, L. and Wittek, R. (2015) 'The impact of humanitarian context conditions and individual characteristics on aid worker retention', *Disasters*, 39(3): 522–45.

Kumar, M. (2017) *Digital Security of LGBTQI Aid Workers: Awareness and Response*, Manchester: Global Interagency Security Forum.

Leach, A. and Laville, S. (2015) 'Raped by a colleague then fired: the aid worker who refused to keep quiet', *The Guardian*, 19 October. Available from: www.theguardian.com/world/2015/oct/19/raped-by-a-colleague-then-fired-the-aid-worker-who-refused-to-keep-quiet (accessed 30 October 2023).

Loftsdóttir, K. (2009) 'Invisible colour: landscapes of Whiteness and racial identity in international development', *Anthropology Today*, 25(5): 4–7.

Martin, S. (2017) 'Holier than thou: MSF needs its own #metoo moment', *Cassandra Complexity*, 12 May. Available from: https://cassandracomplexblog.wordpress.com/2018/05/12/holier-than-thou-msf-needs-its-own-metoo-moment/ (accessed 30 October 2023).

Martin, S. (2023) '8 points to consider about safeguarding and PSEA investigations', *Resource and Safeguarding Hub Eastern Europe*, 11 April. Available from: https://easterneurope.safeguardingsupporthub.org/blog/eight-points-consider-about-safeguarding-and-psea-investigations (accessed 30 October 2023).

Mazurana, D. and Donnelly, P. (2017) *STOP the Sexual Assault against Humanitarian and Development Aid Workers*, Boston, MA: Feinstein International Center.

McClintock, A. (1995) *Imperial Leather: Race, Gender and Sexuality in the Colonial Conquest*, London: Routledge.

Mears, E.S. (2009) *Gender and Aid Agency Security Management*, SMI Professional Development Brief No 2, Geneva: Security Management Initiative.

Michelis, I. and Kisa, F. (2022) *Pocket Guide: Safeguarding LGBTQI+ Individuals Working in Civil Society Organisations (CSO)*, London: Resource and Support Hub.

Mukundi, R. and Flummerfelt, R. (2023) 'More women accuse aid workers in Ebola sex abuse scandal', *The New Humanitarian*, 8 March. Available from: www.thenewhumanitarian.org/investigations/2023/03/08/more-women-accuse-WHO-aid-workers-ebola-sex-abuse-scandal (accessed 30 October 2023).

Naik, A. (2022) 'Tackling sexual exploitation and abuse by aid workers: what has changed 20 years on?', *Humanitarian Exchange*, 81: 20–4.

Newey, S. and Lovett, S. (2023) 'Top WHO scientist fired after allegations of sexual misconduct', *The Telegraph*, 7 September. Available from: www.telegraph.co.uk/global-health/women-and-girls/maurizio-barbeschi-who-sexual-misconduct-fired/ (accessed 30 October 2023).

Partis-Jennings, H. (2019) 'The "third gender" in Afghanistan: a feminist account of hybridity as a gendered experience', *Peacebuilding*, 7(2): 178–93.

Paton, D., Smith, L. and Violanti, J. (2000) 'Disaster response: risk, vulnerability and resilience', *Disaster Prevention and Management*, 9(3): 173–80.

Ragins, B.R. and Cornwell, J.M. (2001) 'Pink triangles: antecedents and consequences of perceived workplace discrimination against gay and lesbian employees', *Journal of Applied Psychology*, 86(6): 1244–61.

Redfield, P. (2012) 'The unbearable lightness of ex-pats: double binds of humanitarian mobility', *Cultural Anthropology*, 27(2): 358–82.

Rengers, J., Heyse, L., Otten, S. and Wittek, R. (2019) '"It's not always possible to live your life openly or honestly in the same way" – workplace inclusion of lesbian and gay humanitarian aid workers in Doctors Without Borders', *Frontiers in Psychology*, 10. doi: 10.3389/fpsyg.2019.00320

Report the Abuse (2017) *Humanitarian Experiences with Sexual Violence: Compilation of Two Years of Report The Abuse Data Collection*, Bern: Report the Abuse.

Rutazibwa, O. (2019) 'What's there to mourn? Decolonial reflections on (the end of) liberal humanitarianism', *Journal of Humanitarian Affairs*, 1(1): 65–7.

Save the Children (2010) *Safety First: A Safety and Security Handbook for Aid Workers* (2nd ed), London: Save the Children.

Smirl, L. (2008) 'Building the other, constructing ourselves: spatial dimensions of international humanitarian response', *International Political Sociology*, 2(3): 236–53.

Stoddard, A. (2020) *Necessary Risks: Professional Humanitarianism and Violence against Aid Workers*, New York: Palgrave Macmillan.

Stoddard, A., Harvey, P., Czwarno, M. and Breckenridge, M. (2019) *Speakable: Addressing Sexual Violence and Gender-Based Risk in Humanitarian Aid*, London: Humanitarian Outcomes.

Stoler, A.L. (2010) *Carnal Knowledge and Imperial Power: Race and the Intimate in Colonial Rule* (2nd ed), Berkeley: University of California Press.

Tatum, A., Formica, L. and Brown, S. (2017) 'Testing a social cognitive model of workplace sexual identity management', *Journal of Career Assessment*, 25(1): 107–20.

Wekker, G. (2016) *White Innocence: Paradoxes of Colonialism and Race*, Durham, NC: Duke University Press.

Westendorf, J.K. (2020) *Violating Peace: Sex, Aid, and Peacekeeping*, Ithaca, NY: Cornell University Press.

Westendorf, J.K. (2023) 'Sex on mission: care, control and coloniality in peacekeeping and humanitarian operations', *International Affairs*, 99(4): 1653–72.

Westendorf, J.K. and Searle, L. (2017) 'Sexual exploitation and abuse in peace operations: trends, policy responses and future directions', *International Affairs*, 93(2): 365–87.

Wood, E. (2014) 'Conflict-related sexual violence and the policy implications of recent research', *International Review of the Red Cross*, 96(894): 457–78.

11

'We Don't Have a Word for That': Issues in Translating PSEA Communication

Emily Elderfield and Ellie Kemp

Introduction

Preventing, or protecting from, sexual exploitation and abuse (PSEA) starts with knowing how to listen to the needs and preferences of survivors and communities. Yet managing multilingualism and addressing the risk of language-related exclusion remain systemic gaps in humanitarian action. As a result, humanitarians are not equipped to design PSEA strategies that communicate on sexual exploitation and abuse (SEA) in culturally, contextually and linguistically comprehensible ways. Organizations also do not adequately understand or address the intersections between language and other factors of vulnerability that increase individuals' exposure to SEA and decrease their access to support and safe reporting channels.

In this chapter, we first explore the role of multilingualism in humanitarian assistance and how language influences power dynamics. We then examine systemic gaps in language awareness in PSEA communication, including conceptual and terminological issues underpinning PSEA; difficulties communicating and translating technical terms; contextual, cultural and gendered differences around the topic of sex; and issues of access to information and reporting mechanisms. We conclude by considering how organizations can adopt a language-aware approach to better listen to those affected by SEA as a basis for support and prevention.

Linguistic diversity and linguistic power

Multilingualism in humanitarian assistance

Humanitarian emergencies are almost always multilingual. In many countries, a colonial language is the official language, yet people use one of several local, regional or non-colonial national languages as their first (or only) language. People displaced by conflict or disaster relocate to areas where they may share no language with host communities. International organizations employ staff speaking a combination of English and one or a handful of languages relevant for the specific context. The linguistic diversity of affected people means humanitarians rarely have the skills to provide services in all their languages; a widespread lack of language use data keeps them largely unaware of that gap. Even local and national organizations, whose staff share a first language with some service users, face challenges understanding and communicating in the languages of all those needing assistance.

In such contexts, humanitarian translators and interpreters fulfil a crucial role. They enable two-way communication between service providers and service users, different levels of the humanitarian architecture, and humanitarian actors and other key stakeholders. Yet despite the integral role of language, language skills are often undervalued (Roth, 2012), and language remains largely overlooked in how the sector understands PSEA (Robinson and Conilleau, 2022). Key international organizations acknowledge the critical role of managing language issues in PSEA, including through culturally appropriate terminology (CHS Alliance, 2018; International Organization for Migration, 2020),[1] diverse languages, formats and channels, especially audio (Inter-Agency Standing Committee – IASC, 2016a; Foreign, Commonwealth and Development Office, 2021), and multilingual access to reporting mechanisms (IASC, 2016a, 2016b; CHS Alliance, 2022). Research with linguistically diverse communities in Ghana, Myanmar and Iraq has also yielded insights on how language issues intersect other barriers to reporting (Oxfam, 2021). Yet in practice, efforts to embed language-related recommendations are rare, and a sector-wide failure to account for language-related barriers and challenges persists. Where efforts exist, the focus is skewed towards lingua francas – (assumed to be) common languages – over the first languages of communities affected by humanitarian crises (Gleasure, 2020). Thus, information is available in some national and international languages but is inaccessible to anyone not speaking a dominant language – in some contexts, this is the majority of the population.

Language as power

There is insufficient attention to the role of linguistic power in multilingual aid settings (Roth, 2019). As a result, PSEA guidance largely conceptualizes language as a practical or technical issue rather than intrinsically linked to power dynamics. Given that power dynamics of aid already skew power away from community members (Samarasekera, 2021), understanding how power manifests through language and communication practices can help organizations redress the balance in their PSEA communication strategies.

Because hierarchies place small local organizations furthest 'downstream', to succeed they are often obligated to adapt to the language practices of more powerful organizations. This includes the prevalence of English (and to a lesser extent other colonial languages); in the international aid system, monolingual English speakers can easily enter, operate in and derive income from multilingual spaces (Roth, 2019). Yet monolingual speakers of other languages do not have the same possibility. The ability to speak English also reasserts linguistic power as it is the main language used in donor communication and, therefore, facilitates access to funding (Abu-Assab and Nasser-Eddin, 2021).

Because crisis contexts are multilingual, organizational decision makers are not likely to speak the same language as survivors of SEA. Even when the survivor can report, the perpetrator is likely to speak a more dominant language, giving them more power in the eyes of the organization and investigative authorities; this linguistic power imbalance can dissuade survivors from reporting (Social Science and Analytics Cell – CASS, 2021). Interpreters are critical to reducing language barriers, yet rarely receive guidance or training to perform their role accurately (Delgado Luchner and Kherbiche, 2018). The resulting risk of information distortion or loss compounds survivors' vulnerability when humanitarians receiving the report do not speak the survivor's first language.

Language dynamics also compound the risk of gender exclusion, as women and girls are both more exposed to SEA and more likely to experience language barriers. Women's lesser educational access makes them less likely than men to be literate and to be comfortable using a national or dominant language. In many contexts, societal gender norms restrict women's ability to receive information and communicate with humanitarians. PSEA interventions that disregard women's relative lack of linguistic power therefore risk silencing survivors and reinforcing the power of perpetrators.

Challenges in understanding and translating terminology and concepts

Defining core PSEA concepts

PSEA information and awareness campaigns draw on terms and ideas about prohibited conduct laid out in the United Nations Secretary-General's 2003 Bulletin on 'special measures for sexual exploitation and abuse'. Yet the central concepts – sexual abuse, sexual exploitation and sexual harassment – risk misinterpretation even in their original language. The United Nations (UN) definition of sexual abuse focuses on acts of a physical nature (UN, 2017), which excludes non-physical acts that can also constitute sexually abusive behaviour, such as emotional abuse (Abu-Assab and Nasser-Eddin, 2021). The definition of sexual exploitation covers abuses of power for sexual purposes (UN, 2017), which may not align with how people perceive or make decisions about engaging in sexual relationships, especially in situations of extreme economic precarity. By contrast, sexual harassment is defined by its location – the workplace – rather than the nature of the act (UN, 2017).

Critiques of the word choices used in PSEA highlight that it conceptualizes humanitarians and those impacted by a crisis as two distinct groups of people. This generates the idea of a singularizing imbalance of power in which one group is positioned as always more powerful – and always in the same ways – than another. This masks the complex power dynamics at play and risks obscuring instances of SEA when dominant narratives about SEA are subverted, such as when the survivor is male (Westendorf, 2023b) or when power relations between humanitarians threaten efforts to challenge harmful norms and behaviours. These definitions also constrain nuanced discussions about local staff who have pre-existing relationships with community members or whose social circle includes people now receiving assistance (Bys, 2022; Satke et al, 2022; Westendorf, 2023a).

Translating core PSEA concepts

The conceptual lack of clarity in the Bulletin compounds translation issues when organizations try to communicate on PSEA in a language other than English. In some languages, one word covers some or all the terms 'sexual abuse', 'sexual exploitation' and 'sexual harassment'. In others, the concepts simply do not exist in the way the UN definitions describe. For example, it has been shown that Kurdish Badini- and Kurdish Sorani-speaking men and women in Iraq consider the three terms to be synonymous, and instead find terms like 'assault' clearer (CLEAR Global, 2022a). In Arabic, some terms used to describe sexual misconduct may also be used to talk about non-sexual misconduct. This has led to complications in reporting and investigations; someone accused of misconduct termed as 'sexual harassment' in English may be found to have committed acts more accurately described as 'bullying' (Abu-Assab and Nasser-Eddin, 2021). In Lingala, the term for 'sexual abuse' is the same as the term for 'sexual violence'; one translation of 'sexual exploitation' was 'to love a woman or a man with the promise of money or employment' (CASS, 2021: 8).

Abbreviations are widely used in humanitarian communication, but anyone unfamiliar with what PSEA or SEA stand for cannot engage with the abbreviations. Abbreviations also rarely translate well between languages. In some languages, they are simply not common; in Arabic, for example, they are a relatively new feature derived largely from globalization processes and not innate to Arabic-speaking contexts (Altakhaineh, 2017). To resolve this, organizations either leave the abbreviation in English or translate the full phrase. Both risk miscommunication; many struggle to decode the English abbreviation, even if they know English, and the resulting translation can be vague, inconsistently applied or simply incorrect.

This lack of clarity and openness to misinterpretation in the central concept of PSEA puts all related communication at risk. Humanitarians need to understand how to clearly communicate what they mean by sexual exploitation, abuse and harassment, that it is concerned with behaviour of humanitarian workers, and who risks misunderstanding due to the language they speak.

Understanding contextual drivers

Perceptions of sex in exchange for material goods

Research has found that PSEA strategies often do not adequately explore the contextual and cultural factors in people's choice, or lack of choice, in engaging in sex acts, or design communication strategies on that basis (CASS, 2021; Oxfam, 2021; CLEAR Global, 2022a). For example, communication that stigmatizes transactional sex or survival sex often reinforces blame- and shame-based narratives about sexual conduct, whether or not those involved consider these activities to be exploitative. This can further entrench stigma about reporting SEA. In this chapter, we do not examine the validity, morality or legality of transactional sex (on this, see Kathleen Jennings in Chapter 9 of this volume). But we do contend that language is fundamentally a social tool, so communication needs to be informed by and embedded in the social context in which it occurs.

Though discourses diverge on transactional sex, its prevalence in humanitarian settings is undeniable. For example, more than 50 per cent of women surveyed in Liberia said they had engaged in transactional sex; more than 75 per cent of those had done so with UN personnel (Beber et al, 2016). Jennings and Bøås (2015) argue that transactional sex is part of a larger 'peacekeeping economy' that proliferates alongside an international humanitarian presence, which includes sex workers alongside domestic work, security guards and drivers. Better language awareness would support PSEA communicators to recognize how contextual factors shape all forms of sexual interaction and to use that to clarify the rights and support available to those who define their experiences as exploitative or abusive.

Economic vulnerability and cultural perceptions of violence also shape how people interpret PSEA messages. In the Democratic Republic of

Congo (DRC) – widely considered one of the world's most complex humanitarian crises and one of the highest-risk countries for SEA – some people only perceived abuse as 'real' if it was perceived as violent (IASC, 2016a). Further research in the DRC illustrates how contextual factors significantly impact what behaviours and acts are perceived as acceptable or abusive, and to what extent people living through humanitarian crises feel that reporting would benefit them. In a context of economic precarity, some community members in the eastern region expressed positive views of relationships that are deemed exploitative in the PSEA discourse, because they considered that the associated access to resources was necessary for their survival (CLEAR Global, 2022c). And in Equateur province, some female community members said they would only consider themselves exploited if the male humanitarian worker did not uphold promises of material support (CASS, 2021). And even if women perceive behaviour to be sexually coercive towards them, their economic precarity may outweigh any desire to disengage or report (World Health Organization, 2021). This is exacerbated when social norms about being pregnant while unmarried pressure or force people to remain in relationships (Blau, 2016). Research in the eastern region also found that PSEA materials focused on telling people which relationships were prohibited rather than addressing practical concerns that influenced whether they felt empowered to report (CLEAR Global, 2022c). Community members wanted to know what would happen to them, their families (including children conceived from rape) and the assistance they received if they reported. They also wanted organizations to reassure them their report would remain confidential and that they would not face reprisals from the perpetrator and other community members.

Translating sex, gender, power and violence

People's experiences of gender, sex and agency inform their understanding and expectation of how organizations govern staff members' sexual conduct (Westendorf, 2023a). In conflict-affected settings with higher rates of other forms of violence, some forms of sexual violence are likely to be more common (Stark et al, 2017). Perceptions of SEA may intersect with perceptions about forced marriage, child abuse and child trafficking, sexual exploitation of combatants and sexual slavery (International Trade Union Confederation, 2011; McAlpine et al, 2016). Yet international organizations frame SEA through an external lens that oversimplifies narratives of violence (Autesserre, 2012). Rather, SEA communication should be developed from the understanding that SEA is embedded in broader intersecting narratives about sex, gender, violence and power that inform people's experiences of all forms of sexual conduct and sexual violence.

People also talk about sex and sexual abuse in different ways between cultures, contexts and even groups within the same community (Resource and Support Hub, 2021). Terminology testing in Kurdish found that 'protection', 'vulnerability' and 'affected population' elicited frustration among some men as they evoked memories of times when they experienced a lack of protection. Women either did not understand or were uncomfortable using the term 'rape', tending to use terms like 'aggression' instead (CLEAR Global, 2022a). In Rohingya, sex can be described differently depending on whether it is deemed 'religiously permissible' (*jaiz*) or 'impermissible' (*na-jaiz*). Words for what is referred to in English as 'rape' vary, and coded terms are common, such as 'being dishonoured' (*beizzot goron*) or 'black deed' (*kala haam*; Translators without Borders – TWB, 2019). Humanitarians unaware of these nuances risk not hearing when someone discloses a sexually violent experience. This has critical implications for the effectiveness of reporting and investigations (CHS Alliance, 2018).

Even common terms in English pose a significant translation challenge. 'Gender' is central to discussing power and sex, but especially difficult to translate. Research on disaster response communication found that the concept of gender does not resonate well in some Pacific Island cultures, especially when used with men; related vocabulary such as 'women's rights' unintentionally generates defensiveness, whereas framing issues in terms of 'women being taken care of in disasters' is more acceptable (Sutton et al, 2019: 13). In Rohingya, there is no direct equivalent for 'gender'; as a result, at the onset of the refugee response in Bangladesh, untrained interpreters translated the concept of 'gender-based violence' as 'violent women' (TWB, 2017). International terminology is not always relevant or well translated, and it can be divisive (Sutton et al, 2019). People may also use coded language when talking about abuse (Stark et al, 2017) or where being understood by others presents a safety risk, such as if the survivor risks persecution if they are perceived to have had sex – consensual or not – with someone of the same gender (Chynoweth et al, 2017).

Topics unconnected to sex may also inform perceptions and translations. For example, some Haitian Creole speakers connoted 'exploitation' with colonialism and economic exploitation more than with sexual exploitation, even when used in a PSEA context.[2] In Polish, the direct translation of 'victim', *ofiara,* can be considered stigmatizing and is not used with the same legal connotations as the English equivalent. Instead, some Polish humanitarians prefer to use *osoba pokrzywdzona*, literally meaning something closer to 'harmed person'.[3] Understanding these nuances in each context is crucial to understand how people talk about relationships, coercion and all forms of abuse, especially abuse that is not interpreted as violent.

Barriers to information and support

Gendered access barriers

Organizations often do not fully understand or account for gendered differences in access to information and services in their PSEA communication. In certain contexts, women show higher awareness of SEA than men due to targeted interventions aimed at women (CLEAR Global, 2022a; Inter-Agency Ethiopia PSEA Network, 2022). Yet in most cases, women have markedly lower access to information, instead relying on male spouses or relatives (TWB, 2022b), or gossip (Inter-Agency Ethiopia PSEA Network, 2022). Religious and cultural barriers may exclude women from information shared in public spaces (TWB, 2021a).

Although SEA predominantly affects women and girls, men and boys are also at risk. Yet shame, stigmatization and a lack of targeted services mean male survivors almost never report (Dolan, 2014). Lack of understanding about what influences men's and boys' reporting of SEA undermines organizations' ability to provide support. For example, Rohingya concepts of sexual violence do not easily facilitate explanations of the penetration of male bodies; basing communication on concepts about sex and violence that work in English compounds the challenges in discussing rape openly with male survivors (Women's Refugee Commission, 2021). Terminology research to identify these conceptual gaps is the necessary first step to ensuring communication is relevant for all survivors, especially where risks of language-based exclusion already impact the overall effectiveness of the response (CLEAR Global, 2023).

This problem is by no means unique to the Rohingya language or culture. Aid workers in many contexts are often either unaware that men and boys experience sexual abuse or unsure how to address the issue; when societal beliefs about sexual violence uphold gendered narratives about who enacts and who experiences sexual violence, men and boys struggle to speak up (Chynoweth et al, 2017).

Dissemination of PSEA policies

Policies addressing sexual violence in crisis contexts proliferated in the years after the release of the Bulletin (Spangaro, 2013; Matti, 2015). Though international PSEA guidance recognizes the importance of language in addressing SEA, as outlined, research demonstrates a lack of meaningful and systematic implementation. This is partly due to communication barriers that reduce awareness of and access to PSEA policy and guidance documents.

Guidance is often designed at an international or headquarters level, then shared to national and local staff, yet awareness among local-level staff varies greatly. In the DRC, Augustin and Mapenzi (2022) found that even where organizational policies existed, most staff either did not know about them or did not know how to apply them. This meant they could not then tell community members how and what to report to their organization. This issue is not unique to PSEA guidance; a multi-country study on education and child protection guidance found that local and national staff faced barriers accessing guidance intended to support them, including limited reading time, poor connectivity and difficulty navigating the documents on phone screens, which was how many staff were accessing documents (TWB, 2021c). Once accessed, guidance was rarely available in the languages practitioners preferred and was not localized to the context in which they worked (TWB, 2021c).

Access to reporting mechanisms

Even when they exist, recommendations on language inclusion in reporting mechanisms are not routinely applied. Most PSEA interventions are considered a technical exercise (Westendorf and Searle, 2017; Gleasure, 2020). As a result, they fail to recognize and address the complexity of communication dynamics that influence an SEA survivor's decision to report. When reporting mechanisms are not available in local languages, the survivor may not be able to report at all. An independent review following widespread reports of SEA by the World Health Organization and other UN and NGO personnel during the tenth Ebola outbreak in the DRC found a systematic tendency to reject reports of SEA that had not been made in writing (World Health Organization, 2021). In such low-literacy contexts, this practice is totally incompatible with how people communicate. Language exclusion also compounds other factors of exclusion to further restrict access to reporting mechanisms (TWB, 2022a).

Visual materials such as posters are popular for overcoming language and literacy barriers. Yet humanitarians often assume that images are more universally understood than they actually are. Clothing style, skin colour, uniforms and other physical attributes in visual material all influence whether the viewer correctly interprets the message.[4] Some internally displaced community members in north-east Nigeria found camp signage ineffective because the faces and landscapes were not from an African context (TWB, 2021b). Community members in eastern DRC largely understood identifiers like utility vests to denote humanitarian staff, but misinterpreted some images intended to show examples of SEA as depicting non-sexual interactions instead (CLEAR Global, 2022c). Failing to test and contextualize these materials leaves people confused or disengaged; this threatens efforts in the short term to achieve basic information provision, and in the long term it can undermine trust and relationships between aid providers and communities.

Even when reporting mechanisms are available, people mostly prefer to report through familiar community justice structures or, to a lesser extent, the police (Independent Commission for Aid Impact, 2022). This is not unique to humanitarian emergencies; reporting sexual abuse is challenging everywhere, and trust and interpersonal relationships matter. Survivors often prefer disclosing their experiences to confidants over authorities (Middleton et al, 2016). The social acceptability of narratives about abuse also influences reporting; in a group setting people may be less likely to disclose abuse by family members and neighbours, instead talking about being assaulted by strangers or 'bandits' (Stark et al, 2017).

Stigma and fears about how others will react and a lack of information about the outcomes of investigations also discourage people from reporting SEA (Spangaro et al, 2013; Blau, 2016). Often, people never hear back about the results of their report; sometimes this is due to a valid anonymity concern, though in many cases poor communication is at fault. Providing information in more languages and improving communication with those who do choose to report would increase use of reporting channels as a first step (Blau, 2016; Independent Commission for Aid Impact, 2022), but addressing the underlying conceptual shortcomings in PSEA communication remains imperative. Recognizing the emotional and psychological resonance of language is also vital; some women in north-east Nigeria felt safer when they could report SEA in their own language, even if they had second language skills (TWB, 2021a).

Conclusion

This chapter has argued that a lack of attention to language issues has undermined PSEA efforts to date, and language awareness needs to play a central role in PSEA communication. Inattention to language exacerbates failures to understand how context influences the way people perceive and discuss sexual conduct. This begins with knowing the right words in the right language to adequately convey the intended message. Yet translation is far more complex than word choice; words rarely have direct equivalents between languages, especially for abstract concepts central to PSEA, such as gender and exploitation. In some languages, certain concepts may be conflated or lacking altogether. This makes translating information related to PSEA intricate at best and rife with miscommunication at worst.

The need for a language-aware approach to PSEA is part of a wider need to systematize multilingual approaches to humanitarian assistance. This starts with increasing humanitarians' awareness of linguistic diversity through data on language use in countries experiencing or at risk of disaster (CLEAR Global, 2022b). Organizations then need to prioritize contextually embedded PSEA communication strategies. This includes finding out what terms people use and avoid, which groups use terms differently, and how context and power dynamics shape the communication choices we make. Clear, accurate communication that informs those at risk of SEA about their rights and available support is possible, and it starts with a conversation – one in which humanitarians do not talk first.

References

Abu-Assab, N. and Nasser-Eddin, N. (2021) *Organisational Safeguarding Best Practices and Procedures: A Toolkit Towards Transnational Intersectional Feminist Accountability Frameworks to Respond to Exploitation, Assault, Abuse, Harassment and Bullying*, Centre for Transnational Development and Collaboration and Women's International League for Peace and Freedom. Available from: https://ctdc.org/content/wp-content/uploads/2021/08/Toolkit-English-final-WEB.pdf (accessed 27 February 2023).

Altakhaineh, A. (2017) 'The linguistic features of acronyms in Arabic', *SAGE Open*, 7(4): 1–14.

Augustin, G. and Mapenzi, T. (2022) 'How many more years before we walk the talk? Translating safeguarding and localisation into action in DRC', *Humanitarian Exchange*, 81: 42–50.

Autesserre, S. (2012) 'Dangerous tales: dominant narratives on the Congo and their unintended consequences', *African Affairs*, 111(443): 202–22.

Beber, B., Gilligan, M., Guardado, J. and Karim, S. (2016) 'Peacekeeping, compliance with international norms, and transactional sex in Monrovia, Liberia', *International Organization*, 71(4): 1–30.

Blau, L. (2016) 'Victimizing those they were sent to protect: enhancing accountability for children born of sexual abuse and exploitation by UN peacekeepers', *Syracuse Journal of International Law and Commerce*, 44(1): 121–48.

Bys, C. (2022) 'What kind of feminism is behind efforts to address sexual exploitation and abuse?', *Humanitarian Exchange*, 81: 34–41.

CASS (Social Science and Analytics Cell) (2021) *Perceptions around Sexual Exploitation and Abuse (SEA) and Barriers to Community-Based Reporting: Equateur Province, DRC*, New York: Unicef. Available from: https://www.unicef.org/drcongo/media/5901/file/COD-CASS-Equateur-PSEA-EN-correction.pdf (accessed 3 March 2024).

CHS Alliance (2018) *How Change Happens in the Humanitarian Sector: Humanitarian Accountability Report 2018*, Geneva: CHS Alliance. Available from: www.chsalliance.org/get-support/resource/2018-humanitarian-accountability-report/ (accessed 7 March 2023).

CHS Alliance (2022) *Sexual Exploitation, Abuse and Harassment Investigation Guide: Recommended Practice for the Humanitarian and Development Sector*, CHS Alliance. Available from: www.chsalliance.org/get-support/resource/sexual-exploitation-abuse-and-harassment-seah-investigation-guide/ (accessed 27 February 2023).

Chynoweth, S., Freccero, J. and Touquet, H. (2017) 'Sexual violence against men and boys in conflict and forced displacement: implications for the health sector', *Reproductive Health Matters*, 25(52): 90–4.

CLEAR Global (2022a) *Finding the Right Words: PSEAH Terminology Testing in Dohuk and Kirkuk, Iraq*, CLEAR Global. Available from: https://clearglobal.org/resources/finding-the-right-words-pseah-terminology-testing-in-dohuk-and-kirkuk-iraq/ (accessed 14 September 2023).

CLEAR Global (2022b) 'Global language data review', *CLEAR Global*, 10 August. Available from: https://clearglobal.org/global-language-data-review/ (accessed 13 September 2023).

CLEAR Global (2022c) *Insights into Community Needs and Wishes*, CLEAR Global and TWB. Available from: https://clearglobal.org/wp-content/uploads/2023/03/CLEAR-TWB-DRC-WHO-PSEAH-English-Report-4.pdf (accessed 13 September 2023).

CLEAR Global (2023) *Knowledge to Action*, CLEAR Global/TWB. Available from: https://clearglobal.org/resources/learning-review-of-language-inclusion-in-the-rohingya-response/ (accessed 14 September 2023).

Delgado, L. and Kherbiche, L. (2018) 'Without fear or favour? The positionality of ICRC and UNHCR interpreters in the humanitarian field', *International Journal of Translation Studies*, 30(3): 408–29.

Dolan, C. (2014) *Into the Mainstream: Addressing Sexual Violence against Men and Boys in Conflict*, A briefing paper prepared for the workshop held at the Overseas Development Institute, London, 14 May. Available from: https://reliefweb.int/report/world/mainstream-addressing-sexual-violence-against-men-and-boys-conflict (accessed 1 September 2023).

Foreign, Commonwealth and Development Office (2021) *Humanitarian Funding Guidelines for NGOs Applying for CHASE Humanitarian Response Funding*, London: Foreign, Commonwealth and Development Office.

Gleasure, N. (2020) *The Translatability of Safeguarding Terminology: Linguistic and Cultural Challenges for Non-Governmental Organisations*, Presentation for Dóchas Safeguarding Working Group, 20 October. Available from: www.dochas.ie/assets/Files/Safeguarding-Resources/The-Translatability-of-Safeguarding-Terminology_-Presentation-to-Dochas-Safeguarding-Group.pdf (accessed 16 March 2023).

IASC (Inter-Agency Standing Committee) (2016a) *Guidelines: Inter-Agency Community-Based Complaints Mechanisms*, Geneva: International Organization for Migration. Available from: https://interagencystandingcommittee.org/system/files/2021-03/Best%20Practice%20Guide%20Inter%20Agency%20Community%20Based%20Complaint%20Mechanisms.pdf (accessed 10 September 2023).

IASC (Inter-Agency Standing Committee) (2016b) *Standard Operating Procedures: Inter-Agency Cooperation in Community-Based Complaint Mechanisms*, IASC. Available from: https://interagencystandingcommittee.org/iasc-task-team-accountability-affected-populations-and-protection-sexual-exploitation-and-abuse/iasc-global-standard-operating-procedures-inter-agency-cooperation-community-based-complaint (accessed 14 September 2023).

Independent Commission for Aid Impact (2022) 'The UK's approach to safeguarding in the humanitarian sector: a review', *Independent Commission for Aid Impact*. Available from: https://icai.independent.gov.uk/review/the-uks-approach-to-safeguarding-in-the-humanitarian-sector/review/ (accessed 30 September 2022).

Inter-Agency Ethiopia PSEA Network (2022) *Communicating with Communities on PSEA*, New York: United Nations.

International Organisation for Migration (2020) *Deployment Package for PSEA Coordinators*, International Organisation for Migration and IASC. Available from: https://psea.interagencystandingcommittee.org/resources/deployment-package-psea-coordinators (accessed 7 March 2023).

International Trade Union Confederation (2011) *Violence against Women in Eastern Democratic Republic of Congo: Whose Responsibility? Whose Complicity?* Brussels: International Trade Union Confederation.

Jennings, K. and Bøås, M. (2015) 'Transactions and interactions', *Journal of Intervention and Statebuilding*, 9(3): 281–95.

Matti, S. (2015) 'Governing sexual behavior through humanitarian codes of conduct', *Disasters – Overseas Development Institute*, 39(4): 626–47.

McAlpine, A., Hossain, M. and Zimmerman, C. (2016) 'Sex trafficking and sexual exploitation in settings affected by armed conflicts in Africa, Asia and the Middle East: systematic review', *BMC International Health and Human Rights*, 16(34): 1–16.

Middleton, A., McAninch, K., Pusateri, K. and Delaney, A. (2016) '"You just gotta watch what you say in those situations": a normative approach to confidant communication surrounding sexual assault disclosure', *Communication Quarterly*, 64(2): 232–50.

Oxfam (2021) *Barriers to Reporting Misconduct: Understanding Power, Intersectionality and Context*, Oxford: Oxfam. Available from: https://policy-practice.oxfam.org/resources/barriers-to-reporting-misconduct-understanding-power-intersectionality-and-cont-621533/ (accessed 16 January 2024).

Resource and Support Hub (2021) *How to Consider Language When Researching Sexual Exploitation, Abuse and Sexual Harassment*, Resource and Support Hub. Available from: https://safeguardingsupporthub.org/sites/default/files/2021-08/FINAL%20How-to%20Note_Language_2208.pdf (accessed 16 March 2023).

Robinson, M. and Conilleau, J. (2022) *Partnerships and Protection against Sexual Exploitation and Abuse: An Analysis of Recent Case Studies*, Geneva: Steering Committee for Humanitarian Response and International Council of Voluntary Agencies.

Roth, S. (2012) 'Professionalisation trends and inequality: experiences and practices in aid relationships', *Third World Quarterly*, 33(8): 1459–74.

Roth, S. (2019) 'Linguistic capital and inequality in aid relations', *Sociological Research Online*, 24(1): 38–54.

Samarasekera, U. (2021) 'Experts criticise WHO response to sex abuse allegations', *The Lancet*, 398(10308): 1291–3.

Satke, C., Jansen, M., Lacroix, N. and Lakhdar-Toumi, N. (2022) 'Applying policies in practice: preventing sexual exploitation and abuse in humanitarian settings', *Humanitarian Exchange*, 81: 84–90.

Spangaro, J., Adogu, C., Ranmuthugala, G., Powell Davies, G., Steinacker, L. and Zwi, A. (2013) 'What evidence exists for initiatives to reduce risk and incidence of sexual violence in armed conflict and other humanitarian crises? A systematic review', *PLOS ONE*, 8(5): e62600.

Stark, L., Sommer, M., Davis, K., Asghar, K., Assazenew Baysa, A., Abdela, G., Tanner, S. and Falb, K. (2017) 'Disclosure bias for group versus individual reporting of violence amongst conflict-affected adolescent girls in DRC and Ethiopia', *PLOS ONE*, 12(4): 1–12.

Sutton, K., Flint, J., Lees, J. and Kenni, L. (2019) *Protecting People in Locally-Led Disaster Response*, Humanitarian Policy Group and Humanitarian Advisory Group. Available from: https://humanitarianadvisorygroup.org/insight/protecting-people-in-locally-led-disaster-response/ (accessed 2 September 2023).

TWB (Translators without Borders) (2017) 'Rohingya Zuban: a Translators without Borders Rapid Assessment of Language Barriers in the Cox's Bazar Refugee Response', *TWB*. Available from: www.arcgis.com/apps/Cascade/index.html?appid=683a58b07dba4db189297061b4f8cd40 (accessed 29 August 2023).

TWB (Translators without Borders) (2019) *Building a Better Dialogue around Gender Issues*, TWB. Available from: https://translatorswithoutborders.org/wp-content/uploads/2019/03/RohingyaLanguageGuidance_Gender_Final.pdf (accessed 29 August 2023).

TWB (Translators without Borders) (2021a) *Effective Communication is Essential for True Accountability*, TWB. Available from: https://translatorswithoutborders.org/wp-content/uploads/2021/07/TWB-Nigeria-AAP-assessment-findings-2021.pdf (accessed 1 March 2023).

TWB (Translators without Borders) (2021b) *In the Loop*, TWB. Available from: https://clearglobal.org/wp-content/uploads/2021/11/Research-brief_In-the-loop_-developing-effective-complaints-and-feedback-mechanisms.pdf (accessed 1 March 2023).

TWB (Translators without Borders) (2021c) *Navigating Global Guidance*, TWB. Available from: https://translatorswithoutborders.org/wp-content/uploads/2021/09/Navigating-Global-Guidance-Report.pdf (accessed 10 August 2023).

TWB (Translators without Borders) (2022a) *Complaint and Feedback Mechanisms are Missing the Voices of Women and People with Restricted Mobility*, Garden City, ID: CLEAR Global/TWB. Available from: https://clearglobal.org/resources/complaint-and-feedback-mechanisms-are-missing-the-voices-of-women-and-people-with-restricted-mobility/ (accessed 24 February 2023).

TWB (Translators without Borders) (2022b) *Imams' Role in Sharing Information in the Camps*, Garden City, ID: CLEAR Global/TWB. Available from: https://clearglobal.org/resources/imams-role-as-sharers-of-information-in-the-camps/ (accessed 10 August 2023).

UN (United Nations) (2017) *Glossary on Sexual Exploitation and Abuse* (3rd edn), New York: United Nations.

United Nations Secretary-General (2003) *Secretary-General's Bulletin: Special Measures for Protection from Sexual Exploitation and Sexual Abuse*, UN Doc ST/SGB/2003/13.

Westendorf, J. (2023a) 'A problem of rules: sexual exploitation and UN legitimacy', *International Studies Quarterly*, 67(3): 1–13.

Westendorf, J. (2023b) 'Sex on mission: care, control and coloniality in peacekeeping and humanitarian operations', *International Affairs*, 99(4): 1653–72.

Westendorf, J. and Searle, L. (2017) 'Sexual exploitation and abuse in peace operations: trends, policy responses and future directions', *International Affairs*, 93(2): 365–87.

Women's Refugee Commission (2021) *Addressing Sexual Violence against Men, Boys, and LGBTQ+ Refugees: Learnings from Pilot Projects in Bangladesh, Kenya, and Italy/Bulgaria*, New York: Women's Refugee Commission. Available from: www.womensrefugeecommission.org/research-resources/addressing-sexual-violence-against-men-boys-and-lgbtq-refugees-learnings-from-pilot-projects-in-bangladesh-kenya-and-italy-bulgaria/ (accessed 14 September 2023).

World Health Organization (2021) *Final Report of the Independent Commission on the Review of SEA during the Response to the 10th Ebola Virus Disease Epidemic in the Provinces of North Kivu and Ituri in the Democratic Republic of the Congo (DRC)*. Available from: www.who.int/publications/m/item/final-report-of-the-independent-commission-on-the-review-of-sexual-abuse-and-exploitation-ebola-drc (accessed 10 September 2023).

12

From 'Cultural Sensitivity' to 'Structural Sensitivity'

Nour Abu-Assab

Introduction

Over the past two decades, international organizations have increasingly introduced policies designed to prevent sexual abuses of power. Central to many of these initiatives is the need for 'cultural sensitivity', a term that has been mainstreamed by many international and intergovernmental organizations. However, there remains a distinct lack of consensus around what cultural sensitivity entails in practice, leading to its misuse and misapplication in cases of sexual exploitation and abuse (SEA). In this chapter, I weave together philosophy, personal reflections based on field experiences, and policy analysis in order to argue that there is a need for an alternative to the concept of cultural sensitivity in safeguarding frameworks exported by international organizations and donor agencies to local civil society organizations.

I begin by borrowing from Giddens' ontological theory of structuration (elaborated later) to examine how agency works across social practice and to think through obstacles impeding safeguarding and protection against sexual exploitation and abuse (PSEA) work. Although international organizations claim that their safeguarding systems are culturally sensitive, those systems are usually built around the experience of those inside the international organizations rather than being based on nuanced understandings of local contexts and dynamics. I propose the concept of 'structural sensitivity' as an alternative to cultural sensitivity and provide examples of how focusing on structures over culture offers a more nuanced approach to SEA work.

Epistemology and ontology

Our knowledges are 'situated' (Haraway, 1988), and as such it is important to question how we know what we know or, in other words, to explicitly define our epistemological approach. For this reason, I want to provide some background to how I came to recognize the need for an alternative paradigm to cultural sensitivity. Broadly, I draw my insights from my work at the Centre for Transnational Development and Collaboration, which I co-founded with my colleague Dr Nof Nasser-Eddin (author of Chapter 13). This experience began with us managing funded projects on gender, sexuality and sexual violence, which addressed various aspects of safeguarding and accountability. Later, we accumulated further experience in safeguarding through consulting work. This work initially started in the Palestinian territories, then expanded across Arabic-speaking countries. In 2021, we published *Organisational Safeguarding Best Practices and Procedures* (Abu Assab and Nasser-Eddin, 2021), in which we identified gaps in prevailing safeguarding and PSEA frameworks and proposed alternatives. Since then, our work has expanded beyond the Arabic-speaking regions, across Africa and into South Asia.

By adopting a political lens to interrogate epistemology, I strive to 'address the entwinement of the cultural politics of science with the political economy of knowledge as a bridge between the structural analysis and the political comprehension of science' (Omodeo, 2019: 1). Harding (1993) argues that 'strong objectivity' can be achieved through a systematic examination of all social values affecting the research project; however, I argue that this examination should also explore emotions and relationalities, and acknowledge the informal unexpected revelations, or 'aha!' moments, the researcher comes across.

For example, personal, professional and geographic factors gave me a unique insight into the February 2023 Syria–Turkey earthquake. My personal connections with people in the earthquake-affected areas in both countries meant that I was emotionally driven to respond and to understand the problems. It was through specific listening moments that I have come to deeply understand that part of the inadequacy of humanitarian interventions is their inability to respond to people's varying needs. For instance, I learned from a casual conversation with a friend that humanitarian aid arriving in affected areas in Syria was not providing women's clothing that is respectful of people's different dress codes. For me, that reflected *in*sensitivity, whether we call it contextual or cultural. It also made me realize that an essential tool for improving humanitarian response – and one that is currently missing – is to encourage humanitarian workers to question their own epistemologies, or in other words, to ask themselves:

- How do I know what I know?
- Is my knowledge based on former assumptions?
- Is my knowledge biased? In an implicit or explicit way?

Asking these questions is important for addressing SEA cases, particularly at the stage of receiving a complaint or carrying out an assessment/investigation into an alleged case. Our epistemology, whether we practise it consciously or not, informs the way we choose to respond to SEA cases, as does our ontological position.

In addition to epistemology, ontology can also be a useful tool to respond to SEA cases, as it allows us a broader understanding of the dynamics at play within the social world, and thus we can better respond to victims and survivors. Here, I use ontology to mean the way we understand how the social world operates, the agency social actors have and the structures that are at play when we address SEA or safeguarding cases. I borrow from and build on Giddens' ontological position, which suggests that '[t]he basic domain of study of the social sciences ... is neither the experience of the individual actor, nor the existence of any form of societal totality, but social practices ordered across space and time' (1984: 2). In other words, while Giddens acknowledges the agency of social actors, he suggests that this agency is exercised through social practices that may differ across time and space, implying that agency is contextualized and the way it operates changes according to time and space (and, I would add, structures of oppression). In relation to safeguarding issues, this is particularly important, as abusive practices, including SEA, are not isolated problems, but rather reflect our societies. To respond appropriately, an in-depth understanding of how society operates is essential. However, this in-depth understanding of agency and social practice is often taken by practitioners in the field to be simply culture or context sensitivity, which represents only a narrow conceptualization of the social world. As we live in an interconnected world, understanding context specificity is not enough, as I discuss later.

Giddens encourages relying on 'the same sources of description (mutual knowledge)' to be able to communicate across cultures (1984: 285). Although his proposal is for sociologists, I argue that it is just as relevant to safeguarding and PSEA. Language is also very important, as it plays a role in society and social actors utilize it to communicate. Language has a formative effect on our understanding of different phenomena (Oyewumi, 1997; Tinsley, 2018). Language also affects and influences structures of oppression, as proposed by structural linguists. People understand and talk about abuse differently, and for this reason many SEA cases fall through the cracks (Abu-Assab and Nasser-Eddin, 2021). In addition, as SEA frameworks themselves are often translated from English into local languages, they do not rely on 'mutual knowledge', but rather on framings and terminologies developed elsewhere – almost always in the Global North by international organizations and NGOs. These gaps cannot be identified without bringing ontology into question. Ontology pushes us to ask the following questions:

- What is the social world? What does it look like?
- What are the structures at play in the contexts we are working in, and how are they linked to other contexts?
- How much room does the agency of social actors have in relation to influencing structures of oppression?

Although epistemology – how we know what we know – and ontology – how we understand the world – may be seen as 'academic', 'theoretical', 'complex' and 'complicated', they can still be useful tools for practitioners, as they do not minimize SEA to isolated incidents, cases or problems, but rather allow us to contextualize them within wider structures, so we become more able to address them across 'cultures'.

Cultural sensitivity

The term 'cultural sensitivity' is a buzzword in many fields, although there is no clear consensus on precisely what it means (Swendson and Windsor, 1996; Resnicow et al, 1999; Ruddock and Turner, 2007; Foronda, 2008; Sahpiro et al, 2008). Foronda (2008), for instance, suggests cultural sensitivity includes knowledge, consideration, understanding, respect and tailoring. Caligiuri and colleagues (2011) attempted to establish guidelines for *Training, Developing, and Assessing Cross-Cultural Competence in Military Personnel*. However, these fall short of embracing the complexity of our lives. Instead, cultural sensitivity has become shorthand for the regulation of the relationship between a 'dominant' group and a 'subordinated' group, reflecting colonial power dynamics. This is particularly relevant in the humanitarian context given that the majority of humanitarian, aid, human rights and development work is carried out in colonial/postcolonial or Global South contexts, meaning that power dynamics are built into the very structures of this kind of work. One of the ways in which these power dynamics manifest is around the relationship between those usually portrayed as the 'saviours' and 'givers' and those usually portrayed as the 'affected', the 'poor' or 'in need'. The disparity in power is also evident in patterns of SEA. Current approaches to cultural sensitivity can therefore reproduce the colonial imaginary, meaning that many well-intentioned organizations indirectly contribute to the maintenance of colonial structures.

Within this field, culture has been central to understanding and approaching specific groups of people or communities. The term 'culture' is sometimes used to describe the way of life of specific groups of people;

other times it is used to describe the heritage of human evolution. We may hear someone being described as 'cultured', or we may be told that a certain organization does not have a good culture. Culture can therefore be used to mark certain groups and distinguish them from one another, and it assumes that people who share a cultural context are alike in their qualities, values and characteristics. We might feel pressure to abide by the standardized norms of a culture to avoid the repercussions of patriarchy or classism, for example; in other cases, we might believe in cultural norms and feel strongly about them, reproduce them and reinforce them. However, culture – ethnic or national, for example – is only one structure of many that we interact with every day. An overemphasis on the role of culture leads us to miss out on the complexity of the context and the cases we are dealing with.

Some claim that ethnic groups have shared ancestry, shared cultural tradition and shared language (Drury, 1994; Song, 2003; Cornell and Hartmann, 2007; Jenkins, 2008). However, as Fenton (2010: 3) puts it 'claims to sharing descent and culture are decidedly questionable'. This is not to say that 'culture' as the shared values, ways of organizing, customs and traditions, norms, modes of governance and ways of life does not exist; rather, it means that we need a deeper understanding of culture that imagines new forms of grouping which do not revolve around identity categories, such as ethnicity or nationalism, or other categories of othering. This is particularly important when dealing with safeguarding cases, as it would allow us to understand the multilayered complexity of someone's assumed culture and, thus, be able to respond better.

Instead of focusing on culture, it can instead be fruitful to consider groups organized by shared values. If we look at how society is organized around us, we can clearly identify that people organize themselves around values. Groups of friends often share similar values. Members of the same organization often share the same values. Instead of using 'cultural sensitivity' to understand the complexities of human life, placing values at the centre of the conversation would bring us one step closer to working effectively *across* cultures. In cases of safeguarding, this would mean refraining from cultural assumptions and stereotyping, and shifting the conversation to values, as a 'mutual language', at all stages of the case handling process. In practice, then, a meaningfully culturally sensitive approach needs to acknowledge individuals' agency within culture as a structure, rather than assuming sets of characteristics based on culture alone.

Structural sensitivity in safeguarding

Structuration theory offers a useful way to think through what safeguarding might look like if we moved away from 'cultural sensitivity' towards 'structural sensitivity'. The central tenet of structuration theory is that social structures are inseparable from social action – they exist because of social action – and their repeated patterns constitute structural reality (Giddens, 1984). Culture is only one structure that has an impact on SEA; other relevant structures include the legal system, patriarchy, class and even borders. I argue that to be able to create transformative change and appropriately address SEA, practitioners need to broaden their understanding of the role structures play in people's lives and the agency (social action) they exercise. This is especially important if we truly seek to tailor our responses to the needs of victims and survivors as they define them on their terms (see Nof Nasser-Eddin, Chapter 13).

A structural understanding could also enable us to appropriately assess risks within safeguarding frameworks, as it broadens our horizon and thus sharpens our responses to abuse. However, this needs to be carried out through a transnational lens, or in other words a lens that enables us to see the way structures of oppression operate across borders, though they affect our lives differently. This will push us to stop shying away from addressing structures of oppression across cultures, no matter how different we are, as we all share global structures of oppression, whether it be violence, exploitation, marginalization, powerlessness or cultural imperialism (see Young, 1993). The repeated nature of the patterns, created by both social actors and structures of oppression, points towards the need for a transnational perspective – one that understands oppression and violence as shared global phenomena and concerns, with no culture being exceptional or more 'advanced'.

In cases of SEA investigations, it is important to contextualize the case and understand the structures at play. A few instances in the Arabic-speaking region, where an alleged SEA case went public and received media attention, demonstrated that several structures are at play to make these cases visible. Some accusations levelled against the organizations were fuelled by racism and embedded in nationalist discourses, while other accusations were patriarchal and yet others were fuelled by classism and regionalism. In such cases, it is inadequate and can even do more harm if all these structures are not interrogated and unpacked (Abu-Assab and Nasser-Eddin, 2022). One of the cases that entered the public domain in the Arabic-speaking region was publicized and investigated informally by feminists, targeting a specific alleged 'harasser' under the 'expose a harasser' social media campaign. Whereas some felt that exposing the person was a form of justice, the exposure itself had repercussions for the person's family within their local community, and it also endangered the lives of his family members. In this case, not understanding the structures at play within that specific community, such as tribalism, jeopardized people's lives. This demonstrates how a failure to consider structures can result in material harm. In this case, an approach driven by structural sensitivity, instead of cultural sensitivity, would have allowed for a more comprehensive risk assessment process.

Examples from outside the SEA literature show similar patterns and exemplify how harm can be caused by a failure to consider structural sensitivity when responding to abuse. In 2012, an organized crime of a sexual nature drew public attention, particularly as the accused were from ethnic minority backgrounds (Salter and Dagistanli, 2015). At the time, the role of the police was placed under public scrutiny, as it became evident that authorities had ignored repeated calls about abuse of children.[1] The police at that time were portrayed in conservative media as having failed to act due to 'political correctness' around ethnicities (Doyle, 2012).

A further example can be found in research by Milani and colleagues (2018) on Muslim women's experiences of intimate partner violence. They found that '[c]ulturally informed practices need to go beyond cultural and language sensitivity; they need to explore cultural, social, political, and historical forces that shape women's experiences, their definitions, and responses to abuse, as well as the sources of support, disclosure patterns, and the processes of leaving abusive marriages' (Milani et al, 2018: 71). They pointed out that barriers to accessing services were one of the main reasons cases of abuse were not dealt with adequately – which reflects structural rather than cultural barriers. This again demonstrates how culture is only one element of many that need to be considered when dealing with SEA, and that all the structures at play – whether political, sociocultural, economic, environmental, legal, geographical/locational or international, among others – need to be taken into account when formulating responses to SEA.

Conclusion

In this chapter, I argued that the overemphasis on cultural sensitivity can actually impede practitioners' responses to SEA, as it limits their understanding of the broader dynamics at play, which operate at a global level – colonialism, neoliberalism and racism, for example. In some cases, 'cultural sensitivity' can even be used in a way that inadvertently creates further harm. Instead of focusing on culture, I propose a need to focus on *structures* in safeguarding cases. I therefore call for a paradigm shift in our approach to SEA and safeguarding, particularly in postcolonial and colonial contexts. This rethinking of approach has relevance for decolonial and feminist research and knowledge production and for the humanitarian, aid, development and human rights fields in relation to safeguarding and PSEA and beyond. The shift from culture to structure is not difficult, but it requires us to fundamentally re-examine our understanding of the world and our positionality. It means that we need to acknowledge how our social actions (agencies) interact with structures, and to understand how the social actions of others do so as well. It means that we must recognize how our social actions affect others, and how social actions affect the structures themselves.

References

Abu Assab, N. and Nasser-Eddin, N. (2021) *Organisational Safeguarding Best Practices and Procedures: A Toolkit Towards Transnational Intersectional Feminist Accountability Frameworks to Respond to Exploitation, Assault, Abuse, Harassment And Bullying*, London: Centre for Transnational Development And Collaboration.

Abu-Assab, N. and Nasser-Eddin, N. (2022) *Accountability and Safeguarding Assessment for Ma3azef*, London: Centre for Transnational Development and Collaboration.

Caligiuri, P., Noe, R., Nolan, R., Ryan, A. and Drasgow, F. (2011) *Training, Developing, and Assessing Cross-Cultural Competence in Military Personnel*, Arlington, VA: United States Army Research Institute for the Behavioral and Social Sciences. Available from: https://apps.dtic.mil/sti/tr/pdf/ADA559500.pdf (accessed 30 October 2023).

Cornell, S. and Hartmann, D. (2007) *Ethnicity and Race: Making Identities in a Changing World*, London: Sage.

Doyle, J. (2012) 'Don't let PC brigade bury ethnic links to sex gangs, warns Children's Minister', *Mail Online*, 4 July. Available from: www.dailymail.co.uk/news/article-2168365/Tim-Loughton-Political-correctness-way-police-social-workers-investigating-child-sex-abuse.html (accessed 12 March 2023).

Drury, B. (1994) 'Ethnic mobilisation: some theoretical considerations', in J. Rex and B. Drury (eds) *Ethnic Mobilisation in a Multi-Cultural Europe*, Aldershot: Avebury.

Fenton, S. (2010) *Ethnicity*, Cambridge: Polity Press.

Foronda, C. (2008) 'A concept analysis of cultural sensitivity', *Journal of Transcultural Nursing*, 19(3): 207–12.

Giddens, A. (1984) *The Constitution of Society: Outline of the Theory of Structuration*, Cambridge: Polity Press.

Haraway, D. (1988) 'Situated knowledges: the science question in feminism and the privilege of partial perspective', *Feminist Studies*, 14(3): 575–99.

Harding, S. (1993) 'Rethinking standpoint epistemology: what is strong objectivity?', in L. Alcoff and E. Potter (eds) *Feminist Epistemologies*, London: Routledge, pp 49–82.

Jenkins, R. (2008) *Rethinking Ethnicity*, London: Sage Publications.

Milani A., Leschied, A. and Rodger, S. (2018) '"Beyond cultural sensitivity": service providers' perspectives on Muslim women experiences of intimate partner violence', *Journal of Muslim Mental Health*, 12(1): 49–75.

Omodeo, P. (2019) *Political Epistemology: The Problem of Ideology in Science Studies*, New York: Springer.

Oyewumi, O. (1997) *The Invention of Women: Making an African Sense of Western Gender Discourses*, Minneapolis: University of Minnesota Press.

Resnicow, K., Baranowski, T., Ahluwalia, J. and Braithwaite, R. (1999) 'Cultural sensitivity in public health: defined and demystified', *Ethnicity and Disease*, 9(1): 10–21.

Ruddock, H. and Turner, S. (2007) 'Developing cultural sensitivity: nursing students' experiences of a study abroad programme', *Journal of Advanced Nursing*, 59(4): 361–9.

Salter, M. and Dagistanli, S. (2015) 'Cultures of abuse: "sex grooming", organised abuse and race in Rochdale, UK', *International Journal for Crime, Justice and Social Democracy*, 4(2): 50–64.

Shapiro, J., Ozanne, J. and Saatcioglu, B. (2008) 'An interpretive examination of the development of cultural sensitivity in international business', *Journal of International Business Studies*, 39: 71–87.

Song, M. (2003) *Choosing Ethnic Identity*, Cambridge: Polity Press.

Swendson, C. and Windsor, C. (1996) 'Rethinking cultural sensitivity', *Nursing Inquiry*, 3(1): 3–10.

Tinsley, T. (2018) 'Language education in the era of Brexit: three challenges for the schools' sector', *Languages, Society and Policy*. doi: 10.17863/CAM.25410

Young, I. M. (2011). Justice and the politics of difference. Princeton University Press.

PART III

Looking Forward: Where to from Here?

13

Agency and Affect in PSEA: Understanding Agency through a Transnational Intersectional Lens

Nof Nasser-Eddin

Introduction

In the past few years, we have witnessed the protection from/prevention of sexual exploitation and abuse (PSEA) take centre stage in the fields of humanitarian aid and development, following the emergence of several scandals about corruption and abuse. International organizations, with great enthusiasm, felt the need to address this abuse and, in many cases without thinking through the repercussions, created frameworks, principles, codes of conduct and criteria to ensure sexual exploitation and abuse (SEA) cases are prevented. They have set these as universal and binding in the sense that if local community organizations in different parts of the world do not follow them, they are not granted funding and partnerships. Those frameworks put forward by the Inter-Agency Standing Committee and Core Humanitarian Standards Alliance (CHS Alliance),[1] among others, have become the only reference for many in the 'field' when it comes to PSEA. Yet these frameworks, put forward by organizations and institutions in the Global North, frequently fail because their approach to PSEA has proven to be top-down, not considering context nor other perspectives and different lived realities. But believing that such policies and standards are adequately addressing SEA, these organizations started promoting themselves as pioneers in PSEA.

Many community organizations adopting these standards have also taken for granted that they can be universally applied. This copying and pasting of Global North frameworks is being done by community organizations to satisfy donor requirements and attain donor funding. It is beyond the scope of this paper to discuss this issue in greater detail, but it is imperative to scrutinize the relationship and think about how community organizations become complicit in those structures of oppression (Abu-Assab et al, 2020). My argument is that 'internationalist' methods that are built on the premise of 'universalism' fail to address SEA, and instead we need an intersectional transnational approach that centralizes difference and acknowledges our interconnectedness and the power dynamics at play between us all at the global level. One of the main issues with the prevalent PSEA frameworks is that their understanding of a victim-centred approach – which they also view as allowing victims the right to self-determination – revolves around specific lists and standards for services they assume all victims and survivors need. This does not take into consideration that victims and survivors experiences of abuse are not uniform, which denies their *agency* and undermines different *affect* and *emotions*. Based on that, I advance a paradigm to address PSEA and avoid singling out victims and survivors as a unified group. It is worth noting that I am not using the terms 'victim' and 'survivor' interchangeably, because not all victims are survivors. In other words, many people who were exposed to abuse in its different forms did not survive the abuse, while others have. Therefore, we should not treat people who are subjected to abuse as a homogenous group.

This chapter sequentially constructs a theoretical framework that draws on a materialist/class analysis of lived experiences within PSEA frameworks to dismantle identity politics, othering and the homogenization of victims to centre emotions and their relationship to affect. First, I put forward an intersectional paradigm to understand intersecting structures of oppression in relation to SEA. Second, I integrate a transnational imperative to view our global interconnectedness in any such structures. Finally, I layer the sociological imagination concept to practically apply the intersectional transnational approach to (re)imagine the different ways people deal with abusive practices and how they are affected differently.

Many of the insights in this chapter are based on works I have carried out through the Centre for Transnational Development and Collaboration (CTDC) with my colleague Dr Nour Abu-Assab (see Chapter 12). Through these, I have worked with different communities, grassroots groups and national and international organizations across varying fields – development, advocacy, humanitarianism and education – in the Democratic Republic of Congo, Ethiopia, Iraq, Italy, Jordan, Kurdistan, Lebanon, Libya, Mali, Morocco, Myanmar, Nepal, Pakistan, Palestine, Rwanda, Somalia, South Sudan, Sri Lanka, Sudan, Syria, Thailand, Tunisia, Turkey, Uganda, the UK and Yemen. Due to the nature of my work, and the gaps that I see in traditional standardized internationalist frameworks, I critique these paradigms because I see how they are failing to address root causes of social, political and economic problems in practice. These frameworks often fail because the starting point of their development assumes that they will be a panacea across the world.

The chapter is divided into two main sections. The first presents an intersectional, materialist analysis of the experiences of people in relation to SEA. In other words, I argue that for us to achieve *just* outcomes for victims and survivors, PSEA frameworks need to be developed based on people's differential *lived* experiences in their own contextualized realities that centre agency, emotions and affect. The second section is about centralizing people's *agency* and *emotionalities* in relation to PSEA. I argue that interventionist frameworks need to further explore people's different needs and emotions when it comes to aiding victims and survivors. To better address such needs, standardized services and assistance must attend to people's agency and emotions.

Materiality of experiences

The reason why internationalist PSEA frameworks cannot be a panacea across the world is that they are formulated around the assumption that victims and survivors share the same experience of abusive practices. Referrals and assistance are an important and necessary component in PSEA frameworks, meaning that victims are provided with access to different material provisions, such as financial, legal, psychosocial, medical and, in some cases, housing support. PSEA frameworks, at the same time, claim that they centre victims' and survivors' right to self-determination throughout the process. For example, the United Nations has set a standard protocol on providing support and assistance to victims of SEA (see United Nations, 2019). However, because of institutional politics and limitations, the measures of self-determination that victims and survivors are granted through PSEA responses are restricted to a list of specific services and standardized processes and procedures (see Jane Connors in Chapter 6). Even though these services are very important and provide a lifeline for some victims and survivors, they still do not satisfy victims' and survivors' visions of justice, as these services are treated as an end goal. For example, a survivor of SEA might not need financial, legal, psychosocial or medical support if they already have access to capital because of their positionality. In this case, material forms of support might not satisfy the survivors' expectations, and therefore might not achieve the justice they imagined. This mainstream approach further stereotypes victims and assumes that they do not have alternative options and that they always require material assistance. It creates a glass ceiling for victims and groups as one homogenous group.

This tendency to homogenize, categorize and define groups has been termed 'identity politics' in the social sciences (Crenshaw, 1991). Identity politics as such is inconsistent with both intersectional and transnational visions of justice. Young (1990) discusses the concept of the 'logic of identity' in her book *Justice and the Politics of Difference*. She explains that the logic of identity revolves around reducing, universalizing, grouping and treating entities as one category by insisting on the similarities between them and ignoring the differences. According to Young, 'the logic of identity tends to conceptualise entities in terms of substance rather than process or relation' (1990: 98). She argues that 'the irony of the logic of identity is that by seeking to reduce the differently similar to the same, it turns the merely different into the absolutely other. It inevitably generates dichotomy instead of unity' (Young, 1990: 99). If we investigate the way victims and survivors are treated within PSEA frameworks, we see that their grouping into one singular category, while providing them with material support as an end goal, further undermines their agency, the dynamics, processes and relationalities at play in SEA cases, and the role of systems of oppression and how they produce different experiences for victims and survivors.

In this context, it is very important to adopt an intersectional lens, beyond identities, which integrates a class analysis and examines the lived material experience of people; this is what I seek to do in this chapter. Internationalist discourses on 'victim-centred approaches' can overlook the lived material experiences of victims and survivors, and produce a set of stand-alone services to be provided if and when needed by people. The tendency towards identity politics that contributes to grouping people, without understanding and responding to the lived material experience of individuals and communities, compartmentalizes struggles and creates a binary of the 'good' and the 'bad', the 'victim' and the 'saviour'. However, to understand survivors' experiences and their agency and affect, we need to incorporate a class analysis, as this allows us to understand survivors' different needs, wants and imaginations or visions of justice.

As Salem puts it, a 'Marxist feminism that takes into account intersectionality's initial point about the primacy of multiple social categories poses one important way of deploying intersectional analysis and taking it further by showing how these categories are created, how they exploit and not simply oppress, and why they intersect' (2016: 6). Salem, in her brilliant article, emphasizes that looking at the lived material experiences of individuals helps us further understand how intersectionality as a framework operates, so we can better understand systems of oppression and their actual impact on people's lives in general and, more specifically, when they are subjected to abusive practices.

To apply this to PSEA, it means that practitioners need to refrain from grouping victims and survivors as if they are homogeneous and instead interrogate the systems of oppression that intersect to enable SEA cases, as these cases do not emerge from a vacuum. Instead, they reflect deeper social, economic and political structures. Standardized systems of assistance and referrals, as such, only help to address 'symptoms' of the deeper social problems that intersectional analysis can uncover. Instead, the intersectional framework can help us understand how violence is systematic and systemic; meaning that we cannot overlook structural oppression and violence when dealing with SEA cases (see Nour Abu-Assab in Chapter 12). This reminds us of the Combahee River Collective (1977) statement, which highlighted 'interlocking' systems of oppression and insisted people are actively engaged in the fight against oppressions such as colonialism, capitalism, racism and sexism. They too rejected the compartmentalization of struggles, as '[i]t leaves out far too much and far too many people, particularly Black men, women, and children. We have a great deal of criticism and loathing for what men have been socialized to be in this society: what they support, how they act, and how they oppress' (Combahee River Collective, 1977).

Moreover, an intersectional *transnational* approach allows us to see our interconnectedness and interdependence across all the world (Hochschild, 1983). This is particularly important when dealing with abusive practices, including SEA cases, as it pushes us to realize that these cases do not operate in a vacuum and are not isolated occurrences. This also means that we need to move away from critiquing structures of oppression in binary terms, meaning that we should acknowledge that systems of oppression operate globally and are experienced not just by one group, but by all, and that those structures intersect and make their manifestations on people's lives different. For us to build transnational solidarities that go beyond alliances of 'shallow taps on the shoulder' or mere material assistance, we need an approach that does not detach anyone and positions us all within structures of oppression. No one is outside such structures, because we are all part of those systems, and we all bargain with those structures in different ways. I argue that to understand SEA cases and how they occur, we need to interrogate how different groups also have structural differences among them based on class, race, sexuality, citizenship and so forth, allowing them to resist systems and structures of oppression sometimes, while at other times they are complicit with them. This broader understanding of how the world works enables us to better imagine and envision solutions.

The 'sociological imagination' concept, as coined by C. Wright Mills (1959), states that in order for us to understand societies, we need to explore the relationship between individuals and systems of oppression. He argues that for us to understand 'private troubles', we need to explore their intersection with 'public issues', or 'social problems'. This sociological imagination, in the context of an intersectional transnational framework addressing SEA, allows us to look beyond our own daily 'traps' and draw connections with overall structures of oppression. In other words, it pushes us to look at our daily issues as part of a bigger overall structural problem, rather than isolated cases. For instance, through adopting this lens, we start looking at SEA cases as part and parcel of bigger problems, and therefore dealing with them becomes part of our collective responsibility, which is also transnational and intersectional. The sociological imagination pushes us to critique the whole idea of a uniformed form of assistance to victims and survivors. Wright Mills (1959) argues that we need to look at societies as heterogeneous and challenge and contest the whole idea that an identical homogenous society is possible.

Therefore, equipping the sociological framework within the intersectional transnational paradigm allows us to (re)imagine the different ways people deal with abusive practices and how they are variously affected. This can help us to (re)imagine types of support and assistance while at the same time understand people's differential material lived experiences, needs, powers and agency. This imagining needs to happen collectively, as current standardized approaches are not able to take these aspects into consideration. Instead, it is very important to always keep in mind that each case needs its own tailored response strategy. Exploring PSEA through a transnational, intersectional framework that equips a sociological imagination is a first step to creating more just and transformative accountability frameworks that (re)imagine and go beyond mainstream approaches that privilege uniformity and overlook the differences between people.

Emotions and affect

In our research at the CTDC in relation to SEA cases within organizations, we found that traditional policies and general safeguarding frameworks do not contain systematic methods for thinking about power and agency. Such methods should be based on the notion that each of us has agency and the ability to make decisions regardless of our position in hierarchies of power. They should also conceive of sociopolitical influence such that it is not considered the sole purview of state penal systems, those occupying positions of power and authority, or the political, social and cultural elite. Accordingly, we must respond to cases of sexual exploitation, assault and harassment without further victimizing survivors by denying their agency (Abu-Assab and Nasser-Eddin, 2021). However, we cannot understand agency fully until we understand emotions and affect, as our agencies and material realities are deeply shaped by our emotions.

To adequately acknowledge agency, which is central to the intersectional transnational framework, with all its forms, it is essential to explore emotions, as they do not operate in a vacuum separate from the social, political and economic contexts under which people live (Ahmed, 2010). If we go back to my main argument in relation to safeguarding, we can see that our emotional responses to SEA cases have been 'institutionalized', through normative and standardized 'victim-centred approaches'. Åhäll and Gregory state that 'emotions in this respect do not refer to a particular state or disposition but are part of an exclusionary process that produces certain subjects to the detriment of others, reinscribing the boundary between the human and the non-human, the loved and the unloved, and the terrorized and the terrorist' (2013: 117).

Emotions are influenced by, and at the same time influence, the social world. They are not simply physical reactions to the external environment, but also linked to the mind, or the way we understand the world, just like the body. As Fischer puts it: 'emotions unfold transactionally in our daily lives. We are actively engaged in and productive of our affective experiences in accordance with the ever-changing contexts of our environments' (2016: 821). In addition, emotion has an 'intellectual content' (Dewey, 1895). It is a very important step to link emotions to cognition and to the mind, because once we do that, we start linking emotions to the broader contexts around us and start politicizing them. As Satre states, 'a cognitivist view would suggest that emotions involve appraisals, judgements, attitudes or a "specific manner of apprehending the world"' (in Ahmed, 2004: 5). Emotions are related to our values and how we relate to the outside world (Slaby and Wuschner, 2014). This means that although emotions are subjective, they are also shaped and informed by the world we live in. Slaby and Wuschner state that

> two interlocking aspects are central to this perspective: (a) emotions are relational; that is, they are constituted by a dense phenomenal coupling to the agent's environment; (b) they are dialogical in that their acting-out as an engagement with the environment helps to shape the space of possible further ways of acting them out and thus partly determines how the emotion will subsequently unfold. (2014: 212)

Based on that, one can argue that our agency and affected realities are shaped by the emotions that we experience, and that our emotions may affect the world we live in. Emotions can 'shape the world around us' (Åhäll and Gregory, 2013: 117).

Conceptualizing emotions as active components in our lives allows us to acknowledge that they can have great influence on us and others around us. And if we do not take emotions into consideration, we are 'complicit in normalizing acts of violence, justifying oppression and masking forms of economic and political subordination' (Åhäll and Gregory, 2013: 118). For example, in cases of SEA, to fight narratives that lay blame on victims and survivors, organizations have been attempting to promote the 'we believe survivors' slogan, and in some cases that can be emotionally driven and influence the process. Through research and consulting work at the CTDC, we have come across cases where community organizations that feel strongly about the 'we believe survivors' slogan have taken extreme measures against alleged perpetrators without carrying out due diligence processes in the form of assessments and investigations. On the other hand, and at the same time, responses to victims and survivors are expected to be institutionalized, not taking into consideration the emotionality of victims and survivors. For example, organizations and institutions dealing with SEA cases have standardized approaches to the assistance and support offered to victims and survivors, and in many cases it is just a 'tick the box' exercise. Those fixed procedures do not consider the different *emotionalities* that victims and survivors have, and do not acknowledge that assistance simply in the shape of services (social, psychological, material and legal) is not the only way to respond to victims' and survivors' needs. As discussed previously, emotions are the product of the contexts we live in and they influence, and are influenced by, the world we live in, as well as intersecting systems of oppression. Therefore, our emotions are active and proactive components of our beings and shape our own *realities*. Thinking through the lens of emotionality would allow us to go beyond the victimhood narrative that is usually used by organizations, where victims and survivors are perceived as 'vulnerable' and 'passive'; instead, it is important to think of our 'vulnerability' as political and shaped by the different power(s) in the world (Daoust and Dyvik, 2022).

Åhäll and Gregory (2013: 118) argue that

> Pity, for example, is often invoked as part of a humanitarian discourse designed to move us to donate money or speak out against acts of violence. Yet, pity might also function to hide past injustices and mask responsibility for the suffering of others; thus, emotions function to reinforce the hierarchical relationship between 'us' and 'them' by locating agency with the international community whilst denying others the capacity to act.

Although pity as an emotion may have an *affect* on humanitarian agencies, it still is not the only emotion at play – fear, guilt or sadness may be equally involved. It is beyond the scope of this chapter to explore the kind of emotions that do *affect*, but I wholeheartedly agree that certain emotions can create power dynamics and have an affective turn on how people and individuals deal with violence. When victims and survivors are treated as a uniform group, practitioners are denying them agency and ignoring their intrinsic and intimate power as well as their emotional authority. This type of power and authority is rarely, if ever, accounted for when addressing SEA cases. Research and PSEA organizational assessments have demonstrated that when organizations are accused of not having dealt appropriately with SEA cases, ranges of emotions emerge among organizational members and the community, and these may include anger, fear, shame and embarrassment. Often in these cases, the emotional responses to accusations result in organizations either becoming defensive or being completely unable to respond, meaning that emotions greatly influence responses to SEA. For this reason, it is very important for practitioners in the field and responders to ask themselves three key questions: What emotions are being triggered? What kind of affect do these emotions have? Who are the most affected?

The intersectional transnational framework developed in this chapter can also help us understand the relevance of emotions to SEA better, since emotions are experienced differently as people have different positionalities and experiences. From a class perspective, even emotions are assigned social values within society and are affected by biopolitics. As Beattie and colleagues state, this relates to 'who gets to express emotions, what emotions are perceived as legitimate or desirable (and conversely which should be repressed or are illegitimate), how emotions are circulated and under what circumstances' (in Gustafsson and Hall, 2021: 974). As emotions are assigned values, and the politics of emotions dictate that there are hierarchies of emotions, this means that 'to give value to things is to shape what is near us' (Ahmed, 2010: 31). It is important to note that we cannot separate emotions from affect (Ahmed, 2014; Åhäll, 2018), as they are heavily interrelated. As people process emotions differently and affect, and are affected by, the political, social and economic contexts, it is essential for safeguarding frameworks to adapt responses to meet the individual and individualized needs of victims and survivors.

Attending to affect and emotions consequently leads to questioning normative assumptions and what is taken for granted as 'known' (Pedwell and Whitehead, 2012). Affect and emotions as such are considered a methodology on their own (Åhäll, 2018). In other words, they allow us to ask questions about the world that we live in, create room for self-reflection and open the door for us to imagine more suitable alternative responses and fairer visions of justice. An intersectional transnational lens is also compatible with affect theory and methodology. Affect allows us to take into consideration people's agency and enables us to understand how they interact with structures of oppression and how they can be affective at a transnational level. Practically, this would allow us to build accountability frameworks *from* the perspective of people and not *about* the people. This approach would allow people to be part and parcel of designing policies and procedures from their lived material realities rather than having those policies imposed on them. It would allow us to be more sensible, responsible and sensitive to victims and survivors. In relation to intersectionality, this framework also acknowledges that although we share systems of oppression, the ways they manifest in our lives are different, and for this reason we cannot rely on grouping people into categories in relation to SEA. Affect theory is incompatible with identity politics. As Massumi puts it: 'affect is not the opposite of thought. It is the movement *of* thought. It is the force of thought, embodied' (in Ferrington et al, 2019: 113).

Conclusion

In this chapter, I introduced a novel framework to address the needs of victims and survivors of SEA, which centres their agency. I argued that an intersectional transnational lens allows us to understand people's lived material experiences. To be able to adequately address the needs of victims and survivors, we must investigate the dynamics, processes and relationalities that are at play in the world we live in. This framework also allows us to move beyond identity politics and binary ways of thinking, which create processes of grouping and othering people. As we live in a transnational world, this framework also enables us to recognize our interconnectedness and interdependence across borders. In addition, I illuminated the importance of scrutinizing root causes of systems of oppression, not just addressing symptoms. We need to deal with abuse not as daily 'traps', or isolated problems, but rather as symptomatic of larger issues. Just as Wright Mills (1959) urged social scientists to imagine alternative worlds, we need to question normative assumptions and standardized procedures and processes to deal with victims and survivors of SEA, which in fact deprive them of the right to self-determination. Finally, the sociological imagination imbued within the intersectional transnational paradigm encourages us to bring out differences rather than similarities, to understand the complex ways through which people interact with(in) systems of oppression and to engender different imaginations of agency.

Agency is an important component when we want to address issues of SEA, as it determines how people deal with abuse. To truly create victim-centred approaches, understanding agency needs to be mainstreamed into PSEA frameworks. However, to understand agency, we need to understand affect and emotions, which we can consider both a methodology and a process. Emotions and affect within PSEA frameworks can be integrated on two levels: addressing our own emotional responses as PSEA practitioners and the way they influence the process; and attaining and understanding victims' and survivors' emotions and emotional *affect*. It is very important to clarify that when speaking of visions of justice for victims, I mean to refer to justice as a process rather than merely an end goal or an outcome. For this reason, I have highlighted the limits of PSEA frameworks for attaining justice, as they do not perceive responding to SEA as a process, but as a target.

References

Abu Assab, N. and Nasser-Eddin, N. (2021) *Organisational Safeguarding Best Practices and Procedures: A Toolkit Towards Transnational Intersectional Feminist Accountability Frameworks to Respond to Exploitation, Assault, Abuse, Harassment And Bullying*, London: CTDC.

Abu-Assab, N., Nasser-Eddin, N. and Seghaier, R. (2020) 'Activism and the economy of victimhood: a close look into NGO-ization in Arabic-speaking countries', *Intervention: International Journal of Postcolonial Studies*, 22(4): 481–97.

Åhäll, L. (2018) 'Affect as methodology: feminism and the politics of emotion', *International Political Sociology*, 12(1): 36–52.

Åhäll, L. and Gregory, T. (2013) 'Security, emotions, affect', *Critical Studies on Security*, 1(1): 117–20.

Ahmed, S. (2004) *The Cultural Politics of Emotion*, Edinburgh: Edinburgh University Press.

Ahmed, S. (2010) 'Happy objects', in M. Gregg and G. Seigworth (eds), *The Affect Theory Reader*, Durham, NC: Duke University Press, pp 29–51.

Ahmed, S. and Schmitz, S. (2014) 'Affect/emotion: orientation matters: a conversation between Sigrid Schmitz and Sara Ahmed', *Freiburger Zeitschrift für GeschlechterStudien*, 20(2): 97–108.

Combahee River Collective (1977) *The Combahee River Collective Statement*, Combahee River Collective. Available from: www.blackpast.org/african-american-history/combahee-river-collective-statement-1977/ (accessed 26 October 2023).

Crenshaw, K. (1991) Mapping the margins: intersectionality, identity politics, and violence against women of color, *Stanford Law Review*, 43(6): 1241–99.

Daoust, G. and Dyvik, S.L. (2022) 'Reconceptualizing vulnerability and safeguarding in the humanitarian and development sector', *Social Policy*, 29(1): 355–78.

Dewey, J. (1895) 'The theory of emotion', *Psychological Review*, 2(1): 13–32.

Ferrington, J., Parsons, J. and Hechler, A. (2019) 'Affect and immediation: an interview with Brian Massumi', disClosure: A Journal of Social Theory, 28: 13. doi: 10.13023/disclosure.28.09

Fischer, C. (2016). 'Feminist philosophy, pragmatism, and the "turn to affect": a genealogical critique', *Hypatia*, 31(4): 810–26.

Gready, P. and Robins, S. (2014) 'From transitional to transformative justice: a new agenda for practice', *The International Journal of Transnational Justice*, 8(3): 339–61.

Gustafsson, K. and Hall, T. (2021) 'The politics of emotions in international relations: who gets to feel what, whose emotions matter, and the "history problem" in Sino-Japanese relations', *International Studies Quarterly*, 65(4): 973–84.

Hochschild, A. (1983) *The Managed Heart: Commercialisation of Human Feeling*, Berkeley: University of California Press.

Pedwell, C. and Whitehead, A. (2012) 'Affecting feminism: questions of feeling in feminist theory', *Feminist Theory*, 13(2): 115–29.

Salem, S. (2016) 'Intersectinality and its discontents: intersectionality as traveling theory', *European Journal of Women's Studies*, 25(4): 403–18.

Slaby, J. and Wuschner, P. (2014) 'Emotion and agency', in S. Roeser and C. Todd (eds) *Emotion and Value*, Oxford: Oxford University Press, pp 212–28.

United Nations (2019) *United Nations Protocol on the Provision of Assistance to Victims of Sexual Exploitation and Abuse*, 12 December. Available from: www.un.org/en/pdfs/UN%20Victim%20Assistance%20Protocol_English_Final.pdf (accessed 26 October 2023).

Wright Mills, C. (1959) *The Sociological Imagination*, Oxford: Oxford University Press.

Young, I. (1990) *Justice and the Politics of Difference*, Princeton, NJ: Princeton University Press.

14

Empowered Aid: Transforming Gender and Power Dynamics in the Distribution of Humanitarian Aid

Alina Potts

Introduction

For over two decades, the aid community has expressed shock when large-scale abuses have come to light – from the widespread abuse of children by peacekeepers and aid workers brought to light in West Africa in 2002 (IRIN, 2012) to the abuse by World Health Organization and NGO staff responding to Ebola in the Democratic Republic of Congo, uncovered by journalists in 2020 (The New Humanitarian and Thomson Reuters Foundation, 2020). It is clear that those sent to help people affected by conflict and disaster can sometimes harm them. Why, despite efforts to hold offending individuals and organizations accountable, does it persist?

Unequal power on the basis of heteronormative gender roles – with men generally having more access to and control over resources than women – is a root cause of sexual exploitation and abuse (SEA) and other forms of gender-based violence (True, 2012). These power imbalances are further entrenched in systems of humanitarian aid, in which the people affected by crisis and dependent on aid for their survival have the least say in how it is delivered and the least ability to hold aid actors to account. Displaced women and girls fall at the intersection of these inequities, with their voices often missing even when crisis-affected communities *are* consulted by aid actors. Yet working with diverse women and girls to shift power and recentre their experiences – and their solutions – is necessary to confront these underlying power imbalances and address the root causes of SEA.

This chapter details what these shifts in power and recentring look like in practice, drawing on participatory work undertaken in Lebanon and Uganda, which are among the largest refugee-hosting countries in the world. I start by providing an overview of the Empowered Aid approach and how it offers advantages over less dynamic methods of engaging with crisis-affected communities. I then explore three of these advantages in detail, illustrating how participatory, feminist, ethnographic approaches to risk assessment help to shift power, harness community-based knowledge and break down barriers to reporting abuse. I conclude with notes on how practitioners can apply these approaches to the contexts in which they work, summarizing key implications for policy and programming.

The Empowered Aid approach to contextual safeguarding

Empowered Aid is a multi-year, multi-country project based at the Global Women's Institute at George Washington University that began in 2018. It uses participatory action research and implementation science to examine the mechanisms through which humanitarian aid is delivered and how these processes might inadvertently increase the risks of SEA within affected populations, in order to address them. Its goal is to mitigate SEA risks through the creation or adaptation of aid delivery models that work to actively reduce power disparities and give women and girls a sustained voice in how aid is delivered (Potts et al, 2022b). Empowered Aid is carried out in partnership with local and international aid actors in refugee-affected countries, as well as refugee co-researchers and advisory boards. The focus is not on individual incidents, but rather on identifying the contexts conducive to abuse being perpetrated and taking action to address these unsafe settings or situations. By taking this ecological approach, also known as 'contextual safeguarding' (Gender and Development Network, 2018), aid actors are accountable for monitoring their programmes for known SEA risks and taking action to address them rather than waiting for a report of abuse to come forward, at which point it is very likely that many more abuses have occurred, as investigations in the aftermath of numerous recent scandals have demonstrated. This shifts the onus of responsibility away from survivors – who may choose not to report for reasons such as fear of retribution, loss of aid, shame and stigma – to organizations, which should not be free to assume that a lack of SEA reports means that abuse is not occurring.

Empowered Aid is grounded in participatory action, feminist and ethnographic research methods, which centre women and girls and their lived experiences and recognize them as experts: they are the ones who know best the SEA risks they face and how to make aid safer for them (Ackerly and True, 2019). These methods seek to share power – in this case, supporting refugee women and girls to safely take an active role in asking and answering questions about their own lives and the ways aid intended for good may do harm. Participatory action research emphasizes the active engagement of those normally considered the 'subjects' of research, and uses findings for social change (Edwards et al, 2022; Cornish et al, 2023). Empowered Aid's participatory action research took place over the first year and a half of the project. In total, 26 Syrian and 29 South Sudanese women and adolescent girls were engaged as co-researchers, and they examined SEA risks associated with accessing five types of aid: food; water, sanitation and hygiene (WASH); shelter; fuel and firewood; and cash and voucher assistance. They selected these areas of focus deliberatively and spent two weeks conducting field observations of SEA risks related to accessing each, meeting every fortnight over three months to systematically record their observations. Participatory group discussions were held with refugee men and boys; host community men, women, girls and boys; and people living with disabilities. Key informant interviews were held with community leaders and humanitarian personnel. In total, 278 interviews or participatory group discussions were conducted and 197 people were engaged in the research.

The study examined risks of SEA throughout the entire process of humanitarian aid distribution: from how crisis-affected people find information about aid, to eligibility and verification exercises, to travelling to and from access points to the point of distribution, to safely storing the aid received. Qualitative findings highlighted SEA risks across all types of aid studied and at all points of the distribution process. For example, an adolescent refugee girl in Uganda described SEA in relation to food aid:

> 'At times you find that we girls or women, we find difficulties with the distributors. They come and tell [us] that "if you fall in love with me, I will add you more food, or for the cooking oil you will get a big share". So, you end up ... after they have realized the food is about to come, they move around corning[1] girls or women, [saying] that "if you really fall in love with me, I will add you food". So those are big challenges.'

Based on the findings, refugee co-researchers prioritized a set of recommendations for aid actors to address the risks that were identified. The second phase of Empowered Aid used implementation science to test these recommendations in small-scale pilots in ongoing humanitarian aid operations in both countries, in partnership with aid distributors (Global Women's Institute, CARE in Lebanon and URDA, 2021; Global Women's Institute, IRC Uganda and World Vision Uganda, 2021). This was done to increase research uptake and test the assumption made by some aid actors that safer programming comes at the cost of other programming outcomes or that it is slower or more expensive to implement.

Monitoring tools already in use by aid actors – such as safety audits, surveys and focus groups – were modified to better capture SEA risks and identify further points for action, based on aid recipients' responses (Global Women's Institute, 2021). The results showed increased feelings of safety – in part, due to respondents observing the protective measures put in place – as well as a greater ability of the monitoring and evaluation tools to detect SEA risks. This approach holds aid agencies accountable to affected populations for proactively identifying and addressing SEA risks in their programming, rather than waiting for a case of SEA to be reported, thus making aid delivery safer and potentially preventing abuses from occurring.

Shifting power

If methods of engaging crisis-affected people do not explicitly address the unequal power dynamics at play, they may inadvertently replicate or even further reinforce them. For example, focus groups are considered participatory, but the questions to be asked may be decided without input from communities, and the final analysis or actions taken may not be shared with participants. The same set of questions may be posed in all groups, without adapting them to the particular interests or expertise of the participants and how they would like to direct the discussion. Discussions are often conducted as one-off, unidirectional data collection activities in which aid actors do not provide space for crisis-affected communities to help shape the questions being asked or play a role in how their responses are used to inform programmes and policy (Rass et al, 2020). Empowered Aid sought to shift power through the participatory, feminist and anthropological methods used in three ways: by allowing space for co-creation of the research design, including contextualizing key terms and definitions in women's and girls' own words; by including reflexivity as an explicit part of the research process, with a pause for reflection halfway through the research process; and by allowing ample time for these processes and relationships to unfold.

The research design phase took a co-creation approach (Potts et al, 2022a), with workshops in which international, national and refugee co-researchers developed research tools together. Visual methods such as drawing, community mapping, body mapping and drama were used so that literacy was not a barrier to participation. The full methodology for these co-design workshops with NGO partners and refugee co-researchers has been shared to encourage others to adapt and utilize similar processes (Global Women's Institute, 2020b).

To engage refugee research team members, as experts with important knowledge to contribute in the research design phase, time was allowed during the co-design workshops for the exchange of ideas and concepts. When discussing key terms and definitions, refugee co-researchers were encouraged to explain their understanding or offer alternatives. For example, in Uganda one of the adolescent girl co-researchers defined 'consent' in the following way: "You say from the mouth but not from the heart." Exploring local understandings allows for contextualization of research as well as programme activities, with the potential to make them more effective. In addition to consent, the workshops included ample time for discussions of power, covering experiences of power being misused, of women and girls using their innate personal power, and of joining together to make change. Sharing examples of the power women and girls hold supported a collective recognition of how women and girl co-researchers are freely *sharing their power with us* as part of this work. They are not passive recipients of a project that 'empowers' them; they are agents of their own, and others', empowerment.

Reflexivity is a key aspect of ethnographic work, also emphasized in feminist methodologies (Ackerly and True, 2019). In the midst of the participatory data collection process, we included a 'pause' for those involved to meet and reflect on power dynamics – this took place both among the international and national staff working on the project as researchers, caseworkers and translators, and between these groups and the refugee co-researchers (Global Women's Institute, 2020d). Exercises further explored where members of the team felt supported to use their power, and where they did not. One issue that arose in both countries was around the timing and notice given for participating in project activities. While the schedule had been agreed in advance, changes were sometimes necessary due to NGO staff being unavailable or experiencing transport delays. Refugee women noted that they were not always given much notice in these situations, and they had at times been asked to reschedule during times when important events, such as food distributions, were happening. Aid staff, in turn, shared how they felt powerless when supervisors or managers asked them to prioritize other activities. The team identified ways aid staff could ensure that more notice and options for rescheduling were provided, while project managers also fed back to their supervisors the need to maintain time for the project within their work plans. This may seem mundane, but the act of providing feedback and seeing it being taken seriously and put into effect served to build trust with the refugee co-researchers and build confidence that the NGOs would also be responsive when it came to sharing more sensitive feedback.

Processes for shifting power are best employed over multi-year timelines spanning various funding cycles and partnership arrangements. In both countries, six years after the project started, Empowered Aid continues to work with many of the same refugee women and girls. While initially engaged as co-researchers, at the end of the research phase they were asked whether they would like to remain engaged in the implementation phase. They chose to form refugee advisory boards, which were engaged in adapting the tools used to monitor aid distributions and reviewing the findings of the pilots. Aid actors often dismiss as unrealistic the idea of engaging community actors over longer periods of time. While humanitarian funding is often provided on short-term cycles of a year or less, this is not the reality of displacement: World Bank estimates, cited by the United Nations High Commissioner for Refugees, indicate that about a third of people forcibly displaced have been so for five to nine years, and over a quarter for more than ten years (Beltramo et al, 2023). This is the reality in both Lebanon – which has hosted large numbers of Syrian refugees since 2011 and Palestinian refugees since 1948 – and in Uganda – which is home to Africa's oldest refugee settlement, Nakivale, formed in 1959 (Easton-Calabria, 2021). Many of the South Sudanese people currently living in Uganda as refugees fled during the waves of conflict that have occurred periodically since 2016. In these protracted displacement settings, engaging crisis-affected people at one point in time should not be considered 'participatory'. Time for processes of reflection are vital to address a form of abuse that is made possible by the same system that wants to end it.

Harnessing community-based knowledge

Listening to affected people is a crucial first step; accountability means putting their words into action. In order to shift power, this process of using results for change should also be participatory, with those closest to the problem of SEA playing active roles in making meaning out of the data collected about it. To explore the harnessing of community-based knowledge, in this section we share the visual and participatory data analysis methods developed within Empowered Aid and look at the specific recommendations resulting from them as well as the ways we sought to decolonize how knowledge was documented, shared, taught and published.

Analysis of monitoring and research data – whether quantitative or qualitative – often takes place in isolation from community conversations and uses computer-based methods that are inaccessible to those without computers or language literacy. While computing tools are necessary to process large amounts of data, there are other ways in which women and girls who are not computer-literate or able to read and write can participate. Empowered Aid's 'action analysis workshops' involved the refugee co-researchers feeding back on the preliminary themes identified through software-based qualitative data analysis undertaken by the NGO- and university-based co-researchers (Global Women's Institute, 2020a). Findings were illustrated (Figures 14.1 and 14.2) and grouped thematically, and women and girls (workshops were age segregated) rotated in small groups, in a round robin format, to share whether the findings accurately reflected their data collection and to further develop the thematic analysis. The use of visual

Figure 14.1: Visual for the recommendation in Uganda for women travelling in groups

Figure 14.2: Visual for the recommendation in Lebanon for distribution in mixed-sex groups at household level

Table 14.1: Recommendations of women and girls for making aid distribution safer in both Uganda and Lebanon

---

Separate lines at distribution points for women/girls and men/boys to avoid women/girls being pushed out of line, harassed or targeted

More **women aid workers** or women's committees involved in aid distribution processes

Formal/informal **accompanying systems** when women and girls collect/receive aid, and information sharing on moving in groups

Transportation support to collect food, WASH and other items, especially for vulnerable groups

More security at distribution points (particularly for WASH and fuel/firewood in Uganda and cash withdrawal points in Lebanon)

Sessions for **community sensitization** to gender-based violence and SEA, and better knowledge and communication on SEA complaint and reporting mechanisms

---

and movement-based methods during this workshop helped remove literacy as a barrier to participating in data synthesis and analysis processes. As Lady Aminah,[2] a South Sudanese co-researcher in Uganda, shared: "Actually, the findings were exactly like what was happening in our communities. ... After the team asked us about their findings, we agreed [and] then from there they asked us about the recommendations. We came up with very many recommendations."

At the conclusion of the workshops, a participatory voting exercise was held, in which women and girl co-researchers chose the three most important recommendations from among the protective strategies that came out of the analysis and were further developed by them. As noted, the resulting set of recommendations were shared back to aid actors for action and formed the basis for testing programme adaptations during the implementation science phase. While the participatory research took place in very different settings – in the urban and peri-urban setting of Lebanon's second-largest city, Tripoli, and in the rural Bidi Bidi and Imvepi refugee settlements of north-west Uganda – a surprising number of the recommendations women and girls put forward were very similar (see Table 14.1).

These findings and recommendations, along with the participatory processes used to develop them (see GWI, 2020c), have been documented and shared through a library of free tools, guides and resources on the Empowered Aid website.[3] These include a toolkit and training on monitoring for SEA risks in distribution processes as well as a free online course, available in five languages, to help humanitarian actors better prevent SEA in aid distribution. The course is co-taught by the refugee co-researchers, highlighting their expertise and centring it in training and capacity sharing.

In addition, within each country, and globally, technical advisory groups were formed to engage key aid actors from local and international NGOs, the United Nations, government, civil society and national research or academic institutes so that the findings of this work could be both informed by and able to inform other initiatives to address SEA. These groups not only share resources but also provide avenues through which to amplify and utilize community-based knowledge within national, regional and global discussions.

Local actors, in particular, benefit from explicit efforts to share power through capacity sharing. Empowered Aid sought to do this by: offering skills trainings on conducting safe gender-based violence research, monitoring and evaluation; providing technical support to implement the Empowered Aid tools and approaches across local programming; giving support to secure funding as well as to hold international actors to account; and providing support to publish in international fora, where local actors are often under-represented. Setting aside time to support local partners to co-author publications, including as first author, was part of sharing power in the knowledge production process with those who are often left out of the Global North- and English language-centric publication system (Kaisi et al, 2021).

Breaking down barriers to reporting abuse

Women and girls identified multiple barriers to reporting cases of SEA and seeking help from informal or formal sources. These barriers and their effects on reporting SEA are described in this section. Barriers are numerous and include: lack of knowledge or awareness; lack of faith in reporting mechanisms managed by the same aid structures that employ or empower perpetrators; confusion around the perpetrator's role (as a staff member or volunteer or contractor, and with which agency); and normalization of SEA, which many see as the cost of receiving life-saving assistance. Another barrier is the perception that the sexually exploitative relationship is of benefit to a survivor; simply put, she may fear that aid will be taken away if she moves to end the sexually exploitative relationship. For victims, sharing what has happened with others in their community may be met with either a positive response that supports survivors' healing or with stigma, victim blaming and shaming that causes further harm. As one of the Syrian refugee women shared: "I don't think that she referred to anyone. How can she make a complaint about him if it was consensual? Of course, he asked for something in return for installing a water tank for her."

In participatory group discussions with refugee and host community women, girls, men and boys, vignettes, or 'open-ended stories', were used to discuss where survivors of SEA turn for help and what the response is.

This approach does not require individuals to share personal stories. The participants shared that family member responses could be both helpful and harmful: some may offer support to the survivor and help connect her to services or reporting mechanisms, while others may blame or shame her, limit her freedom of movement, express disbelief, or even force her to marry the perpetrator or further abuse her. Women and girls noted that families who are economically vulnerable may neglect female family members and encourage or force them into relationships because they need assistance and/or money. For example, at the conclusion of an open-ended story about a girl who is exploited, the question was posed: If the girl tells her parents that someone took advantage of her, what would their reaction be? A Syrian refugee woman responded: "Some people don't mind, if they're in need. Things like that happen a lot by the way. Some people refuse to be taken advantage of, even if they're poor and in need, but a lot of people accept because they need money to provide for themselves and pay the rent."

For these reasons, SEA survivors tend to be fearful of reporting abuse or seeking services to help them recover. Refugee women, girls, boys and men spoke of the negative mental health effects survivors of SEA may struggle with, including depression and suicidal thoughts or attempted suicide. During participatory group discussions in Lebanon, refugee women and host community girls (separately) shared how perpetrators may threaten the survivor or her family with violence or spreading rumours to "spoil her reputation". Fear of being gossiped about in the community can be a powerful deterrent to coming forward. As a discussion with adolescent girls in Uganda surfaced, "Sometimes you tell your friend, your friend then tells her friend, her friend also goes and tells the other one and just they go talking about your name." Women and girls may feel unsafe reporting to police, as some police officers are perpetrators. These fears, combined with a perceived lack of accountability for perpetrators and lack of knowledge of reporting mechanisms, contribute to a chilling effect on reporting. The gendered power imbalances at play in silencing survivors were perhaps best captured in a participatory group discussion with adolescent boys from the host community in Uganda, with one participant saying:

> 'She cannot tell anyone because she is using that as an opportunity for adding her food ration so she will not tell anyone about her situation, because if she tells anyone about her situation this person will follow the person who is doing that to her and the person may lose [their] job, which will make her also lose her addition of food ration.'

As described by Bian and colleagues in Chapter 10 and Phoebe Donnelly and Dyan Mazurana in Chapter 4, impunity is rampant and lack of confidence that SEA complaints will be pursued or taken seriously further discourages reporting. When reports are met with stalling (for instance, numerous requests for further proof or information), inaction or inept action (for example, moving the perpetrator to another location or firing them only to have another organization rehire them), or outright denial and retribution, this sends a strong signal throughout aid-dependent communities to stay silent (Westendorf, 2020). One of a group of Syrian refugee men shared:

> 'We went to the organization and told them about what happened [SEA], but the employee did not believe us. He said he worked with honourable people that wouldn't do such a thing. We insisted that we were telling him the truth and we took the woman to talk to him. We convinced her to trust him and tell him what happened, but when he grabbed her, she yelled at him and went outside where she cried. Even the manager didn't believe her.'

A Ugandan woman living in the 'host community' surrounding the refugee settlement described what happened to a known perpetrator in her community: "They did nothing to him, there was nothing that was done to him ... he also applied to another organization and is now working with another group." Conversely, seeing or hearing examples of a perpetrator being held to account builds trust.

When a survivor comes forward, she often confides in friends, female family members and religious or community leaders first, to seek counsel on next steps. Refugee women and girls identified women's centres, women refugee leaders, complaints desks, the organization in charge of the aid worker or distributor, and hotlines as places where they could report. Women and girls also reported a preference for accessing services from NGOs that support women, including local and women-led organizations; specific mentions of trusted helpers included caseworkers. This underscores the importance in humanitarian responses of funding, from the outset, local women's rights organizations and gender-based violence services. Their presence is key to SEA prevention and response, as they provide supportive and confidential spaces to ask for help, and ensure survivor-centred processes are in place.

Conclusion

Empowered Aid's focus on prevention calls on aid actors to proactively take steps to address known SEA risks, even in the absence of reports of SEA. Many of the recommendations formulated for safer aid distributions build on steps women and girls are already taking to protect themselves, like 'sounding an alarm' or moving in groups. They make visible the ways in which communities know what puts them at risk and work with the tools they have to mitigate those risks. They also highlight the relatively straightforward steps aid agencies can take to play a more active role in addressing known risks. There is no 'silver bullet' to ending SEA, but at the same time none of the recommendations are high-tech or overly complex. Something as simple as setting up sex-segregated lines at distribution points – which should be in place, but in many cases are not – protects against SEA and other forms of gender-based violence. Several women described that in order to avoid being groped and harassed, they stepped aside to let men go ahead of them. Then, as they arrived home from the distribution point later than expected, their partners accused them of wasting time or adultery, and perpetrated domestic abuse. SEA does not occur in a vacuum; it affects how women and girls navigate aid systems and violent situations – hence the need to safeguard the context. A distribution system that does not meet women's and girls' needs for aid in safe ways inadvertently opens up this space for exploitation and abuse.

Empowered Aid supports aid agencies to provide safer access to humanitarian aid for all crisis-affected people, including women and girls in all their diversity. This chapter described how Empowered Aid uses feminist, participatory and ethnographic methods within research and programming to shift power, harness community-based knowledge and break down barriers to reporting abuse. In essence, these approaches are about actors acknowledging their own power over crisis-affected communities and the multiple ways it may be misused. While this misuse of power does not always amount to 'violence', failing to use one's power as an aid actor to proactively address known risks for SEA can be considered negligence, given the imperative to 'do no harm'. Empowered Aid's resources offer a roadmap for actively seeking input and feedback, in multiple ways, from those who live closest to the problem we are trying to address, namely SEA by aid workers. They offer a less extractive and protectionist way to interact with communities, particularly women and girls, whose voices are marginalized by patriarchal power systems in which male leaders are often trusted intermediaries for distributing aid. By applying these tools and approaches, organizations across the sector can embed ongoing community-based risk identification and response into aid programming. It is not the responsibility of women and girls to make aid agencies do better. It is the responsibility of aid actors to consult women and girls and to show that they are listening by deferring to them in programming and policy decisions. Without such structural power shifts, the cycle of abuse will continue.

Reducing the massive power imbalance between aid actors and the local populations they serve is crucial in building trust, which is often sorely lacking. Listening to women and girls and working with them to put their ideas and recommendations into action builds trust. When women's rights groups and gender-based violence services are funded and supported, this trust is met with a supportive infrastructure in which to come forward and seek help. As Lama Sibaii, one of the Syrian refugee co-researchers in Lebanon, shared: "We went through the distribution cycle as refugees, so we know better than anyone the risks we face across distributions. Our role was to provide the solutions to the problems we were facing." By critically engaging with power structures – including reflecting on their own position within them – aid practitioners and researchers can create an enabling space for many more women and girls to voice their solutions in ways that are heard and acted on.

References

Ackerly, B. and True, J. (2019) *Doing Feminist Research in Political and Social Science* (2nd edn), London: Bloomsbury Publishing.

Beltramo, T., O'Riordan, A., Hesemann, J. and Gagnon, J. (2023) 'Collecting data on the forcibly displaced is essential for better inclusion'. Available from: https://www.unhcr.org/blogs/collecting-data-on-the-forcibly-displaced-is-essential-for-better-inclusion/ (accessed 15 September 2023).

Cornish, F. et al (2023) 'Participatory action research', *Nature Reviews Methods Primers*, 3(34).

Easton-Calabria, E. (2021) 'Uganda's long history of hosting refugees', *Yes! Magazine*, 1 September. Available from: www.yesmagazine.org/social-justice/2021/09/01/uganda-history-hosting-refugees (accessed 31 October 2023).

Edwards, K.M. et al (2022) 'Engaging Native American youth and their caregivers in sexual violence research: a case study documenting challenges, opportunities, and lessons learned', *Journal of Interpersonal Violence*, 37(23–24): NP22273–99.

Gender and Development Network (2018) *Safeguarding and Beyond – Recommendations from the Gender and Development Network*, London: Gender and Development Network.

Global Women's Institute (2020a) *Empowered Aid: Action Analysis Workshop Facilitation Guide for Women and Girl Researchers*, Washington, DC: George Washington University.

Global Women's Institute (2020b) *Empowered Aid: Participatory Action Research Workshop Facilitation Guide*, Washington, DC: George Washington University.

Global Women's Institute (2020c) *Empowered Aid: Participatory Action Research with Refugee Women and Girls to Better Prevent Sexual Exploitation and Abuse – PAR Toolkit*. Washington, DC: The Global Women's Institute at The George Washington University.

Global Women's Institute (2020d) *Empowered Aid: Research Reflection Workshop Facilitation Guide*, Washington, DC: George Washington University.

Global Women's Institute (2021) *Empowered Aid: Toolkit for Planning and Monitoring Safer Aid Distributions*, Washington, DC: George Washington University.

Global Women's Institute, CARE in Lebanon, and URDA (2021) *Empowered Aid Phase 2 Pilot Reports in Lebanon: Applying Findings from Participatory Research on how to Reduce Sexual Exploitation and Abuse in Aid Distribution*, Washington, DC: The George Washington University.

Global Women's Institute, IRC Uganda, World Vision Uganda (2021) *Empowered Aid Phase 2 Pilot Reports in Uganda: Applying Findings from Participatory Research on how to Reduce Sexual Exploitation and Abuse in Aid Distribution*, Washington, DC and Kampala: The George Washington University, IRC, and World Vision.

IRIN (2012) 'West Africa: sexual exploitation and abuse 10 years on', *PeaceWomen*, 4 July. Available from: www.peacewomen.org/content/west-africa-sexual-exploitation-and-abuse-10-years (accessed 15 September 2023).

Kaisi, J., Haddad, R., Fattal, L. and Potts, A. (2021) 'Localising knowledge generation during a pandemic to make distributions safer', *Humanitarian Exchange Magazine*, 79: 105–9.

Potts, A., Fattal, L. and Kolli, H. (2022a) 'Engaging refugee women and girls as experts: co-creating evidence on sexual exploitation and abuse in humanitarian crises using creative, participatory methods', *Evidence & Policy*, 18(2): 311–35.

Potts, A., Kolli, H. and Fattal, L. (2022b) 'Whose voices matter? Using participatory, feminist and anthropological approaches to centre power and positionality in research on gender-based violence in emergencies', *Global Public Health*, 17(10): 2530–46.

Rass, E. et al (2020) 'Participation by conflict-affected and forcibly displaced communities in humanitarian healthcare responses: a systematic review', *Journal of Migration and Health*, 1–2: 100026.

The New Humanitarian and Thomson Reuters Foundation (2020) 'EXCLUSIVE: More than 50 women accuse aid workers of sex abuse in Congo Ebola crisis'. Available from: https://www.thenewhumanitarian.org/2020/09/29/exclusive-more-50-women-accuse-aid-workers-sex-abuse-congo-ebola-crisis (accessed 15 September 2023).

True, J. (2012) *The Political Economy of Violence against Women*, New York: Oxford University Press.

Westendorf, J.-K. (2020) *Violating Peace: Sex, Aid, and Peacekeeping*, Ithaca, NY: Cornell University Press.

15

Rethinking PSEA: Reflections for Policy Makers

Jasmine-Kim Westendorf

Two decades on from the adoption by the United Nations (UN) of the zero tolerance policy, the chapters in this volume have collectively presented broad investigations into the efforts to address sexual exploitation and abuse (SEA) by peacekeepers and humanitarian aid workers. The contributors have bought into conversation theory, research and practice in analysing the effectiveness and unintended consequences of efforts to prevent and respond to SEA. In doing so, they have clearly identified the structural and systemic obstacles facing effective prevention of and accountability for SEA and drawn out the often-missing links between the pursuit of protection from sexual exploitation and abuse (PSEA) and broader processes of decolonization, anti-racism and localization in peacekeeping and aid. Critically, they have also laid out the implications of their analysis for policy makers, practitioners and scholars working in this area.

In this final chapter, I build on the discussions in preceding chapters to highlight the overarching policy implications this collection has for how we might better understand and respond to SEA in peacekeeping and aid. I reflect on the fault-lines that have emerged in PSEA and the potential for new ways of making sense of, and responding to, SEA perpetrated by peacekeepers and humanitarian aid workers against those populations in conflict and crisis, in which they live and work.

Challenges: the missing pieces of prevention

A key theme that has emerged across the chapters in this collection is that structural and systemic obstacles continue to hamper effective, grounded local PSEA work, despite both significant progress and investment in building stronger integrity systems across the UN and humanitarian sectors and the elevation of victim-centred approaches as a cornerstone of PSEA. As Naik and I illustrated, policy developments have often been reactively pursued in response to major SEA scandals, in attempts to both plug the holes such scandals reveal in accountability mechanisms and salvage credibility in the eyes of the public for the critically important work of peacekeeping and humanitarian missions. However, these developments often tend to prioritize procedural accountability rather than prevention of the occurrence of SEA in the first place through addressing the factors that give rise to it in different ways in different operational contexts. For example, Kihara-Hunt showed how the focus on getting the systems right for UN Police to play a role in SEA accountability was not matched by attention to *who* those police are and their own practices and behaviours that contribute to SEA perpetration, while Donnelly and Mazurana illustrated the factors that contribute to SEA as they operate within organizational cultures, creating conditions for the perpetration of, and impunity for, SEA both inside and outside peacekeeping and humanitarian organizations.

Jennings then demonstrated how the complex dynamics of interactions between peacekeepers and the communities they work within creates the conditions in which sexual interactions occur with varying levels of abuse, exploitation and agency. Elderfield and Kemp showed how the intersections between language and other factors of vulnerability, such as economic desperation and sociocultural/gendered circuits of violence, increase the exposure to SEA of individuals in communities in conflict and crisis, and decrease their access to support, including reporting pathways. Potts illustrated how these collections of factors that give rise to SEA have been identified and articulated by refugee women and girls in Uganda and Lebanon, and how they remain unaddressed by dominant PSEA approaches, which sideline these grounded analyses of risks and causes of SEA. Furthermore, the prioritization of procedural accountability in PSEA has not only detracted from systemic and structural prevention efforts, but also come at the expense of substantive redress for victims, as White demonstrated in her analysis of the genesis and implementation of the UN's new victim-centred approach.

Providing further insight into the structural and systemic obstacles to effective PSEA efforts, several chapters delved into the way inequitable, sexist and colonial power dynamics operate in practice, with effects on both local/mission levels and system levels. Martin illustrated how these dynamics work within organizations to discourage reporting and sideline whistleblowers – issues further elucidated through Donnelly and Mazurana's analysis of their surveys of peacekeepers and humanitarian workers on patterns of SEA against both local communities and colleagues. Bian, Daigle, Martin and Myrttinen further picked apart the gendered and racialized power imbalances, practices and structures that operate in the humanitarian sector, and how these enable SEA in practice, particularly against marginalized groups including individuals of diverse sexual orientation, gender identity and sex characteristics. At the local level within missions, these power dynamics contribute to creating the conditions for both the commission of SEA and impunity for it. At the system level, these contribute to the lack of political will to properly resource and institutionalize PSEA.

These manifest particularly clearly in relation to the victims' rights agenda, which, as White and Nyambeki demonstrated, has struggled to deliver on its promise as a result of inadequate political will to properly resource victim support mechanisms to deliver on the transformative promises of the agenda. As Connors' detailed reflections on her work as the UN's first Victims' Rights Advocate highlight, although the victims' rights approach is now embedded across the UN system, the Office of the Victims' Rights Advocate continues to face a multitude of challenges in delivering victim support and appropriately tailored accountability to meet the expectations and needs of those victims (and their children) who are brave enough to report in the first place. This was reinforced by Elderfield and Kemp in their chapter on language-based exclusion in the humanitarian system, which demonstrated, among other things, the need for victim-centred approaches to focus on meeting victims' material needs. It was also reinforced by Nasser-Eddin, whose chapter highlighted the critical importance of meeting victims' *immaterial* needs for victim-centred justice.

Opportunities: rethinking SEA

So where does this assessment of the significant structural and systemic obstacles to a local, grounded, effective PSEA response leave us? Collectively, the chapters in this book have provided a range of avenues for policy makers and practitioners to explore in support of rethinking and reorienting PSEA responses. First, several chapters have highlighted the centrality of the narratives dominant in the peacekeeping and humanitarian sectors that contribute to the intractability of SEA. On the one hand, I showed that the dominant narratives about the causes of SEA, which centre masculinity, are shaped and propelled by institutional imperatives in ways that reinforce a 'bad apple' narrative. This produces momentum for individualized compliance responses while simultaneously rendering invisible the intersecting local, international, normative and systemic factors that create the conditions in which some peacekeeping and humanitarian personnel choose to perpetrate SEA against local people. Jennings showed that this is also bolstered by the narratives and assumptions of consent and agency that have roots in the Secretary-General's Bulletin establishing zero tolerance for SEA within the UN system. She demonstrated how this flattens the complex realities of power relations between peacekeepers and locals, undermining the policy's legitimacy and complicating its implementation in practice. Bian, Daigle, Martin and Myrttinen added another layer to this understanding of the narratives at play, showing how the dominant self-image of the humanitarian sector – which assumes humanitarian workers to be resilient, noble and well intentioned, and positions the threats they face as coming from outside their organizations, from the chaotic local context – intersects with the colonial, heteronormative foundations of the system to enable SEA. Rethinking and redressing the policies and practices that these narratives produce would be a critical step in shifting the foundations from which SEA is understood and addressed. As these chapters have shown, that could encompass, for example, reconsidering the scope and framing of sexual exploitation and 'relationships with beneficiaries', or security trainings and practices to provide a better base from which to make sense of and tackle the power imbalances that give rise to SEA.

Building on this, there is significant scope for rethinking how PSEA can be communicated to host communities in culturally, contextually and linguistically comprehensible ways, as Elderfield and Kemp illustrated in their chapter. By shifting focus from what institutions can do to what communities need, we can better centre victims and their needs, and focus on locally appropriate language on SEA. As Abu-Assab laid out, this could in fact be the basis for a contextual safeguarding approach, which would shift attention from 'cultural sensitivity' in PSEA to addressing the 'structural sensitivity' of the work of organizations, through an intersectional perspective. This can in turn contribute to better restorative and transformative justice processes, the likes of which were presented by Nasser-Edin in her vision for a transnationalist approach to SEA that prioritizes empowerment of survivors and creates space to meet not only their material needs, but also their immaterial needs for agency and recognition. While Nasser-Edin provided ways to approach accountability that are centred on victim needs and desires, Potts' exploration of the Empowered Aid approach provided a blueprint for what this might look like in practice in terms of prevention. She laid out in detail how organizations can better adopt recipient-informed models of safer and more empowered aid delivery in ways that not only shift power balances in identifying the risks of SEA, but also address them in a holistic way that is attentive to social, economic and political dynamics in host communities.

Extending the existing SEA architecture to address these structural and systemic obstacles is no easy task, but as the contributions in this volume have demonstrated, it is not beyond the capacity of UN and humanitarian organizations to do so. In fact, the commitment of many individuals and organizations in the sector to localization and decolonization provides a robust foundation for renewed efforts to tackle the root causes of SEA and impunity for its perpetration, and for doing so in a way that centres the voices and needs of local communities. The commitment of many – including those who contributed to this volume – to ensuring lasting victim- and survivor-centred processes and mechanisms of justice highlights that a reoriented vision to address the fundamental, systemic obstacles examined in this volume is not only within organizational capacities, but a necessary imperative.

Notes

Introduction
1. Although the terms 'victims' and 'survivors' are often used interchangeably, we have opted in this book not to do so. We recognize that individuals may not see themselves as both victims and survivors – and that sometimes individuals only recognize themselves as survivors with the passing of time. Across the book, authors have chosen the term that most reflects the dynamics or focus of the specific cases, examples, or patterns that they are writing about.
2. This information is available from the UN website – 'Data on allegations: UN system-wide': www.un.org/preventing-sexual-exploitation-and-abuse/content/data-allegations-un-system-wide

Chapter 1
1. Although 'SEA' is a commonly used acronym, I generally prefer to use 'sexual exploitation and abuse' when referring to the acts of abuse and exploitation themselves, so as not to mask the realities of these acts behind the innocuous acronym. I have used 'SEA' primarily where refererring to the work of addressing sexual exploitation and abuse, including PSEA work.
2. For instance, in the Dominique Strauss-Kahn scandal, the case was settled and he continued his career (Collins, 2021).
3. I am a gender advisor on their board. See more at: www.aapc.legal/
4. 'Himpathy', a term coined by Kate Manne, Cornell philosophy professor, means 'the inappropriate and disproportionate sympathy powerful men often enjoy in cases of sexual assault, intimate partner violence, homicide and other misogynistic behaviour' (Chotiner, 2020).
5. On 13 October 2023, news came that PSEA positions in Romania and Poland were being cut.

Chapter 2
1. While there is no set definition of UN 'stabilization', it is clear that stabilization missions work alongside the government and national forces against peace spoilers, and thus do not stay impartial to conflict parties. Naturally, it allows more use of force than peacekeeping. A potentially problematic trend of stabilization missions is that they can be never-ending, as the more stability is achieved, the less incentive exists among conflicting parties for political transition. International presence benefits political and economic elites, which adds to the reluctance of political leaders to seek political solutions. This may have implications for the establishment of the rule of law and delivering accountability.
2. They are subject to exclusive criminal jurisdiction of the contributing state, as agreed in the status-of-forces agreement between the UN and host countries.

NOTES

3   This source of information can come through means of either receipt or discovery (OIOS, 2015: 36).
4   The Secretary-General reported that 'if the rule of law means anything at all, it means that no one, including peacekeepers, is above the law' (Annan, 2004: 11).

Chapter 4

1   We found the description of toxic work cultures in an article from *MIT Sloan Management Review* helpful, specifically its use of five key attributes of toxic cultures: disrespectful, non-inclusive, unethical, cut-throat and abusive (see Sull et al, 2022).
2   The data from our two studies revealed a pattern of sexual abuse perpetrated against peacekeepers and aid workers who identify as women. However, research has shown that men in military and conflict settings have also been victims of sexual abuse, and this tends to be under-reported (see, for example, Sivakumaran, 2007).
3   We use the term 'men' to indicate a gender identity of an individual, but we use 'masculinity' to refer to a type of behavior associated with men and males (though not displayed only by them) and a characteristic that is frequently seen as superior to other gendered behaviors.
4   We are aware of the patterns of under-reporting of sexual abuse for LGBTQ+ populations and men. However, even with under-reporting, we still expect women to be the largest category of victims.
5   Woman former police peacekeeper, interviewed 22 April 2021.
6   Man international humanitarian worker interviewed 29 August 2016.
7   Woman police peacekeeper, interviewed 6 April 2021.
8   Woman humanitarian worker, interviewed 25 August 2016.
9   Woman former police peacekeeper, interviewed 22 April 2021.
10 Woman security professional, interviewed 1 September 2016.
11 Woman police peacekeeper, interviewed 2 June 2021.
12 Woman former UN official, interviewed 5 May 2021.
13 Woman humanitarian worker, interviewed 26 August 2016.
14 Only one person in our study of peacekeepers identified as LGBTQ+, and thus our data are too limited to make any conclusions about LGBTQ+ persons' experiences of sexual abuse in peacekeeper missions.
15 Man humanitarian worker, interviewed 29 August 2016.
16 Woman humanitarian worker, interviewed 17 August 2016.
17 Woman humanitarian worker, interviewed 6 March 2017.
18 Woman former UN official, interviewed 5 May 2021.
19 Man former police peacekeeper, interviewed 29 June 2021.
20 Woman NGO worker, interviewed 7 April 2021.
21 Man peacekeeper, interviewed 20 April 2021.
22 Woman former UN official, interviewed 5 May 2021.
23 Woman humanitarian worker, interviewed 10 August 2016.
24 Woman humanitarian worker, interviewed 1 September 2016.
25 Woman humanitarian worker, interviewed 6 March 2017.
26 Woman humanitarian worker, interviewed 1 September 2016.
27 Man humanitarian worker, interviewed 29 August 2016.
28 Woman humanitarian worker, interviewed 15 August 2016.
29 Woman reporter, interviewed 5 August 2016.
30 Man trainer and counsellor, interviewed 17 August 2016.
31 Woman humanitarian worker, interviewed 6 March 2017.

³² Woman security professional, interviewed 8 August 2016.
³³ Woman reporter, interviewed 5 August 2016.

Chapter 5
1. See, for example, the investigative reporting by industry news outlet *The New Humanitarian* on SEA globally.
2. See the UK Foreign, Commonwealth and Development Office's complaints procedure (www.gov.uk/government/organisations/foreign-commonwealth-development-office/about/complaints-procedure) and USAID's Office of Inspector General (https://oig.usaid.gov/)
3. See the Girls' Education Challenge website: https://girlseducationchallenge.org

Chapter 6
1. The body was established by the United Nations General Assembly (UNGA) in 1991 (UNGA, 1991).
2. These are summarized in the annual reports of the Secretary-General on preventing sexual exploitation and abuse, available at: www.un.org/preventing-sexual-exploitation-and-abuse/content/secretary-generals-reports
3. The reports and supplementary statistical information are available at: https://conduct.unmissions.org/sea-data-introduction/
4. The UN system is made up of over 35 entities, including funds, programmes, specialized agencies and related organizations with their own areas of work, leadership and budget (see UN, nd-d).
5. The operations were the UN Multidimensional Integrated Stabilization Mission in the Central African Republic; the UN Organization Stabilization Mission in the Democratic Republic of the Congo; the UN Stabilization Mission in Haiti; and the UN Mission in South Sudan.
6. The approach can be accessed at: https://capseah.safeguardingsupporthub.org/
7. There are federal and state codes in the US, a UK victims' rights code and similar documents in Australia, Canada, Ireland, New Zealand and South Africa. The European Union's 2012 Victims' Rights Directive is reflected in the legal frameworks of most of its Member States; following an evaluation, revisions to the Directive were proposed by the European Commission in July 2023 (see European Commission, nd).
8. For the outcome of one case, see United States Mission to the United Nations (2022).
9. For a recent account, see Hu (nd).

Chapter 6A
1. The statement is available online at: www.un.org/preventing-sexual-exploitation-and-abuse/sites/www.un.org.preventing-sexual-exploitation-and-abuse/files/victims_rights_statement_on_sea_may_2023_web.pdf

Chapter 8
1. Interview with senior UN staff member with experience in multiple peace operations and Office of the Special Coordinator on Improving the United Nations' Response to Sexual Exploitation and Abuse, New York, 31 October 2016.
2. Interview with UN Women official, New York, 2 November 2016.
3. Interview with Paula Donovan, CEO of Aids-Free World, 2017.
4. Interview with senior diplomat to the UN, New York, 4 November 2016.
5. Interview with UN Police official, New York, 31 October 2016.
6. Interview with gender-based violence coordinator at a UN agency, Geneva, 23 September 2016.

7   Interview with senior troop-contributing country military official, Dili, 18 July 2016.
8   Interview with senior staff from a major humanitarian organization, Geneva, 20 September 2016.
9   Interview with senior staff member, UN Conduct and Discipline Unit, New York, 4 November 2016; see also Conduct in UN Field Missions Unit (nd).

Chapter 9

1   For an incisive analysis of the 'strongly discouraged' clause from both conceptual and implementation standpoints that raises many of the same points, see Westendorf (2023a).
2   This is also evident in the fact that if the peacekeeper marries the minor (under the age of 18), they *are* permitted to have sex with them – otherwise forbidden by the ZTP.
3   Including transgender and non-binary people.
4   Local employees of peacekeeping missions occupy a singular position. As UN staff members, they are subject to the rules of their employer, just as their international colleagues are. As locals and as people deriving income from the UN mission, they can also be considered beneficiaries of assistance. The ZTP applies to all staff of the UN, but its application generally reflects the assumption that the staff member/peacekeeper is a foreign national rather than a national of the host country, while the beneficiary of assistance is not someone with a direct employment relationship to the UN. Local employees of missions (and other UN agencies and offices) are, in this way, both written into and written out of the ZTP.
5   See discussion of these differences and relevant references in Jennings (2010, 2014); also see Westendorf (2023b).

Chapter 10

1   While we focus on the perpetration of SEA by humanitarian actors against colleagues, we do not wish to deny or downplay the various other forms of violence that crisis-affected people and humanitarian staff experience. See, for example, research on SEA perpetrated by armed actors, peacekeepers and opportunist civilians in Jenning (2014), Wood (2014) and Harrington (2010).
2   Interviews were conducted by the authors between 2020 and 2023 in the course of several other ongoing research projects. Twenty-one interviewees were from Europe, North America and Australia and White; eight were from the Middle East, East Asia and Asia-Pacific; two were from Europe and biracial or Black; two were from Africa and Black. All were aid workers at the time of interview or or had been previsously.
3   Although LGBTQI (lesbian, gay, bisexual, transgender, queer/questioning and intersex) may have greater familiarity to readers, we prefer the terminology of SOGIESC, which is more comprehensive and not rooted in Western categories and identities.
4   At time of writing, *Good Practice Review 8* is being updated.
5   The Resource and Support Hub, which has been rolled out across many settings, has assisted civil society organizations and national NGOs in developing safeguarding policies and improving their response to SEA. However, many of these documents are translated and introduced into different contexts without much contextual analysis (Westendorf and Searle, 2017; see also Clare and Bys, 2022).

Chapter 11

1   The International Organization for Migration's *Deployment Package for PSEA Coordinators* is currently under revision; at the time of writing, the updated guidance is not yet available.
2   This arose from internal term testing for the development of CLEAR Global's interagency multilingual glossary on PSEA, available from: https://glossaries.clearglobal.org/psea/

3   This was shared during in-person training on language and communication in emergencies, conducted by CLEAR Global in Poland in 2022.
4   This emerged from an internal learning review of the development of PSEA communication material for the project PSEA at the Frontline – Together We Say No, a collaboration between the World Food Programme and the International Organization for Migration in partnership with Translators without Borders. For more information, see: https://psea.interagencystandingcommittee.org/psea-frontline-together-we-say-no

Chapter 12
1   It is worth mentioning that, while the case was used to stigmatize specific ethnic communities, it is beyond the scope of this chapter to discuss the racialized elements that surfaced in this case.

Chapter 13
1   The CHS Alliance is a global alliance of humanitarian and development organizations committed to making aid work better for people. The Inter-Agency Standing Committee (IASC) is the longest-standing and highest-level humanitarian coordination forum of the United Nations system. It brings together the executive heads of 18 organizations and consortia to formulate policy, set strategic priorities and mobilize resources in response to humanitarian crises.

Chapter 14
1   This is a local term that means 'seducing'.
2   All refugee co-researchers were consulted about whether, and how, they would like to be named in public-facing documents.
3   See the Empowered Aid website at: https://empoweredaid.gwu.edu

Index

A

#AidToo movement 7, 22, 28, 30, 156
#MeToo movement 7, 21–22
abbreviations, acronyms 26–28, 63, 172–173
Action Against Prohibited Conduct 25
affect 200–204
agency 4, 13, 115–116, 118, 123, 143–153, 172–174, 195–204, 223
aid distributions 207–219, 224
Aids Free World - Code Blue Campaign, 132
Aid Worker Registration Scheme 86
aid workers 3, 7, 10, 19–30, 62–74, 79–88, 157–165, 224
  alcohol 69, 72, 133, 134, 146, 160
  as victims of SEA 72–74, 156–166
  resilience 159
  security practices 157–162, 224
Akashi, Yasushi 131

B

Bangladesh 175
Barbeschi, Maurizio 156
Bosnia 3, 134
Broström, Martina 24, 28, 156
buzzwords 21, 26, 29

C

Cambodia 3, 37, 98, 122, 131–132
cash and voucher assistance 209–219
Central African Republic 6, 20, 24, 51, 93–94, 96, 97–98, 116, 118, 135
Clear Check 23, 86, 93
coloniality 10, 12, 21, 138–140, 145, 148, 150, 157, 160–161, 165, 170–171, 175, 187, 199, 222, 224
Common Approach to Sexual Exploitation, Abuse and Sexual Harassment (CAPSEAH) 7, 99
community-based complaints mechanisms 51, 101, 121, 125, 212, 218
conflict-related sexual violence 5, 34, 135, 138–139, 162, 174, 176
Connors, Jane 6, 93–104, 108

consent, agency 4, 12, 48, 143–153, 172, 211, 223
contextual safeguarding 185–186, 208–210, 224
Core Humanitarian Standard 82, 100, 195
cultural awareness, cultural sensitivity 13, 161, 169–179, 184–190
culture (see *organizational culture*)
Cyprus 37, 152

D

decolonization 2, 8, 165, 190, 221, 224
Democratic Republic of Congo (see also *United Nations Organization Stabilization Mission in the Democratic Republic of Congo*) 1, 4, 20, 23–24, 25, 50, 80, 85, 96, 118–122, 133, 138–139, 151, 157, 173–174, 176, 177, 207
discourse, institutional 132–133

E

emotions 185, 196–197, 200–204
Empowered Aid 13, 29–30, 207–219

F

food aid 209–219
funding cycles 20–21, 211–2

G

gender 6, 10, 12, 13, 21, 27–29, 42, 64–74, 132, 136–137, 139, 144, 148–152, 156–165, 169, 171, 174–175, 178, 207–219, 222
gender-based violence 19, 21, 41, 50, 64, 87, 103, 118, 158, 162, 175, 190, 218
Guinea 3, 79, 135

H

Haiti 6, 20–21, 37–38, 40, 50, 79, 95–96, 98, 121, 145, 156, 175
heteronormativity 12, 13, 144, 149–150, 158, 162, 165, 207, 224
homosexuality (see also *SOGIESC, LGBTQ+*) 66, 68, 159
hotlines 121, 217
Humanitarian Accountability Partnership Standard 82

Humanitarian Women's Network 65, 162
humanitarianism 159–162, 187, 224

I

Independent Commission for Aid Impact 85, 87, 99
institutional culture (see *organizational cultures*)
Inter-Agency Standing Committee 5, 7, 81, 82, 85, 93, 98, 99, 100, 170
Internally Displaced Persons camps 4, 138, 177
International Covenant on Civil and Political Rights 47
International Planned Parenthood Federation 79
Interpol (see also *Soteria project*) 7, 86
Iraq 170, 172, 175

K

Kompass, Anders 20, 135
Kosovo 37, 133

L

language 12, 20, 26–27, 29, 51, 144, 164, 169–179, 186, 188, 190, 212, 215, 222–223
  rights 51, 111, 173
  vague (see also *abbreviations, acronyms*) 26–27, 133
Lebanon, 98, 207–219
LGBTQ+ (see also *SOGIESC*) 63–74, 158–159, 222–223
Liberia 3, 8, 19–21, 50, 79, 98, 122, 145, 151, 173
linguistic diversity 170, 178
linguistic power 87, 170–172, 186, 215, 223
localization 2, 8, 165, 221, 224
local staff 70, 87, 161–163, 170, 172, 176–78, 186, 211, 215–217, 223
Loures, Luiz 156
love 144, 149, 209
Lubbers, Ruud 81

M

Majumdar, Arnab 28–29
Mali 98, 133
masculinities 11, 42, 64–65, 67, 130–140, 161, 223
  - militarized masculinities 64, 135, 136–137
Médecins Sans Frontières (MSF) 79, 165
Misconduct Disclosure Scheme 7, 86
misogyny 68, 156, 158
modern management techniques 133
Moldova 26–27, 133
Multilateral Organization Performance Assessment Network (MOPAN) 84, 99
multilingualism 169–179

N

Naik, Asmita 3, 79–88
national staff (see *local staff*)
Nigeria 177–178

O

Ombuds mechanism 80, 83, 86
organizational cultures 3, 9–10, 19, 21–22, 28–30, 39, 41–42, 51, 63–74, 80, 99, 156–157, 159, 161, 165, 187–188, 190, 222
Organization for Economic Co-operation and Development (OECD)Development Assistance Committee 84, 99
Oxfam 6–7, 21–22, 29, 79, 82–83, 135, 156

P

Pacific Islands 175
participatory methodologies 207–219
paternalism 146–151, 218
paternity claims 4, 7, 51–54, 98–99, 101, 103, 110–111, 113, 114, 117, 119, 121–123
patriarchy 9, 12, 19, 21, 28–29, 64–66, 130, 132–133, 136–138, 158, 161–162, 165, 187–189, 218
peacekeepers 2–13, 19–24, 48, 50, 62–74, 81, 93–104, 114, 121, 131–136, 145–153, 221–224
  accommodation and living standards, 133
  alcohol, 69, 133, 134
  as victims of SEAH, 62–74
  civilian peacekeepers, 5, 62, 133, 135, 145, 150–151
  fraternization, 133
  from Belgium, 139
  from Chad, 135
  from Equatorial Guinea, 135
  from France, 6, 20, 40, 116, 135, 139
  from Morocco, 138
  from Uruguay, 98, 138
  repatriation, 1, 5, 93–94, 106
  stress, R&R, 69, 133
  women, 64–74, 132, 133
peacekeeping economies 12, 138–139, 144, 148, 150–152, 173
ping-pong tables 133
Plan International 79
Poland 23, 26–27, 175, 226
police (as perpetrators) 216
power 1, 3, 8–10, 12, 62–67, 132, 143–144, 148–153, 169, 171–172, 207–219, 223–224
  imbalances of, 20–21, 28–30, 42–43, 62, 67, 80, 121, 131, 139, 144, 148–149, 164–165, 172, 187, 198–200, 207, 224
Prevention of Sexual Violence in Conflict Initiative 99
protection 34–37, 134, 145, 150

INDEX

protection of civilians (peacekeeping) 37–38
PSEA communication 169–179, 224
PSEA frameworks 46–55, 79–88, 121, 130, 176, 195–204, 222–224

R

race, racism 21, 28, 138–140, 148, 150, 157–158, 161, 190, 199, 222–223
rape 1, 3, 26, 48, 65–69, 71, 73, 75, 132, 135, 138, 141, 162, 174–176
Report the Abuse 21, 162
reputational management 20, 48–49, 73, 85–86, 94, 145, 157, 159, 162–163, 222
Resource and Support Hub 7, 23, 26, 164
Rohingya response (see also *Bangladesh*) 175–176
Rule of law 9, 26, 34, 36–43, 70, 87, 226–227

S

safeguarding 6, 12, 22, 26–27, 47, 83, 87, 99, 119, 164, 184–190, 201–209
Safeguarding Summit 82–83, 84, 99
Save the Children 79, 82–83, 156
SEA 62–74, 94, 145, 158, 172, 174, 215
 'bad apples' 36, 74, 134, 139–140
 'scandals' 1, 3, 6–7, 9, 20–1, 24, 30, 46, 48, 51, 79–85, 88, 120–121, 135, 156, 189, 195, 207, 222
 accountability mechanisms 5, 23, 37–42, 47–51, 71–72, 80, 83, 85–88, 103, 110, 114–123, 134–135, 139, 186, 189, 195, 203, 215–217, 222
 against LGBTQ+ people 68–69, 72
 allegations 7–8, 22, 35–37, 41–42, 46, 50, 54–55, 63, 70, 79–86, 93–94, 103, 116, 118–121, 121–122, 132, 135, 139, 153, 174, 195
 by aid workers 68, 87, 138, 156–165, 208–218
 causes, risk 11, 63–74, 130, 135, 136–137, 139–140, 169, 174, 176, 187, 198–200, 204, 208–210, 215–218, 222–223
 code of conduct (see also *zero-tolerance policy*) 20, 48, 134, 137, 139
 compliance approaches 11, 52–53, 79–88, 139, 203, 222–223
 deterrence 23, 139
 discouraged relationships 148–151, 174, 215, 224
 false allegations 8, 49–51, 87
 funding 20, 22, 25–26, 29, 53–55, 83–84, 101–103, 119–121, 164, 171, 195, 211–212, 215
 impunity 3, 6, 10, 25, 51, 64, 70–73, 80, 82, 94, 134, 135, 162–163, 216–217, 222–223, 225
 integrity systems 47–48
 involving children 3, 6, 10, 20, 24, 26, 46, 48, 64, 79, 132, 135, 138–139, 143, 176
 narratives of 130–136

perpetrators 5, 7, 11, 22–24, 40–43, 64–73, 80, 83, 86, 132, 133, 150, 159, 164, 171, 202, 215–217
prevention (see also *PSEA*) 23, 49, 84, 137, 139, 169, 195, 217–219, 221, 224
remedial action, access to justice 9, 25, 46–55, 72, 83, 112, 118–121, 197, 216–217, 222, 224
reporting 5–8, 20, 23–25, 28, 51, 71–72, 81, 86–88, 94, 121–122, 143, 158–159, 174, 176, 178, 186, 208, 215–217
retaliation 49, 51–52, 83, 86–87, 97, 112, 116, 121–122
stigma, victim blaming 25, 27, 51–2, 54, 72, 81, 94, 97, 121, 138, 173, 175–176, 178, 201, 208–215, 216
survivor-centered approach 13, 24, 54, 71, 85–86, 96, 99, 169, 177–178, 198, 202, 217, 224
training 5–6, 20–21, 23–24, 26, 35, 37, 73, 87, 99–100, 134, 137, 139–140, 151, 164, 176, 214–215
victim-centered approach 39, 93–104, 186, 196–204, 223–224
securitization 160–162
security training 160–163
sex industry/prostitution 3, 131, 132, 133, 138, 144, 146–147, 152, 173
sexism 21, 28, 68, 140, 199
sexual assault (see *rape*)
sexual harassment 7, 21, 23–28, 52, 65–67, 81, 82, 84, 87, 98, 100, 122, 156–158, 170, 172
sexual harm framings 135, 146
sexuality 64, 66, 68, 138, 150, 156–163, 175, 185, 199
shelter, fuel and firewood aid 209–219
Sierra Leone 3, 20, 40, 79, 133, 138
SOGIESC 63–74, 158–159, 222–223
Soteria project (Interpol) 7, 86
South Sudan 23, 32, 50, 95–96, 98, 118, 162
Srebrenica 134
structural sensitivity 184–190
structuration theory 188–190
Syria-Turkey earthquake (2023) 185
systems of oppression 137, 187, 189, 196, 198–204

T

technocratic fixes 20, 27–28, 140, 164
technology 27–28
The Global Fund 46
The Grand Bargain 165
The New Humanitarian 80, 85, 138
Timor-Leste 37, 122
trafficking 1, 3, 23, 27, 42, 47–48, 134–135, 174
transactional sex 1–3, 8, 20, 34, 48, 110, 132, 135, 138, 146, 149, 151–152, 173–174
translation practices 169–179

U

Uganda 196, 207–219
UK Government 82–83, 84, 86, 99
Ukraine response 23, 27–28, 164, 175
UNAIDS 24, 79, 131, 156
UNHCR 3, 79, 81, 100, 102
UN Misconduct Tracking Scheme 86
UN Office of the Special Coordinator on Improving the UN Response to SEA 6
UN Police 1, 34–43, 222
  accountability 38, 40
  as perpetrators of SEA 37–43
  investigations 37
  personnel 40–41
UN Population Fund (UNFPA) 79
UN Secretary General Antonio Guterres 5, 6, 10, 36, 39–39, 43, 82, 93–94, 118–121
UN Secretary General Ban Ki-Moon 6, 41
UN Secretary General Kofi Annan 3, 81
UN Stabilization Mission in the Democratic Republic of Congo (MONUC) 1, 4–5, 138–139
UN Transitional Authority in Cambodia 37, 131
UN Trust Fund in Support of SEA 6, 23, 29, 101, 119–120, 122
UN Victims' Rights Advocate 6, 11, 52, 93–104, 118
  Office of the Victims' Rights Advocate 6, 93–103, 114, 118–123, 223
  Senior Victims' Rights Officers 40, 94–102, 118
UN Victims' Rights Statement 11, 85, 100, 108–113
UN Women 79, 132

V

victim advocacy 93–104, 115–123
victim blaming 25, 27, 51–52, 159–160, 215
Victim Care Officers 102
victim-centered approach (see also *SEA victim-centered approach*) 5–6, 9–11, 13, 39–40, 46–55, 82–83, 93–104, 114–123, 198, 201, 222–223
victims
  funding 53, 54, 119–120
  rights (see also *UN Victims' Rights Statement*) 46–55, 93–104, 108–113, 223
  support/assistance 10–12, 23–25, 39, 46–55, 85, 93–104, 108, 110, 114, 117–123, 174, 179, 197–198, 200, 202, 216, 222–223
Victims' rights advocates (non-UN) 9, 46–52

W

Water, Sanitation and Hygiene (WASH) 209–219
whistle-blowers 19–25, 28, 81–83, 135, 222
whiteness 23, 29, 139, 157–158, 160–162
Women, Peace and Security 132, 165
women's inclusion 28–29, 207–219
World Health Organization 23–24, 80, 85, 102, 156–157, 177, 207

Z

Zeid report 4–5, 48–49, 119
Zero tolerance bulletin 43, 48–49, 62, 93, 143–153, 171–172, 176, 195, 223
  background 2–4, 81, 93
  definitions 2

www.ingramcontent.com/pod-product-compliance
Lightning Source LLC
Chambersburg PA
CBHW051537020426
42333CB00016B/1964